Caring for School-Age Children

SECOND EDITION

Caring for School-Age Children

SECOND EDITION

PHYLLIS CLICK

Delmar Publishers

an International Thomson Publishing company I(T)P®

Albany • Bonn • Boston • Cincinnati • Detroit • London • Madrid
Melbourne • Mexico City • New York • Pacific Grove • Paris • San Francisco
Singapore • Tokyo • Toronto • Washington

NOTICE TO THE READER

Cover Design: Timothy J. Conners

Delmar Staff
Publisher: William Brottmiller
Administrative Editor: Jay Whitney
Associate Editor: Erin O'Connor Traylor
Project Editor: Marah Bellegarde
Production Coordinator: James Zayicek
Art and Design Coordinator: Timothy J. Conners
Editorial Assistant: Mara Berman

COPYRIGHT © 1998
By Delmar Publishers
an International Thomson Publishing Company

The ITP Logo is a trademark under license.

Printed in the United States of America

For more information, contact:

Delmar Publishers
3 Columbia Circle, Box 15015
Albany, New York 12212-5015

International Thomson Editores
Campos Eliseos 385, Piso 7
Col Polanco
11560 Mexico D F Mexico

International Thomson Publishing Europe
Berkshire House
168-173 High Holborn
London, WC1V 7AA
England

International Thomson Publishing GmbH
Konigswinterer Strasse 418
53227 Bonn
Germany

Thomas Nelson Australia
102 Dodds Street
South Melbourne, 3205
Victoria, Australia

International Thomson Publishing Asia
221 Henderson Road
#05-10 Henderson Building
Singapore 0315

Nelson Canada
1120 Birchmount Road
Scarborough, Ontario
Canada, M1K 5G4

International Thomson Publishing—Japan
Hirakawacho Kyowa Building, 3F
Chiyoda-ku, Tokyo 102
Japan

1 2 3 4 5 6 7 8 9 10 XXX 03 02 01 00 99 98 97

Library of Congress Cataloging-in-Publication Data

Click, Phyllis.
    Caring for school-age children / Phyllis Click. — 2nd ed.
      p. cm.
    Includes bibliographical references and index.
    ISBN 0-8273-7692-8
    1. School-age child care — United States. I. Title.
HQ778.6.C55   1997   97-20831
305.234 — dc21   CIP

Contents

Preface

This book is meant to be an easy-to-read guide for those who spend time with school-age children. It is written in a format that can be used in a course for those who are preparing to work with children or as a reference for those who are already employed as teachers, aides, caregivers, leaders, or recreational supervisors. It will also help those in administrative positions, such as directors, principals, managers, or coordinators. Parents of school-age children will find help in understanding their youngsters and for participating in the operation of their children's child-care center. Interspersed throughout the book are drawings done by children enrolled in centers. Some of their drawings and comments lend credence to the information being discussed. Other drawings allow us to understand how children perceive themselves, their friends, and their families. The *Instructor's Manual* that accompanies this text is designed for the person who teaches classes to prospective child-care personnel. Included in the manual are an outline of the chapters that can be used for planning class sessions, suggestions for in-class discussions and activities, additional exam questions, and information about videos or films.

The first edition of *Caring for School-Age Children* grew out of a recognition of the need for a comprehensive text for those who were caring for children before and after school. There was a lot of information available for understanding the needs of children under the age of five, but little was written for those who work with older children. The first edition filled that need. This second edition responds to requests for further information to help caregivers understand the development of children during middle childhood and to plan developmentally appropriate programs for their time in child care.

The three chapters in Section I, *How Children Grow and Develop,* are completely new to this edition and contain a fairly extensive review of the developmental stages between the ages of five and twelve. These chapters cover children's physical, cognitive, and psychosocial development. These chapters should help the adults in child-care centers understand how children in the middle childhood years differ from children under the age of five.

Section II, *The People in School-Age Care,* provides information about how children relate to one another and how today's changing families affect children's development. New information in this edition includes the grandparent as caregiver and the impact of poverty on children's development. Chapter 6 presents information about the adults who spend out-of-school time with children, the caregivers. The question of what they should be called is raised and the characteristics of effective child-care leaders are presented. The final chapter in this section is devoted to helping adults understand the best ways to enhance children's self-esteem and effectively change their destructive behaviors. A process for resolving conflicts is also included in this chapter.

Section III, *The Background,* includes a new discussion of developmentally appropriate practices and suggestions for planning activities that support development. Chapter 8 has a new segment that will help caregivers create an environment that supports development. There is also information on creating a place where children can experience the natural environment.

Section IV, *The Curriculum,* covers the activities of a child-care program. New to this section is an emphasis on how each portion of the curriculum affects the development of the children for whom it is designed. Each chapter has a segment on how that part of the curriculum contributes to or supports development and each activity is preceded by statements of its purpose. Each chapter includes ideas for multicultural experiences. A final chapter in this section discusses the use of community resources to support children's development and to expand the program beyond the walls of the child-care center.

It is hoped that this second edition will be a source of help to those who are concerned for the welfare of the thousands of children who spend their out-of-school time in organized care programs. Working with children of any age is extremely rewarding. Working with school-age children presents some special challenges. This book should make that job not only a little bit easier, but also more meaningful as well as enjoyable.

About the Author

Phyllis Click obtained both her bachelor's and masters degrees from the University of California at Berkeley in psychology and child development. Throughout a long career, her interest in providing the best possible environment for young children led her to work in a variety of settings from preschools to summer camp programs for older children. Later, she began working with adults, teaching college classes, administering grant programs, and designing a curriculum for a private college for prospective teachers.

Now retired, she has been a consultant, helping others to start or administer programs, and has published extensively. Her publications include another textbook for child-care personnel, articles in professional journals, and ancillary materials for other authors' texts. She belongs to the National Association for the Education of Young Children and the California School-Age Consortium.

Acknowledgments

I want to thank the helpful staff members and the marvelous children at two child-care centers who worked together to provide me with the charming drawings interspersed throughout the chapters of this book. I wish I could name each of the children, but there were too many. Their real first names are shown below their drawings. Their caregivers and their programs are:

Dawn Borel, Simi Children's World Learning Center Children in the Adventure Club, Simi Children's World Learning Center

Debbie Webster, Great Pacific Child Development Center Children in the Kid's Club, Great Pacific Child Development Center

Thanks also to Delmar Publishers Administrative Editor Jay Whitney who supported the proposal for the first edition of this book and has continued to provide encouragement through the revision. Erin O'Connor Traylor, Associate Editor, has been a source of information and help as the writing progressed and occasionally ran into difficulty. Thanks also to the many staff members at Delmar who carry a project from one step to another until the final pages are put together.

Several reviewers chosen by Delmar to comment on the final version of the manuscript offered many excellent suggestions. I appreciate their thoughtful consideration of the content of this book. They were:

Jann James, Ed.D.
Troy State University
Goshen, AL

Jennifer Lynch
Moorpark College
Moorpark, CA

Karen Peterson, Ph.D.
Washington State University
Vancouver, WA

Joan Sanoff
Wake Technical Community College
Raleigh, NC

Dianne K. Smith
Moorpark College
Moorpark, CA

Section 1

How Children Grow and Develop

1

Development In Middle Childhood: Physical

Objectives

After completing this chapter, the student should be able to:

- Discuss the importance of understanding child development
- Distinguish between development and learning
- Relate major changes and variations in growth patterns among children
- Describe ways in which child-care leaders can enhance children's physical development

Importance of Understanding Child Development

The years between five and twelve bring about changes in children that make them more independent of adult assistance in the conduct of their daily activities. Children master new physical skills fairly easily when they have opportunities to practice those skills. Illnesses and death occur less frequently than during infancy and preschool years or later in adolescence. Gender differences in physical development and ability are minimal. Most children feel competent to manage their school and home lives and still want to perform in ways that earn recognition from adults.

FIGURE 1–1   *School-age children can hop on one foot to play hopscotch.*

A knowledge of the universal predictable stages of growth as well as an understanding of individual patterns of timing are absolutely essential for anyone involved in planning and operating a child-care program. The quality of a program may depend upon a variety of factors, but a major determinant is the extent to which activities and procedures are appropriate for the developmental level of the participating children. The learning environment and program activities should be based on an assessment of children's cognitive, social, emotional, and physical abilities at each stage of their development and also provide challenges to promote further development. A knowledge of child development will enable adults to choose effective techniques for guiding an individual child's behavior and planning strategies for group interactions. Further, a knowledge of child development will enable child-care leaders to communicate more effectively with parents about a child's progress.

Development and Learning

The study of human development examines how individuals grow and change over the period of a lifetime, how they remain the same, and how some individuals may vary from typical patterns. Several characteristics of individuals are programmed by genetic makeup at the time of conception, while others are the result of environmental conditions and experiences. The relative importance of one over the other, known as *nature vs. nurture,* is a topic for debate among developmental researchers.

Nature refers to a variety of characteristics such as eye color and body type, which are inherited from parents. Physical limitations and certain diseases are also inherited, as well as some personality characteristics such as activity level or verbal ability. **Nurture** refers to all the experiences and influences one is exposed to from the moment of conception on throughout a lifetime.

The dichotomy of influences on human development is also portrayed as *maturation vs. learning.* **Maturation** indicates the progression of changes that take place as one ages. **Learning** refers to the processes by which environmental influences and experiences bring about permanent changes in thinking, feeling, and behavior.

The basic question is the same no matter what labels are used. How much of development and human behavior is the result of genetic inheritance and how much is the result of all of life's experiences? Most developmentalists believe that both are important and that in fact the interaction between them is the determining factor in one's pattern of growth.

Physical Development

Height and Weight

Middle childhood is a time when children grow more slowly than they did in the preschool years and they will not experience another growth spurt until they approach adolescence. Typically, children gain about five pounds per year and 2½ inches. By the time they are ten years old most will weigh 70 pounds and be 54 inches tall (Lowrey, 1986). Up to the age of nine, boys and girls are about the same size, but then girls start to pull ahead in both height and weight. Around age nine or ten girls begin a growth spurt that precedes adolescence. By the end of the elementary years girls are generally taller and heavier than boys. School-age children seem slimmer than they did during the preschool years because their body proportions change and they begin to look more like adults. Their arms and legs get longer, their torso elongates, and their faces are thinner.

Yet there are wide variations in their appearance. Variations in body size could be due to malnutrition. Children who are well nourished will be taller than their

FIGURE 1–2   *School-age children master many physical skills.*

contemporaries growing up in poverty. Genetics also plays a large part in determining size as well as rate of maturity. While adults may understand that variations in size and timing of maturity are normal, it is often difficult for children to accept these differences. Physical development can affect peer relationships, since children often choose friends who have a pleasing appearance and are physically, academically, or socially capable (Hartup, 1983). Children who are shorter, taller, or heavier than their peers, as well as those who are less capable, are often rejected.

Obesity

Obesity is a growing problem among children. It can seriously affect a child emotionally as well as physically. A study of 26,371 persons between the ages of five and twenty-four in Louisiana showed a marked increase in overweight individuals (Freedman et al, 1997). During the study period from 1973 to 1994 they found that the prevalence of overweight people increased approximately twofold.

Labeling a particular youngster as obese rather than just childishly chubby depends partly on the child's body type and partly on the proportion of fat to muscle. At least 10 percent of all American children are 20 pounds above the average for their peers. More exact measurements of the percentage of body fat at various points of the body show that the percentage of overweight children may be higher than 10 percent and has increased in the last few years (Gortmaker et al, 1987).

Overweight children may be subject to increased orthopedic and respiratory problems (Johnston, 1985; Aristimuno et al, 1984). In addition, serious psychological distress can occur since these children may be the object of teasing and rejection by their classmates. This results in lowered self-esteem, depression, and various kinds of behavior problems. Their unhappiness leads them to further curtail participation with their peers and to overeat to compensate for their unhappiness. Thus patterns are established that carry over into adulthood; overweight children are frequently overweight adults (Serdula et al, 1993). It is estimated that 60 percent to 80 percent of obese children will become overweight adults (Lucas, 1991).

Causes of Obesity

There is no one cause of obesity, rather, it is an interaction between several possible conditions. Patterns are often established in infancy and continue into adulthood.

- Heredity. Several factors that contribute to obesity are inherited: body type, height and bone structure, the amount and distribution of fat, metabolic rate, and activity level.
- Activity level. Children who are more active are less likely to be overweight since they burn more calories. Although activity level is influenced by heredity, an individual's willingness to engage in active play will also affect weight. For some children, the unavailability of safe places to play will also be a factor.
- Overfeeding in infancy. In the prenatal period and during the first two years of life, the number of fat cells in the body is established. Poor nutrition during the gestation period and in infancy slows down the rate of fat cell multiplication; overfeeding speeds it up. Fat babies are likely to become fat children and adults when the existing fat cells become larger. Even when dieting decreases weight, the same number of cells remain in the body waiting to be filled again.
- Television-watching. Families who watch television frequently have a higher incidence of obesity (Dietz & Gortmaker, 1985). Children are not only inactive when they watch television, but are also bombarded with commercials for foods that are high in fat and sugar. These are the foods they choose to snack on while they watch television.

- Types of food consumed (Albertson et al, 1992). The choices of foods a family prepares and serves is a factor in determining whether or not its members will be overweight. Diets that are rich in fruits, vegetables, and grains do not cause excessive weight, while diets that contain a lot of fat and sugar will. In addition, many of the "junk foods" or special treats children demand and parents provide contain large proportions of high-calorie ingredients. This can lead to dietary cravings that carry into adulthood along with the resulting weight and health problems.
- Attitudes toward food. In some families, children are encouraged to consume large portions of food as a measure of the family's prosperity or their love for their children. Often, too, food becomes a symbol for love and comfort, causing people to overeat when under stress or unhappy. Parents who offer special foods as a reward or comfort set up a lifelong habit that can lead to obesity.
- Specific event. A traumatic event in a child's life can be a precipitating factor in the onset of increased weight gain. Hospitalization, parental divorce, the death of someone close to the child, or even a move to a new neighborhood can all cause distress and a need for a substitute gratification in the form of food.
- Physiological problems. A small number of cases of obesity in children can be traced to abnormalities in the growth process or metabolism (Lowrey, 1986). The obesity is only one part of the problem that usually includes disturbances in normal physical and mental growth. Only about 1 percent of childhood obesity can be attributed to this cause, however.

Implications for Child-Care Staff Members

Within any group of school-age children, particularly if there is a wide age span, there will be children of many sizes and shapes. Children compare their own appearance with their peers' and as a result often think they are too tall, too little, too heavy, or too thin. In addition, children who vary noticeably from their peers tend to get teased and labeled with unflattering names. Differing from the norm can cause a great deal of anguish and loss of self-esteem.

- An important task for adults who have responsibility for children's welfare is to assure them they are accepted no matter how they look and to help their peers be accepting. Further, they need to know that they will change as they grow and develop.
- Obese children need special attention to help them change their eating patterns and activity level. They can learn about good nutrition and how to prepare good-tasting, low-calorie foods. See Chapter 14 for ideas that can be used in child care. Although increased activity is the best way to lose weight, obese children have a difficult time participating in active sports or games. They are often rejected as team members and are teased if they try to join in games. It is important to encourage them to start somewhere: walking to school, bicycling, or participating in the exercises suggested in Chapter 14.

- The children's families need help to change the environment that created the obesity, whether it lies in the foods that are served, in the parental interactions, or in the kinds of activities children are encouraged to engage in. Information on nutrition can be made available. Help parents find ways to discipline or reward children other than with food. They can be provided with suggestions for active things the family can do together.

Health Conditions

During middle childhood children may suffer from a variety of health conditions. According to a 1992 study, 31 percent of children under age 18, or 20 million children nationwide, have chronic health problems (Newacheck & Taylor, 1992). The most frequently reported conditions are respiratory allergies and repeated ear infections. Less common are diabetes, sickle cell disease, and cerebral palsy.

Conditions that are not chronic but are prevalent during the school years are communicable diseases and hearing, vision, or ambulatory limitations. Early sexual behavior leads to preadolescent pregnancies and sexually transmitted disease, including HIV and AIDS. Drug and alcohol abuse are also occurring at the elementary school level.

Poverty contributes to the poor health status of many children. According to the U. S. Bureau of the Census, 14.6 million children under age 18 were living in poverty in 1995. Fifteen percent of these children have no health insurance coverage. Because of their living conditions they are subject to poor nutrition, inadequate prevention care, and little treatment for chronic conditions.

Implications for Child-Care Staff Members

The adults who work with children in a child-care setting can do a great deal to help children learn to maintain a healthy life-style as well as help parents be responsible for ensuring that children's health needs are met.

- Help children evaluate the messages they receive from their environment concerning health. Provide activities that encourage them to question images of people having fun while smoking cigarettes, eating "junk" foods, or consuming alcoholic beverages.
- Include program activities that stress good nutrition. Allow children to participate in choosing and preparing food.
- Offer only nutritious meals and snacks. Offer supplementary nutrition to children who may be undernourished.
- Provide space within the physical facility for activities that encourage health and fitness.
- Model behavior that demonstrates fitness. Do not smoke or consume nonnutritious foods.
- Become informed about community health services and resources. Refer parents to appropriate facilities.

Motor Skills

During the elementary school period children develop a wide variety of motor skills, particularly when they have ample opportunities to practice and are encouraged to try new things. Five-year-olds endlessly practice running, jumping, and throwing. Gradually their timing and coordination increase, enabling them to become noticeably more proficient. They soon learn to judge the time to swing a bat in order to hit a ball or estimate the distance a ball will travel when thrown in order to catch it. Along with developing physical skills, children are also acquiring new ways to get along with their peers and beginning to understand the importance of rules. The interaction of these developing abilities accounts for the popularity of sports during middle childhood.

Gross-Motor Skills

Several skills that are acquired in middle childhood are seen in play activities typical of this period. Developmentally appropriate practices for school-age children should include opportunities to develop both gross- and fine-motor skills (Albrecht & Plantz, 1993).

- **Running.** By age five or six most children have mastered the form and power required to run. They have learned to start, stop, and turn, and can integrate these into their play activities.
- **Jumping.** Jumping requires a complex set of skills including balance, maintenance of equilibrium, and form. Jumping is usually not attempted by children until they have become fairly proficient in basic locomotion, but by age five most children have a good mastery of jumping skills.
- **Throwing.** At age five or six, there is a perceptible change in children's ability to throw. They learn to transfer their weight from one foot to the other during throwing. This weight shift, coupled with a horizontal movement of the arms and body, allows children to efficiently propel a ball forward. Most six-year-olds are able to perform an overhand throw.

Further practice and refinement of gross-motor skills allow children to participate in the popular activities of childhood: swimming, biking, roller-skating, ice-skating, jumping rope, baseball, and basketball.

Fine-Motor Skills

During middle childhood, most children master a variety of tasks requiring the use of small muscles. They learn to cut easily with scissors, draw, write or print accurately, and sew or knit. As their coordination increases further, they can learn to play musical instruments, engage in hobbies such as model-making, or play games such as jacks.

FIGURE 1-3   *"I like to play baseball." Lark, age 8*

Differences in Motor Skills

Boys and girls are fairly equal in their physical abilities during the middle child-hood years except that boys have greater forearm strength and girls have greater flexibility. Boys are often better at baseball, while girls excel in gymnastics. More and more girls are willing to try sports like baseball and when they are given ample opportunities to practice they, too, can catch and throw a ball accurately and hit home runs. Likewise, with training, boys can do well in activities that require flexibility, such as gymnastics.

Certain motor skills do not depend upon the amount of practice a youngster engages in. Some depend upon body size, brain maturation, or inherent talents. A good example of a skill dependent upon brain maturation is reaction time. A child's brain continues to mature into adolescence, therefore, older children usu-ally do better where this skill is necessary.

Inherent traits are also important in determining how well a particular child performs a motor skill. Body size, particularly height, gives some children an advantage when playing basketball. Children also vary in their ability to coor-dinate body movements. Some children find it easy to kick a soccer ball with accuracy while others find it almost impossible. Heredity accounts for children's basic skill at these activities but practice and experience can increase their pro-ficiency.

FIGURE 1–4   With practice, children can participate in difficult sport activities.

Implications for Child-Care Staff Members

Middle childhood is a time when children want to feel competent at whatever they do. In school they must use small muscles to be successful, while out of school they need well-developed gross-motor skills to participate in the sports, vigorous games, and strenuous individual activities that are so much a part of the school-age years. Since practice and experience help children enhance their inherited abilities and acquire new skills, it is extremely important that child care offer as many opportunities as possible. Child-care leaders can:

- provide a wide variety of activities requiring different skills and skills at varying levels.

FIGURE 1–5   Girls have greater flexibility than boys.

- allow children ample time to practice and refine new skills.
- encourage both genders to participate in all activities.
- offer children encouragement for their efforts rather than praise their achievements.
- encourage children to teach their skills to others.

Summary

A knowledge of the universal predictable stages of growth, as well as an understanding of individual patterns of timing, are essential for anyone involved in planning and operating a child-care program. The quality of the program may depend to a large degree on the extent to which all activities, procedures, and interactions are developmentally appropriate for the children who participate.

Human growth is affected both by maturation and learning. Maturation refers to a variety of abilities, characteristics, and limits that are inherited from parents. Learning refers to processes by which environmental influences and experiences bring about permanent change in thinking, feeling, and behavior. Children grow more slowly during middle childhood than they did in the preschool years. They may gain five pounds and 2½ inches. Boys and girls are about the same size up until age nine, when girls begin a preadolescent growth spurt. Variations in size are due to nutrition or heredity.

Obesity is a growing problem among children and can affect a child emotionally as well as physically. Overweight children are often unhappy because they are rejected or teased by their peers.

Causes of obesity are: heredity, activity level, overfeeding in infancy, types of food consumed, and attitudes toward food. In addition, specific events and psychological problems trigger overeating.

Child-care leaders can help children accept the way they look and also to understand that as they grow, they will change. Obese children need special attention to encourage them to change eating habits and to be more active.

School-age children may suffer from a variety of health conditions, both chronic and nonchronic. Child-care staff members can help children and parents learn to be responsible for meeting their health needs.

During middle childhood, children rapidly acquire a variety of new motor skills. Gross-motor skills include running, jumping, and throwing. Fine-motor skills include the ability to cut easily with scissors, draw, write or print accurately, and sew or knit. Boys and girls are fairly equal in their physical abilities during middle childhood except that boys have greater forearm strength and girls have greater flexibility. With training and opportunities to practice, the differences are lessened.

Child-care leaders can provide many opportunities for children to participate in a wide variety of activities requiring the use of large or small muscles. Leaders should also allow plenty of time for children to practice, encourage both genders to participate in all activities, encourage efforts rather than achievements, and encourage children to teach their skills to others.

References

Albertson, A.M., Tobelmann, R.C., Engstrom, A. (1992). Nutrient intakes of 2- to 10-year-old American children: 10 year trends. *Journal of the American Dietetic Association, 92,* 1492–1496.

Albrecht, K., & Plantz, M. (1993). *Developmentally appropriate practice in school-age child care programs.* Dubuque, IA: Kendall/Hunt Publishing Company.

Aristimuno, G., Foster, T., Voors, A., Srinivasan, S., & Berenson, C. (1984). Influence of persistent obesity in children on cardiovascular risk factors—the Bogalusa Heart Study. *Circulation, 69,* 895–904.

Dietz, W. Jr., & Gortmaker, S. (1985). Do we fatten our children at the television set? Obesity and television viewing in children and adolescents. *Pediatrics, 75,* 807–812.

Freedman, D., Srinivasan, S., Valdez, R., Williamson, D., & Berenson, G. (1997). Secular increases in relative weight and adiposity among children over two decades: The Bogalusa Heart Study. *Pediatrics, 99*(3), 420–426.

Gortmaker, S., Dietz, W. Jr., Sobol, A., & Wekler, C. (1987). Increasing pediatric obesity in the United States. *American Journal of Diseases of Children, 141,* 535–540.

Hartup, W. (1983). Peer relations. In Paul H. Mussen (Ed.). *Handbook of child psychology: Vol. 4. Socialization, personality and social development.* New York: John Wiley & Sons, Inc.

Johnston, F. (1985). Health implications of childhood obesity. *Annals of Internal Medicine, 103*(6), 1068–1072.

Lowrey, G. (1986). *Growth and development of children* (8th ed.). Chicago: Year Book Medical Publishers.

Lucas, A. (1991). Eating disorders. In M. Lewis (Ed.). *Child and adolescent psychiatry: A comprehensive textbook.* Baltimore: Williams and Wilkins.

Newacheck, P., & Taylor, W. (1992). Childhood chronic illness. Prevention, severity, and impact. *American Journal of Public Health, 82*(3), 364–371.

Serdula, M., Ivory, D., Coates, R., Freedman, D., Williamson, D., & Byers, T. (1993). Do obese children become obese adults? A review of the literature. *Preventive Medicine, 22,* 167–177.

United States Bureau of the Census. (1997). *Current population reports.* Washington, DC: U.S. Department of Commerce.

Student Activities

1. Ask the children in your child-care group to draw a picture of themselves and one best friend. Do they show themselves as taller or shorter than the friend? Is there any noticeable difference between the attractiveness of their own image and that of the friend's?

2. Write a paragraph describing your appearance when you were six. Include the kinds of activities you engaged in during your out-of-school time. Next, describe yourself when you were eleven. In what ways did your development follow the description in this chapter? In what ways did it differ?

3. Watch two hours of Saturday morning children's television programs. Count and list the commercials for food that are shown. How many are for high-fat, high-sugar, or high-salt foods? Do they show children having fun while consuming these foods? Discuss the impact these commercials might have on children.

4. Survey the neighborhood near your home or child-care center. Are there places where children can play outdoors? How do you think the environment affects the children who live there? What could be done to increase opportunities for physical activities? Share your information with your classmates.

Review

1. Why is it important for child-care leaders to have a knowledge of predictable stages of growth and an understanding of individual patterns of timing?
2. Differentiate between maturation and learning.
3. What is another way to describe the dichotomy of influences on human development?
4. How much will an average well-nourished child gain in weight and height per year? The typical ten-year-old will weigh _____ pounds and be _____ inches tall.
5. Boys and girls are about the same size for part of the middle childhood years. At what age do girls begin to increase in size faster than boys?
6. List the causes of obesity in children.
7. In what ways can child-care personnel help children who are different from the norm in body size or who are obese?
8. List eight motor skills developed by children during middle childhood. In what ways do children use these skills in their daily lives at school or at home?
9. In what ways do the motor skills of boys and girls differ?
10. What can child-care leaders do to help children enhance their inherited abilities and acquire new skills?

CHAPTER

2

Development In Middle Childhood: Cognitive

Objectives

After completing this chapter, the student should be able to:

- Discuss the major principles of several cognitive theories
- List the concerns expressed by critics of each theory as well as the points of agreement
- Describe ways child-care leaders can use each theory to enhance children's development
- Discuss the ways in which children develop and use language

Cognitive Theories

Cognitive theories are used to explain all the mental processes that enable children to think or acquire knowledge and how these processes affect the way they perceive and understand their experiences. How individual children function is dependent partly upon hereditary factors and partly upon their experiences. As children's brains grow and mature, they are able to use different cognitive skills to gather and process information.

The thinking processes of school-age children are markedly different from those of preschoolers. By middle childhood, children can selectively focus on tasks, that is screen out distractions and concentrate on the relevant parts of the

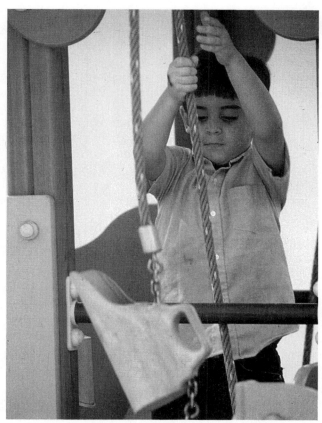

FIGURE 2–1   *Children's thinking changes and they are able to use logic to solve problems.*

information at hand. This capacity helps them to remember and also to reason in logical steps in order to solve a problem. School-age children also learn strategies for increasing memory. These are called storage strategies. They rehearse the information, organize it into memorable units, or use mnemonic devices such as rhymes or mental images to aid in remembering. Language develops rapidly and is used to communicate ideas, interact with others, and develop competencies that are required by the society in which they live. All of these abilities enable children to perform tasks beyond the reach of younger children.

Piaget

Swiss psychologist Jean Piaget is an important contributor to our understanding of how children think and learn. He began his work with children by helping to develop the first intelligence test. Piaget's task was to interview children and find the age at which most children could answer the test questions correctly. Instead, Piaget became curious about children's incorrect responses to items on the test, and observed that children who were the same age gave similar answers. This began a lifelong search to understand children's thought processes and how they change with age. Piaget (1952) concluded that cognitive development follows predictable patterns through four major stages. Each stage has certain characteristics that form the basis for how children approach and process intellectual tasks. Each person proceeds through these stages at his own rate, some slower, some faster, but everyone goes through them. Each stage is built on the skills of the previous stage. Piaget called the period from birth to two years the **sensorimotor** period. During this time infants use all their senses to explore and learn about the world around them. They put objects in their mouths, become attentive to sounds, poke or pat objects, react to tastes, and follow out-of-reach objects with their eyes. The information they gather is experience-based; they can only understand what they experience directly. Limited memory of an object or experience is retained when the object is removed or the experience ended.

By contrast, preschool children, two to seven years old, are in the **preoperational** period in which they can begin to think symbolically. They can remember experiences and objects independently of the immediate encounter. This can be observed in their rapidly developing ability to use language. Words help them to remember past events or to talk about an object. They also begin to engage in pretend play, not always needing the real props to support the play. The preschool child can play out elaborate scenarios in which he relives familiar interactions with parents or with siblings.

Piaget observed that during the preoperational period children often came to the wrong conclusions. He believed that this was because they could not perform "operations." By operations Piaget meant the ability to internalize an action, that is, that it can be carried out in the mind and that it can go in one direction or reverse into the opposite direction. The preoperational child cannot perform these operations.

Piaget observed the difficulty children had with one of his conservation experiments. He placed two identical cylinders with equal amounts of liquid before four-year-olds. He then added two cylinders, one tall and slim, the other short. He poured the liquid from one glass into the tall cylinder and from the other into the short one. When asked which glass had more, most children would indicate the taller one. They could not mentally reverse the event to realize that when poured back into the original containers, the amounts were equal. In addition to an inability to imagine reversibility, children can only focus on one dimension of a form at a time. In the case of the liquids, they focused on the height of the fluid in the glasses. Piaget called this **centering.**

Another characteristic of preoperational children is that they believe everyone thinks and acts the same way they do. They are egocentric, incapable of understanding how others think or feel.

Between the ages of seven and eleven children are in the **concrete operations** stage. They begin to think symbolically and can imagine reversing processes. The word "concrete" means that children can only carry out this process when the

Figure 2–2   Children learn by doing.

information is presented concretely. If a child is asked how many pieces of fruit there are if she has two apples and a friend gives her one, she will be able to figure out the answer. She can imagine two apples and then one additional one. She has experienced apples, can imagine them, and execute the solution. It would be difficult for her to figure out the answer to the question "What is two plus three?"

During this period, children become less egocentric and much more social. Increased language skills enable them to interact more effectively with their peers and to begin to understand the views of others. The need to be a part of a group or to have friends requires discussion and negotiations over play activities. In the process children learn that others do not always think or feel the same way they do.

Piaget's last stage, **formal operations,** occurs between the ages of eleven and fifteen. During this period, adolescents are able to consider hypothetical problems without concrete examples. They are also not limited by having to consider the here and now, but can imagine situations they have not yet experienced or are abstract. Thus, adolescents begin to ponder questions about the effects of global warming or how important is it to preserve wilderness areas for future generations to enjoy.

Several general principles underlie the concepts of Piaget's theory and are important to fully understand his perception of how children think and learn.

1. Children are active participants in the development of their own intelligence. Piaget believed that children actually *construct* their knowledge of the world through their activities. Experiences are the raw ingredients from which they organize and structure their knowledge, implying that the process takes place within the child rather than being transmitted from the outside. Through experimenting with the objects and experiences in their environment, children actually create their own intelligence.
2. The development of intelligence is the result of a progression through stages. Each stage builds a foundation for the next stage. There is no finite division of the stages since each stage may carry vestiges of the previous period.

3. Due to differences in maturation rate, individuals will progress through the stages at different rates. However, each individual goes through the same stages in the same order.

Evaluation of Piaget's Theory

Piaget's ideas changed the way children's intellectual development is perceived, focusing more on how children come to know rather than on what they know (Berger, 1995). Yet, there are criticisms from those who point to the formal nature of his experiments. These critics state that when children are closely watched in everyday situations, different interpretations of their abilities are possible. Some skills that Piaget relegates to later stages are clearly present in earlier ones. Therefore, critics contend that Piaget must have been wrong about just how early some cognitive skills develop.

Another concern of those who have looked closely at Piagetian theory is that children's abilities are not homogeneous within a given stage. In fact, each stage is entered gradually with vestiges of the previous stage remaining for a period of time. Additional factors affect a child's ability to think consistently at an expected level for his stage of development. Hereditary differences in abilities and aptitudes, as well as timing of maturation, play an important part. Environmental factors, such as the kinds of experiences children are exposed to and the kind of education they receive, also influence the rate of intellectual development.

The criticisms of Piaget's theory do not negate the importance of his ideas, however. We do know that children proceed developmentally from one stage to the next, changing their thinking processes as their maturity and experiences dictate. They continue to learn, taking in new information, organizing it, and deciding how it fits in with previous information.

Implications for Child-Care Staff Members

Piaget never claimed to be an educator, yet his theory is widely used to formulate educational programs for children. His theory does provide a framework from which appropriate learning experiences can be designed.

- Provide many different objects and experiences for children to explore so they can incorporate them into their symbolic thinking process at a later time. There needs to be a balance between unstructured materials and guided ones. Art materials, sand and water, and building materials are examples of unstructured activities. Experiences such as cooking, in which children must follow a recipe, and classifying or seriating a group of objects are guided activities.
- Plan activities that are age-appropriate for the level of ability of most members of the group. In addition, add activities that meet the needs of individual children.
- Allow plenty of time for children to explore freely and engage in play activities. Through play children have an opportunity to test out their own ideas and find out what is true and what is not.

FIGURE 2-3   *"Me doing my reading book." Sarah, age 6*

- Provide experiences that allow children to solve their own problems and make decisions.
- Set up situations in which children can exchange ideas, thus learning that others may think differently from themselves.

Behaviorist Learning Theory

John B. Watson (1967) saw the need for a more exact study of psychology. He believed that in order to be a true science, hypotheses should be tested and measured. The only way that could be done was to measure those things that could be observed; behaviors and words rather than feelings or thoughts. His concepts were popular since they were different from the psychoanalytic theory prevalent at the time.

Watson studied Pavlov's (1960) **classical conditioning** experiments with animals and then used those ideas to formulate his own theory of human conditioning. In classical conditioning, a stimulus (anything that elicits a response, either a reflex or voluntary action) is repeatedly followed by a specific response (behavior). Dogs salivate when they see their food. Pavlov added a ringing bell along with the presentation of the food. After several repetitions, the dogs would salivate when they heard the bell. The result is a connection that allows the response to occur without the need of the stimulus. An example is our response to a favorite food. When we are presented with that food, the sight and the smell cause us to salivate in preparation for tasting. When we see pictures of that food in a magazine or on television, we often have the same reaction—we salivate.

Watson was also influenced by the writings of John Locke (1959) who saw human infants as a "tabula rasa," a blank tablet upon which life experiences write a script. According to Watson, human behavior could be shaped by controlling events children were exposed to and by offering rewards for proper responses. Give children appropriate rewards and the desired behavior will follow. A parent who says "You are being so patient waiting while I pay for our groceries" is giving an appropriate reward to her child.

B.F. Skinner (1953) used both Watson's and Locke's (1959) ideas to formulate his theory. He proposed that infants are "empty organisms" that can be filled with carefully controlled experiences. He agreed that behavior could be changed by conditioning, but saw another type of conditioning that plays a larger role. He called it **operant conditioning.** Children play an active part by operating or acting on their environment and are reinforced for their behaviors. When a behavior is followed by a pleasant response (reward), it is likely to be repeated. If the consequence of a behavior is unpleasant, it is not likely to be repeated. Therefore, a system of positive or negative reinforcers can be used to shape an individual's behavior. Teachers who tell children they have done a good job putting away their materials are using a positive reinforcer. At the next cleanup time, the children are more likely to go about the task willingly.

Albert Bandura (1977) contributed another dimension to our understanding of how learning takes place. He felt that some behaviors could not be explained as a simple conditioned response to a direct stimulus but occur through less direct learning. He believes children observe others behaving in given ways and then pattern their own behavior accordingly. This type of social learning is more likely to occur when one is uncertain or unsure in a situation and when the object of observation is admired or is seen as powerful. Called **modeling,** it is a technique used by parents and teachers to increase the likelihood of acceptable behavior in children. In other words, model the behavior that is expected of children. It may also explain why four-year-olds pretend to be Superman or why teenagers want to dress like their favorite rock star. They are imitating the behavior of people they admire.

Social learning changes as individuals mature. One has to be attentive to the behaviors of others, store the information for future retrieval, possibly mentally rehearse the behavior, and then use the information when needed. The consequences of behaviors are also noted. The individual then can test out alternative behaviors and choose the one with the best outcome. A school-age child observes that when he gets mad and leaves a game, his friends do not ask him to play next time. He will try to curb his anger in order to be included.

Evaluation of Behaviorism

Learning theories have contributed a great deal to the study of how behaviors are shaped (Berger, 1995). The emphasis on the connection between stimulus and the resulting observable response allows a different interpretation of some kinds of behaviors. Previous notions that behavior is the result of deep-seated emotional problems could be revised by observing the environmental causes of some behaviors. Behavior can then be changed by changing the environment's response.

Learning theory has also contributed to a more scientific study of human development. Researchers are pressured to refine their hypotheses, define their terms, devise replicable tests for their hypotheses, and avoid reliance on concepts that cannot be tested. On the other hand, there are valid criticisms of learning theory. The emphasis on observable behavior and external influences does not take into account the inner life of children. Some behaviors result from complex relationships between biological maturation, an individual's thought processes, and the struggle to make sense of new experiences. If only observable behaviors are taken into consideration, there would be an incomplete picture of the wide range of influences on human behavior.

When behaviorist learning theory was first proposed, there were claims that behavior modification through a system of rewards and punishments was manipulative. Present-day critics still voice the same concerns and also object to the kinds of reinforcers that are sometimes used by parents or teachers.

Implications for Child-Care Staff Members

Behaviorist theory provides some specific guidelines for adults who work with children.

- Carefully arrange the learning environment. Since the importance of the environment is stressed in behaviorist learning theory, anyone who works with children can use this information to arrange the setting to bring about positive responses. This means that the placement of furniture, the ways in which activities are presented, and the ways in which adults interact with children all have to be carefully considered based upon expected results.
- Use appropriate reinforcers to bring about desired results. Carefully consider the implications of reinforcers and choose those that will enhance positive, rather than negative, behaviors.
- Model the behavior that is expected of children.
- Provide opportunities for social learning to take place among peers. Children are powerful models and can have extensive influence on one another.
- Help children find alternative behaviors to those that are generating negative responses from others.

Sociocultural Theory

Only recently have the writings of Lev Vygotsky (1978, 1987), a pioneer in the study of sociocultural influences of learning, become available. Studying sociocultural aspects of development as a means for helping children in a multicultural society is helpful. Vygotsky's theory assumes that social interaction and children's direct participation in authentic cultural activities is necessary for their optimum development. There are several main ideas that follow this basic assumption.

Cross-cultural Variation.   Cultures differ from one another in the tools they use and the kinds of activities that are important. Cognitive competencies result from the interaction of children with more mature members of their society. Parents and others instruct children in acquiring the knowledge and skills that are valued in their society. A child in a rural area of China will be encouraged to learn vastly different skills from one living in a housing project in New York City.

Scaffolding.   The child is seen as actively constructing himself, constantly adding to his knowledge and skills (Berk & Winsler, 1995). The social environment is the necessary scaffold, or support system, sustaining the child as he moves from one intellectual level to the next. Parents and teachers carefully structure a child's participation in a series of learning experiences so that learning is facilitated.

Language.   Language plays a crucial role in the development of cognitive abilities since it is the basis for social interactions between adult and child or between children. Through communication children can be guided to acquire the practical skills needed in their society. Communication also allows the individual to make mental contacts with others and provides a means for interpreting, storing, and using social experiences.

Zone of Proximal Development.   The zone of proximal development is the hypothetical environment in which learning and development take place (Berk & Winsler, 1995). It can be further described as the region between what a child can learn by himself and what he can learn through the guidance and tutoring of a more competent member of his society. Through carefully chosen and planned activities, the child gradually moves from assisted performance to independent performance. Crucial to this process is sensitivity to the child's level of competence and a means to encourage the child to move to the next level. When teachers or parents help a child to acquire a new skill they may begin with a demonstration, then carefully guide the child through the steps and encourage the child as he performs on his own.

Evaluation of Sociocultural Theory

Sociocultural theory has added a new dimension to the study of children's development, particularly in understanding diversity (Berger, 1995). It has increased knowledge of the ways in which cognitive development varies depending on the values and makeup of different societies. It further emphasizes the importance of understanding each culture's values and beliefs and their effect upon children's competencies.

Although the importance of Vygotsky's theory is recognized, present-day researchers are cautious in trying to generalize research findings from one culture to another (Cole, 1992). On the other hand, there is recognition that children's competencies should be examined through procedures that are relevant within their culture.

One limitation of sociocultural theory is that it does not take into account developmental processes that are not social. Some processes are the result of biological maturation. Another limitation is that Vygotsky did not consider how much children affect their own learning environment. According to Rogoff (1990), children often choose their own activities or their mentors. They often reject or resist help and support from parents or teachers.

Implications for Child-Care Staff Members

Most child-care centers will serve children who come from more than one cultural group and who, as adults, will live in an increasingly diverse society. It is important, therefore, that they learn to function comfortably in a multicultural environment without losing their identity within their own group. Child-care staff members can help them achieve that goal in the following ways:

- Learn more about different cultures and be sensitive to cultural values, ways of interacting, and linguistic differences.
- Include families, integrating their values and culture into teaching and learning experiences.
- Encourage children to learn about and appreciate cultures other than their own.
- Help each child to acquire the competencies that are important in his culture as well as those that are necessary in broader society.
- Carefully choose and plan activities that will gradually move children from assisted performance to independent performance.
- Cultivate each child's communication skills as an important tool of learning.
- Establish a meaningful relationship with every child since it is through the interaction between adult and child that much learning will take place.

Language

Middle childhood is a time when the ability to use language to enhance cognitive skills and to manipulate social situations increases rapidly. Children acquire as many as 20 words a day, achieving a vocabulary of 40,000 words by the fifth grade (Anglin, 1993). The list of words they understand and use may include some they have not experienced directly, but understand through reading, conversation, television, and computers. They deduce the meaning of a word through knowledge of the context in which it is used.

School-age children define words differently than they did as preschoolers. When asked to define a word, preschool children give examples that are based on perceptions. "An orange is something to eat that tastes good." A school-age child will likely be more logical by saying "It's a fruit." Preschoolers also define words by using action-based statements, while older children analyze the relationship to other words. A four-year-old will say, "Under something is where I hide my toys from my brother." A nine-year-old might say, "Under is the opposite of over" (Holzman, 1983).

Children practice their language skills by trying to refine grammatical construction. By age six most children understand and use grammar correctly, but during middle childhood further improvement takes place. Preschool children acquire new language constructions by adapting what they have previously learned. They discover that "ed" is added to make a verb past tense and therefore say, "He goed." Gradually, school-age children learn the variations of verb forms and use them correctly. Older children may not always use correct grammar even though they know it. In conversation with their peers, for instance, they may say, "Me and my mom had a fight." In school they are able to correctly say, "My mom and I had a fight."

School-age children become adept at pragmatic uses of language. They choose words, modify sentences, or change voice inflections to fit the listener in a particular situation. They may use simpler words and shorter sentences when talking to a younger sibling than they would with their friends. The best example of pragmatic use of language is seen in the jokes told by elementary school children. In order to be successful humorists, they need to recognize what the listener will think is funny and to remember the exact words (Yasilove, 1978).

Further indication that school-age children use language pragmatically is the switch to different forms as the occasion dictates. When making a request of possibly reluctant adults, they are careful to use a polite form of request. "Could I please go to the movie with Rachel?" A more extensive switch in language is what is called **code-switching** (Holzman, 1983; Yoon, 1992). This means a complete change of form when addressing adults and another when addressing cohorts. They may use **elaborated code** in the classroom and change to a **restricted code** when they are on the playground (Bernstein, 1971, 1973). Elaborated code has a more extensive vocabulary, is correct grammatically, and is longer. In contrast, restricted code is more limited and may rely on gestures and voice intonation to communicate meaning. While they are required to use standard English in the classroom, children also learn the idiosyncrasies of speech specific to their ethnic group or in common usage in their particular region of the country. Some forms differ in minor ways, such as regional accents or colloquialisms in common usage. Certain speech patterns or accents are so distinctive that they can identify the region where a person lives or grew up. A Southern accent is easily distinguished from a Texas drawl. Another variation is Black English, or Ebonics, which uses double negatives. "Nobody couldn't come to the party." Even greater problems are faced by children for whom English is not their primary language. These children are forced to use a language they may barely understand and get behind in school. They may also be mercilessly teased by other children for their accent or misuse of words.

Implications for Child-Care Staff Members

The importance of language in children's development cannot be underestimated. Good language skills are needed for success in school, and children who can communicate their needs and feelings clearly get along better with their peers and adults. Perhaps even more important, good language skills are needed for many of the jobs these youngsters will pursue in the future.

- Provide a wide variety of reading material: books, magazines, comic books, newspapers.
- Read to children frequently and encourage them to read alone or with others.
- Plan a variety of activities and experiences that help children expand their vocabularies and their ability to communicate clearly with others. Remember that listening is a part of communicating.
- Model correct English when speaking to children, while accepting children's forms of speech.
- Provide opportunities for children to use their primary language in ways that enhance their self-esteem. Encourage them to teach useful words or phrases to others. Allow them to use their speech forms in creative ways when writing stories, plays, or poetry.
- Include written or oral language in culturally based activities.

Summary

The thinking processes of school-age children are markedly different from those of preschoolers. Swiss psychologist Jean Piaget is a major contributor to our understanding of how children think and learn. Piaget believed that intelligence is the result of progression through four stages: the sensorimotor period, from birth to two years, the preoperational period, from two to seven years, the concrete operations period, from seven to eleven, and the formal operations period, from age eleven to fifteen. Another general principle of Piaget's theory is that children are active participants in the development of their own intelligence. A third principle is that differences in the rate at which individuals pass through the stages are due to variations in maturation rate.

Behaviorist theory grew out of a need for more precise studies of human development and was proposed early in the twentieth century by John Watson. Watson's ideas were based on the classical conditioning of Ivan Pavlov and pointed to the connection between a stimulus and response. When a stimulus is followed by a pleasant response, the behavior is likely to be repeated; if the response is unpleasant, the behavior may disappear. B.F. Skinner started with Watson's ideas, but went a step further. He proposed another type of conditioning, operant conditioning. He observed that children operate on their environment and are reinforced. When the reinforcer is pleasant, the behavior will be repeated, and when unpleasant it is likely not to be repeated. Albert Bandura also agreed with behaviorist ideas, but felt that some behaviors could not be explained by simple stimulus and response mechanisms. He saw that some behaviors occur as a result of less direct teaching, through observation of a model and then subsequent imitation of that behavior.

Sociocultural theory, proposed by Lev Vygotsky, has only recently been widely disseminated. Vygotsky assumed that social interaction and children's direct participation in authentic cultural activities is necessary for their optimum development. He pointed to the need to understand cross-cultural variation, the kinds of tools and activities different societies use to help children develop the competencies they will need as adults. Vygotsky believed that children construct themselves, adding to their knowledge and skills. Later researchers labeled this scaffolding. Vygotsky also pointed to the importance of language since it forms the basis of social interactions between adult and child. According to Vygotsky, the zone of proximal development is the hypothetical environment in which learning and development take place.

Middle childhood is a time when the ability to use language to enhance cognitive skills and manipulate social situations increases rapidly. Children acquire as many as 20 words a day, achieving a vocabulary of 40,000 words by the fifth grade.

Children practice their language skills by trying to refine grammatical constructions. They are adept at pragmatic uses of language, choosing words, modifying sentences, or changing inflections to suit particular situations. Children also demonstrate their pragmatic use of language when they switch to different forms as an occasion dictates. Code-switching is a complete change of form when addressing adults and another when addressing peers.

References

Anglin, J.M. (1993) Vocabulary development: a morphological analysis. *Monographs of the Society for Research in Child Development, 58* (10, Serial No. 238).

Bandura, Albert. (1977). *Social learning theory.* Englewood Cliffs, NJ: Prentice-Hall.

Berger, K.S., & Thompson, R.A. (1995). *The developing person through childhood and adolescence* (4th ed.). New York: Worth Publishers.

Berk, L.E., & Winsler, A. (1995). *Scaffolding children's learning, Vygotsky and early childhood education.* Washington, DC: National Association for the Education of Young Children.

Bernstein, B. (1971, 1973). *Class, codes, and control.* Vols. 1, 2. London: Routledge and Kegan Paul.

Cole, M. (1992). Culture in development. In M.H. Holzman, M. (1983). *The language of children: Development in home and in school.* Englewood Cliffs, NJ: Prentice-Hall.

Holzman, M. (1983). *The language of children: Development in home and in school.* Englewood Cliffs, NJ: Prentice Hall

Locke, J. (1959). *Essay concerning human understanding.* Collated and annotated by A.C. Fraser. New York: Dover Publications.

Pavlov, I. (1960). *Conditioned reflexes: an investigation of the physiological activity of the cerebral cortex.* (G.V. Anrep, Ed. and Trans.) New York: Dover Publications.

Piaget, J. (1952). *The origins of intelligence in children.* (M. Cook, Trans.). New York: International Universities Press.

Rogoff, Barbara. (1990). *Apprenticeship in thinking: Cognitive development in social context.* New York: Oxford University Press.

Skinner, B.F. (1953). *Science and human behavior.* New York: Macmillan.

Vygotsky, L. S. (1978). *Mind in society: The development of higher psychological processes.* Cambridge, MA: Harvard University Press.

Vygotsky, L. S. (1987). *Thinking and Speech.* (N. Minick, Trans.). New York: Plenum.

Watson, J.B. (1967). *Behaviorism* (rev. ed.). Chicago, IL: University of Chicago Press. (Original publication dated 1924)

Yasilove, D. (1978). The effect of riddle-structure on children's comprehension and appreciation of riddles. Doctoral dissertation. New York University. *Dissertation Abstracts International, 36,* 6.

Yoon, K. (1992). New perspective on intrasentential code-switching: A study of Korean-English switching. *Applied Psycholinguistics, 13,* 433–449.

Student Activities

1. Observe a group of school-age children. Can you recognize any models the children are using to pattern their own behavior? Are the models real persons (familiar adults or their peers) or characters from television, films, or computer games? Why do you think they have chosen these particular models? In small groups, share your observations with classmates. Discuss the above questions.

2. Visit an after-school program serving children from five to eleven. Record the number of times the adults use positive reinforcers. What types of reinforcers seem to be most effective with this age level? Did they encourage repetition of the behavior? What negative reinforcers were also being used? Did they discourage the behavior? Share your findings with classmates and compile a list of responses that seem effective when working with school-age children.

3. In small-group discussions, ask members to relate their own methods of working with children to one of the theories described in this chapter. Do they choose one theory over others? Or do they tend to use each of the theories in an eclectic approach?

4. Plan two activities for a group of nine-year-olds that will help them increase their vocabulary. Share your plans with classmates.

Review

1. Why did Piaget observe that during the preoperational period children often came to the wrong conclusions?

2. Between age seven and eleven children progress to the stage of concrete operations. What new abilities have they acquired?

3. State three applications of Piagetian theory in the child-care setting.

4. How does operant conditioning, proposed by Skinner, differ from the social learning theory of Bandura?
5. What are some criticisms of behaviorist theory?
6. How is behaviorist theory used when planning an appropriate environment for school-age children?
7. What is meant by "scaffolding"?
8. What is meant by the "zone of proximal development"?
9. How can child-care leaders use Vygotsky's ideas in a multicultural community?
10. State three ways child-care leaders can help children increase their language skills.

3

Development in Middle Childhood: Psychosocial

Objectives

After studying this chapter, the student should be able to:

- Discuss the major principles of several theories of psychosocial development
- List the concerns expressed by critics of each theory as well as the points of agreement
- Develop strategies that enhance children's psychosocial development

Theories of Psychosocial Development

The world of children between the ages of five and twelve expands as they enter school and begin to experience the environment outside their homes. Increased physical and cognitive skills allow them more independence to explore their neighborhoods, visit friends' homes, and use community facilities such as playgrounds or clubs. In the process they have many adventures and encounter new people. Parents are often unaware of and have little control over the kinds of challenges their children face as they maneuver this new territory. How children manage will depend a great deal on how they feel about themselves and the kinds of moral values they have learned within their families. Several theories are used to explain how children develop their sense of identity and learn to be successful members of a society.

Psychoanalytic Theory

Sigmund Freud

Sigmund Freud (1938) was an Austrian doctor and the founder of the psychoanalytic theory of human behavior. While working with persons diagnosed as "hysterics," Freud evolved the theory that irrational behaviors had underlying hidden causes that came from unconscious sexual and aggressive drives that he called libido. He saw the psyche as having three parts: the **id,** the source of pleasure-seeking drives, the **ego,** or the rational aspect of personality, and the **superego,** which controls behavior through the development of a conscience. Freud also proposed that the id is present at birth while the ego and superego develop as one progresses through stages of development. In the process the ego functions as a mediating force between the desire to seek pleasure and the need to yield to the demands of parents and society. Each stage brings with it conflicts that a child must resolve. How well a child is able to do this will be determined by the skills and competencies acquired along the way. Freud delineated five stages of development:

1. **Oral: Birth to one year.**   During the oral stage, infants direct their physical and psychic energy toward gaining pleasure from the mouth. They suck anything that comes in contact with their mouth—breast, bottle, pacifier, blanket, fingers. When they are able to pick up objects, everything goes in their mouths. Gradually, through weaning and gentle urging from caring adults, they learn other ways to find pleasure.

2. **Anal: One to three years.**   During the anal stage, increased awareness of the body and the demands of toilet training focus the individual's attention to the anus as a source of pleasure. At first the child eliminates whenever or wherever he pleases, but gradually learns to meet the demands of his parents to eliminate at specific times and in specific places. Freud believed that personality characteristics formed as a result of how rigid or relaxed parents are during this process.

3. **Phallic: Three to six years.**   During the phallic period, the genital areas are the focus of pleasure and children become aware of physical differences between boys and girls. It is also during this period that children develop attachments to the parent of the opposite sex; boys are attracted to their mothers, girls to their fathers. Eventually they learn that they must control these feelings and resolve the conflict by identifying with the parent of the same sex. This leads to development of gender identity and sexual orientation, as well as internalization of family moral values.

4. Latency: Seven to eleven years.   The latency period, as the name implies, is a period of latent or quiet feelings. Children's sexual urges are unobtrusive and energies are directed toward school activities and sports. During this period children develop competencies and refine their self-images.

5. Adolescence: Twelve years to adulthood.   Adolescence brings changes in sexual organs and physical changes in the appearance of both males and females. Strong sexual urges cause the adolescent to struggle with how to satisfy those urges in socially acceptable and safe ways. Moral values incorporated during earlier stages are re-examined and tested against those of their peers, their religion, and society.

Evaluation of Psychoanalytic Theory

Many of Freud's ideas are so widely accepted that they are no longer attributed to psychoanalytic origins (Berger & Thompson, 1996). There is general agreement that unconscious drives affect some behaviors, although the source of those drives may not be attributed to sexual urges, as Freud proposed. Modified aspects of psychoanalytic theory are evident in research and popular writings about the importance of attachment between mother and infant, gender identity, and adolescent development.

Some facets of psychosexual theory, however, are no longer considered valid. There is little support for Freud's belief that the way in which conflicts during the oral and anal phases are resolved result in specific personality traits. Present-day developmental theory emphasizes that personality and behavior are affected more by a person's heredity, life events, and the culture in which he lives rather than on conflicts that occur in childhood. There is little support as well for Freud's belief in the struggle between the id and the superego. The strongest criticism of psychoanalytic theory is that it cannot be proven through controlled scientific research.

Psychosocial Theory

Erik Erikson

Erikson (1963) studied pyschoanalytic theory with Anna Freud, the daughter of Sigmund Freud. He later moved to Boston, where he started a psychoanalytic practice. Erikson's work included children from a wide variety of backgrounds. Some were from middle-class, professional families, others from poor families and some who were delinquent children. At first he found it difficult to apply psychoanalytic principles to his work with children who were not typically middle-class, but eventually he found that all children have some common characteristics. Erikson expanded Freud's stages of development to encompass the entire life span, with each stage characterized by a challenge or developmental crisis.

FIGURE 3–1   These boys are best friends.

Erikson's first five stages are similar to those of Freud, but Erikson added **three** additional stages of adulthood. The significant difference between the two, however, lies in Erikson's emphasis on one's relationship to the social environment rather than on the body. He called his ideas the psychosocial theory of development. At each stage of development the resolution of a crisis depends upon the interaction between the individual's personality characteristics and the support and guidance provided by the social environment. How successful or unsuccessful one is in resolving these crises will depend a great deal upon competencies and the support and guidance provided by parents and society.

1. Trust vs. Mistrust: Birth to one year.   During the first year babies either learn to trust that others will take care of their basic needs or that others cannot be depended upon. The important factors are the sensitivity to the infant's needs and the love and warmth shown by caregivers.

2. Autonomy vs. Shame and Doubt: One to three years.   The primary focus of this stage is to become independent by gaining control over bodily functions: toileting, feeding, walking, and talking. The crisis arises when the strong drive for autonomy must be balanced by the demands of parents. Too much control by adults results in feelings of inadequacy, followed by shame and doubt.

3. Initiative vs. Guilt: Three to six years.   During this period children want to attempt many tasks they observe their parents or other adults performing. They sometimes attempt activities that are beyond their capabilities or are outside the limits set by their parents. If given support and guidance by their caregivers, the result will be feelings of success and pride in their own initiative. If they are unsuccessful, they will be left with feelings of guilt.

4. Industry vs. Inferiority: Seven to eleven years.   During this middle-childhood period children expend all their energies on mastering new skills at home, in school, on the playground, and in their neighborhoods. When they are successful, they acquire the tools they will need for important societal tasks such as getting a job and getting along with others. When they are unsuccessful, feelings of inferiority set a pattern for possible failure throughout life.

5. Identity vs. Role Confusion: Adolescence.   This period is highlighted by adolescents' search for identity as individuals in a society. They must balance a desire to establish their own uniqueness with a need to conform to the standards set by the society or culture in which they live. Rebelliousness may lead to role confusion, and strict conformity to a stifling of individuality.

Erikson delineated three additional stages that follow the school-age years and extend into adulthood: Intimacy vs. Isolation, Generativity vs. Stagnation, Integrity vs. Despair.

Table 3–1   Psychoanalytic Theories of Psychosocial Development

Approximate Age	Freud	Erikson
3–6	Phallic stage	Initiative *vs.* guilt
	Oedipal situation	Attempt adult activities
	Identification with same-sex parent	Gaining independence
	Superego, conscience	Overstep parental limits, feel guilty
7–11	Latency	Industry *vs.* inferiority
	Quiet period, less sexual tension	Becoming competent is important
	Psychic energy goes into learning skills	Can feel inferior if unsuccessful
Adolescence		Identity *vs.* role confusion
	Genital	Considering own identity
	Seeking sexual stimulation and gratification	Establishing ethnic and career identities

Evaluation of Psychosocial Theory

Erikson's perception of human development is more widely accepted than psychoanalytic theory even though it is based on Freud's ideas (Berger & Thompson, 1995). Erikson's writings are more contemporary, not based on the Victorian culture of Freud's time. Many ideas taken from Erikson are currently applied to issues regarding care of infants, parenting problems, care of children in groups, and training of caregivers.

Implications for Child-Care Staff Members

Two themes are present in both Freudian and Eriksonian ideas about how children develop: the significance of childhood stages in the formation of personality and the importance of the manner in which adults respond to children's behavior during each of the stages. These lead to several specific implications for persons working with school-age children.

- Remember that adults are active participants in helping children resolve the conflicts inherent in each of the stages of development. Provide guidance and support so that the conflicts can be resolved in ways that enhance children's self-image.
- Include families in decisions concerning a child's problem behaviors. The behaviors have been formed within the context of family interactions and will be more easily changed with cooperation from family members.
- Support children's need for competence by providing opportunities for them to acquire new social skills and to practice already acquired skills.
- Support their need to be independent by allowing them freedom to make choices and do things without adult intervention. Let them plan and carry out many of their own activities. Also let them make their own rules within limits that do not interfere with others' rights.
- Let children know their competence and responsibility are valued.

Moral Development

The process of acquiring and using moral values and attitudes continues throughout life. At each step of development children learn that certain behaviors are acceptable while others bring disapproval and rejection. The years of middle childhood are particularly fertile grounds for learning the lessons taught by the family, culture, and society for several reasons. First, peer relationships become extremely important, sometimes taking precedence over family. Children want to be part of a peer group, so they learn to negotiate, compromise, and play "by the rules" in order to be included. Second, they have already acquired cognitive skills that allow them to think logically and even abstractly. They understand concepts of right and wrong and can consider moral issues related to their own behaviors. Lastly, their world has expanded beyond the family into the school and the neighborhood. Toward the end of middle childhood, children begin to look at broad moral issues that affect others: human rights, destructiveness of war, ecological devastation, global hunger.

Jean Piaget

Piaget's (1932) primary concern was the cognitive development of children, but he was also interested in how children begin to understand justice and develop a respect for social order. He believed that children's understanding of rules goes through stages as their thinking processes change. In the earliest stage, the preschool and early school-age years, children consider rules to be created by an all-powerful authority figure and that they are not to be changed. He called this stage **moral realism,** in which justice is whatever the authority decides at a particular time. By age 7 or 8, children reach another level. During this period, they interact with their peers differently, often with give-and-take reciprocity. They also change their ideas about authority, recognizing that punishments may be fair or unfair, depending upon the transgression committed. As children approach adolescence, around age 11 or 12, a new stage emerges. Piaget called this stage **moral relativism.** At this level, children are able to be more flexible, change rules, and discuss moral issues.

Lawrence Kohlberg

The most complete theory of children's moral development was proposed by Kohlberg, who used Piaget's theories as a starting point for developing his own theory of moral development. Kohlberg (1963) believed that children's moral thinking developed in stages along with the development of cognitive skills. As cognitive processes changed, the ability to consider moral questions also changed. To test his theory, he presented children with a set of hypothetical stories about moral dilemmas that required decisions involving human life, property rights, or human needs. He examined children's responses to these situations and concluded that children proceed through the following three levels of moral reasoning.

Level I, Age four to ten. Preconventional: Emphasis on punishment and rewards.

Stage 1. Might makes right   At this level behavior is labeled good or bad based entirely on the consequences of an action. Children obey authority in order to avoid punishment. "If you do that, you'll get in trouble."

Stage 2. Satisfy your own needs   Each person takes care of his or her own needs first and occasionally the needs of others. Children believe that if they are nice to others, others will be nice to them. "I'll invite you to my birthday party if you let me play with you."

Level II, Age ten to thirteen. Conventional: Emphasis on social rules of the individual's family, group, or nation.

Stage 3. Interpersonal concordance   Good behavior is behavior that others approve of and reward. Approval is more important than any other kind of compensation. Children value conformity to stereotyped images of what is majority behavior. A significant change occurs during this stage: children recognize intent that is attached to behavior. "He didn't really mean to ruin your building. He was just trying to help."

Stage 4. Law and order   Emphasis is on authority and obedience to the laws set down by those in power in order to maintain social order. Right behavior means doing one's duty, showing respect for authority, and recognizing the need to maintain social order. "It's not right to take things that don't belong to you. Besides, you might get arrested."

Level III, Age thirteen and older. Postconventional: Emphasis on universal moral values and principles.

Stage 5. Social contract   People understand that laws and rules exist to ensure individual rights. Right action is seen in terms of standards that have been examined and agreed upon by society. Aside from what has been democratically agreed upon, right is also a matter of personal values and opinions. Laws might be changed if a consensus of opinion can be reached. "I think we should change the rules of this game so the little kids can play."

Stage 6. Universal principles   People behave according to universal ethical principles. These principles are abstract, like the golden rule, and involve a basic right for everyone to be treated equally and with dignity. "I don't think anybody should be discriminated against. Everyone should be able to live where he wants or go to school where she wants."

Kohlberg found that individuals progress through the moral hierarchy very slowly. He found that most school-age children function at Stage 1 or 2. He believes that children must be at the cognitive level of adolescents to make moral decisions comparable to Stage 3. Only then will they begin to consider another person's intent before judging behavior as right or wrong. Once that level of thinking is reached, they may be able to go on to question authority and laws in terms of faithfulness to maintaining basic human rights. Each stage must be experienced before progressing to the next level and no level can be skipped. Some individuals may become fixed at a certain level and never move on to a higher one.

Evaluation of Kohlberg's Theory

Although Kohlberg's stages of moral development were praised originally by developmentalists as a way of understanding moral education, several researchers took a closer look.

Carol Gilligan (1982) pointed to the fact that Kohlberg's scheme was validated only on a group of males, ages ten, thirteen, and sixteen. When women were tested, they scored lower than males; women on average were at Stage 3, men at Stage 4. Moral development at Stage 3 is an interpersonal level, with emphasis on gaining

FIGURE 3–2 *"Me." Nicole, age 7*

approval for good behavior. Stage 4 is a more objective acceptance of rules. Gilligan argues that females are socialized differently than males; they are taught to value being considerate and preserving relationships. Therefore, they cannot be judged in the same way as males.

Elliot Turiel (1983; Turiel et al, 1991) pointed out the fact that Kohlberg used hypothetical situations, not the daily circumstances children typically confront. When Turiel used test situations more closely resembling children's own experiences, he found children can reason better about familiar settings. When playing games, for instance, they function at a higher level of moral thinking. Turiel also found that when children have a chance to discuss issues repeatedly, they make wiser decisions.

A further criticism of Kohlberg's theory is that his stages reflect Western values and cannot be applied to other cultures. Barbara Reid (1984, 1989), studying Samoan and European families in New Zealand, found that the needs of family members sometimes take precedence over observing moral principles that apply to everyone.

Implications for Child-Care Staff Members

Since middle childhood is a period when children are learning to find their way in the world outside their home, it is important to facilitate their ability to live within society's rules and to get along with others. Child-care workers can play an important part.

- Involve children in solving moral dilemmas that occur in their everyday experiences. Give them opportunities to discuss possible solutions and what the consequences of each decision might be.

- Provide children with opportunities to interact with children and adults of different age groups, exposing them to higher levels of moral functioning.
- Create an environment in which individual and family value systems are accepted. It is easy to accept value systems that are like one's own, but it takes more practice to accept those that are different.
- Model the kind of behavior expected of children. Behave in ways that are fair and just rather than imposing arbitrary rules that have no relation to values.

Summary

Sigmund Freud's psychoanalytic theory of development is based on the belief that there are hidden causes of behavior that originate in the unconscious. He also believed that libido, general sexual or sensual energy, is the driving force behind all human behavior. He saw the psyche as having three parts: the id, the ego, and the superego. The struggle between the pleasure-seeking id and the conscience-driven superego is facilitated by the mediating force of the ego. Individuals go through five stages during this process.

Erik Erikson based his theory on psychoanalytic principles, but felt that the resolution of the conflicts between the id and the superego takes place in the context of the social environment. How successful one is in resolving the crises of each stage depends upon the support and guidance of parents and society. Erikson delineated eight stages from birth to the end of life.

Although many facets of Freud's theory are widely accepted there are criticisms. Erikson's theory is more easily accepted since it is not based on the Victorian culture of Freud's time.

The process of developing moral values continues throughout life. Jean Piaget related moral development to the development of cognitive abilities. He wrote of the stage of moral realism during the preschool and early school-age years. By age seven or eight children reach another level, moral relativism. At this level children are able to be more flexible, change rules, and discuss moral values.

Lawrence Kohlberg formulated the most complete theory of children's moral development. He used Piaget's ideas as a starting point and related moral development to the acquisition of cognitive skills. Kohlberg proposed three levels of moral reasoning, with two stages at each level. Kohlberg found that individuals proceed through the stages slowly and that most school-age children function at the first level.

Criticism of Kohlberg's theory came from several researchers who noted that his research was done only with preadolescent and adolescent boys. Another criticism was that his test situations were hypothetical, not the actual day-to-day moral dilemmas children actually face. A further criticism is that his theory reflects Western values and therefore should not be applied to other cultures.

References

Berger, K., & Thompson, R. (1995). *The developing person through childhood and adolescence* (4th Ed.). New York: Worth Publishers.

Erikson, E.H. (1963). *Childhood and society* (2nd ed.). New York: Norton.

Freud, S. (1938). *The basic writings of Sigmund Freud.* (A.A. Brill, Ed. and Trans.). New York: Modern Library.

Gilligan, C. (1982). *In a different voice: Psychological theory and women's development.* Cambridge, MA: Harvard University Press.

Kohlberg, L. (1963). Development of children's orientation towards a moral order (Part 1). Sequence in the development of moral thought. *Vita Humana, 6,* 11–36.

Piaget, J. (1932). *The moral judgment of the child.* (M. Gabin, Trans.). New York: The Free Press.

Reid, B.V. (1984) An anthropological reinterpretation of Kohlberg's stages of moral development. *Human Development, 27,* 56–74.

Reid, B.V. (1989). Socialization for moral reasoning: Maternal strategies of Samoans and Europeans in New Zealand. In Jaan Valsiner (Ed.), *Child development in cultural context.* Toronto: Hogrefe and Huber.

Turiel, E. (1983) *The development of social knowledge: Morality and convention.* Cambridge, England: Cambridge University Press.

Turiel, E., Smetana, J., & Killen, M. (1991). Social context in social cognitive development. In William M. Kurtines & Jacob L. Gewirtz (Eds.). *Handbook of moral behavior and development: Vol 2, Research.* Hillsdale, NJ: Erlbaum.

Student Activities

1. Ask several school-age children to discuss some moral dilemmas they are likely to face in their everyday life. The following are some possible scenarios, but you can make up your own.
   a. You and your friend go to the store to buy some candy. You notice that your friend puts a candy bar in his pocket, but pays for a package of gum. What should you do?
   b. Your friend's little sister wants to play a game with the two of you, but you know that it will be too difficult for her. What will you do?
   Write down the responses the children make and then try to put them into one of Kohlberg's stages. Share the results with your classmates during your next class.
2. Ask your parents how they handled the following situations when you were growing up:
   a. toilet training
   b. thumb sucking
   c. questions about gender differences.
   Were their methods influenced by psychoanalytic thinking? If so, in what way?

Review

1. Freud saw the psyche as having three parts. List and define each.
2. How is Erikson's theory related to Freud's ideas and how is it different?
3. Briefly describe children's development according to Erikson during the following stages:
   a. Initiative vs. Guilt
   b. Industry vs. Inferiority
   c. Identity vs. Role Confusion.
4. State some criticisms of psychoanalytic theory.
5. What are some ways child-care leaders can apply Freudian and Eriksonian theory to their work with children and families?
6. Jean Piaget cited two stages in children's development of a sense of justice and respect for social order. What are they?
7. Kohlberg proposed three levels of moral reasoning. He called Level I, age 4 to 10, preconventional. State and describe Stage 1 and 2 at this level.
8. Why did Kohlberg believe that school-age children would find it difficult to make moral decisions having to do with a person's intent behind a behavior?
9. What was the basis for Carol Gilligan's criticism of Kohlberg's theory?
10. Another researcher who criticized Kohlberg's findings is Elliot Turiel. What were Turiel's concerns?

Section II

The People in School-Age Care

CHAPTER

4

The Children

Objectives

After completing this chapter, the student should be able to:

- Discuss the ways in which children develop friendships
- State the factors that are important to children's sense of self
- State the ways child-care leaders can help children form friendships and develop a healthy sense of self

---

Development of Self

Middle childhood is an important period when children develop a sense of who they are, what they can do, and how others perceive them. It is a time when the focus of their daily lives is on school and their self-esteem is closely tied to school success. Most children enter kindergarten eager to learn and are optimistic in their evaluation of self and their expectations for academic success (Stipek & MacIver, 1989). When they first begin reading and writing they have little idea of how successful they will be and cannot accurately assess their own competency. Young children assume they are successful because they put a lot of effort into their activities. As they get older and more experienced, they become more realistic. They

FIGURE 4–1   "Mom, me, Dad, and Rascal, my dog." Carissa, age 6

learn that different people have different abilities, enabling them to achieve at varying levels. They may find they are good at reading but not so capable at math.

A second way children develop a sense of self is in terms of their feelings of power. One source of power is their status with their peers. They measure and compare themselves to others. Are they liked and looked up to? Are they similar to their peers in appearance, in dress, in abilities? If they answer in the affirmative, they feel more powerful. A second source of power is inner control over their own behavior, in other words, being able to behave in ways that are looked upon favorably by their parents and society. They also have good self-esteem if they are accomplishing their goals and expanding their skills.

Acceptance by peers is a third way children refine their sense of self. At times school-age children can be cruel to their peers. Teasing and hostility are ways of testing feelings of power and learning just how much aggression will be tolerated. The ups and downs of childhood friendships are part of growing up, but children who are persistently exposed to cruelty or rejection have a difficult time. Rejected children are likely to develop negative attitudes about themselves, leading them to further unacceptable behaviors that bring derision and exclusion.

A final standard by which school-age children evaluate themselves is in terms of good or bad behavior. In the preceding chapter, moral behavior in middle childhood was described as being nice to others, behaving in ways that others approve of, and obeying rules or laws. These standards are used by teachers and peers to label children as good/nice or bad/not nice. Reputations acquired during middle childhood may affect an individual's behavior into adolescence and adulthood.

Race may also play a part in how children perceive themselves and others. Holmes (1995) studied kindergarten children in several schools in southern California. She found that the content of children's self-concepts and the way children

FIGURE 4–2   "This is me." Sarah, age 6

perceive themselves and convey information about themselves is linked to their cognitive maturation. At the kindergarten level they concentrated on specific, observable characteristics: gender, skin color, eye color, and language. The children described themselves by saying, "I have brown skin" or, "My eyes are brown." According to Holmes, older children at a higher cognitive level will portray themselves as having personal preferences or in terms of personality traits— "I'm pretty good at sports and have a lot of friends."

Holmes found that socialization experiences were important factors affecting children's subjective feelings about themselves. Children who had repeated negative experiences with others from a different group than their own may incorrectly assume that the negativism was due to their being African American or because they spoke Spanish rather than English.

In the same way, when children had limited interactions with others from a different group than their own and those interactions were negative they tended to categorize all persons from that group as being alike. They saw the group as homogeneous even though their experience had been with only a few members. One negative encounter led to a wrong conclusion about the group, thus giving rise to stereotyping and prejudice. "White people are all mean" or, "I don't like Blacks because they're always fighting."

Implications for Child-Care Staff Members

Children's feelings about themselves do not develop in a vacuum, but within the context of their daily experiences and their contacts with others. The importance of adults who are caring, who respond to children's feelings, and who facilitate self-esteem cannot be minimized.

- Provide authentic feedback to children rather than empty praise. Help them to evaluate their own skills realistically and to set feasible goals for themselves.
- Provide supportive intervention to children who have been rejected or are having difficulty being accepted by their peers. Offer special help to upgrade skills that will bring acceptance in the classroom or on the playground. Teach children how to be successful.
- Accept children's feelings rather than deny or belittle their importance. Be a sensitive listener.
- Avoid stereotypes and labels. Build on each child's uniqueness and strengths rather than limiting a child because of preconceived ideas.
- Provide children with positive encounters with persons from different racial and ethnic backgrounds.
- Encourage interracial groups to work together on activities that require cooperation and compromise.

Peer Groups, "The Society of Children"

Beginning in the preschool period, when children first understand the meaning of the word "friend," the need to have friends becomes increasingly important. As children's cognitive abilities change, so does their concept of friendship and its purpose. At first, there is a mutual dependence upon friends to share activities, carry on conversations, and provide support for attempts at independence from parents. Young school-age children choose friends who are the same gender, have similar interests, and share similar values. There is very little cross-gender fraternization and, in fact, even some antagonism toward members of the opposite sex. Girls pal around with girls, tell each other secrets, watch video movies, and talk on the telephone. The leader of a group of girls is chosen for her managerial skills, for having new ideas, and by being thoughtful, friendly, and organized (Edwards, 1994). Boys get together to skateboard, play videogames, or compete in organized sports.

Older school-age children rely upon friends for intimate conversations about problems, dreams, and expectations. Friends are seen as someone who will remain loyal and can be relied upon when life is difficult. The circle of friends gradually becomes smaller as children become more selective about the qualities of a friend. Often, by age 10 both boys and girls have a single best friend, although this exclusivity tends to occur more frequently with girls. By the end of middle childhood many girls have only one best friend upon whom they depend for all their social needs (Gilligan et al, 1990). Around the fourth or fifth grades, children begin to change their perceptions of the opposite gender and intergender interactions are more frequent (Adler, Kless, & Adler, 1992). By age nine everyone knows who is best friends with whom and would not think of trying to disrupt the pair.

This fraternity of friend relationships makes it difficult for children who have not found a companion. It is also heart-wrenching when one of a pair becomes more mature than the other and moves on to other alliances. The deserted partner experiences difficulty in finding a new companion.

Middle childhood is also a period when children form themselves into cliques, clubs, or gangs with the primary purpose of gaining independence from adults. Each group has its own vocabulary, dress code, rules, and activities (Opie & Opie, 1959). The group provides a mutual support system and a sense of solidarity as children learn to sharpen their social skills. Those who belong build self-esteem, but those who are excluded have difficulties socially and often academically as well.

Adler, Kless, and Adler (1992) have been following 200 elementary-age children in their community. Their findings, soon to be published in a book, illustrate the changes in children resulting from historical changes in society. They found that children are very aware of the importance of cliques and the power they give the members who belong. Some of the influence is positive, helping children learn appropriate social behavior and the consequences of misbehavior. Clique members tend to have similar characteristics. During middle childhood, they have similar interests or come from similar backgrounds. When the cliques continue into high school, they are identified as the "jocks," the "nerds," the druggies, the artists, the intellectuals. The clique provides children with a social identity and a sense of belonging.

Adler, Kless, and Adler (1992) found that cliques can be extremely limiting, prescribing very specific ways of behaving, dressing, or associating with others outside the group. Those outside the group can be derided for wearing the wrong clothes, being of a different race or religion, or being too studious. They may even carry on "negative campaigns" against chosen targets, heaping verbal abuse and humiliation on those who have been selected. In order to stay in the group and be accepted, as well as gain the feelings of power that result, members go along with this behavior. The consequence is that bigotry and racism become part of children's value system as well as increase their need to conform to standards that may conflict with values they have been taught at home.

In the case of gangs, the purpose may be even more negative. Not only are they outside the realm of adults, but they may even be antisocial. The result is that members engage in vandalism or criminal activities that put them in legal jeopardy.

The need to form groups may be observed in the child-care setting as well as in the community. The number of individuals involved is usually smaller than in school or in the neighborhood, but the same dynamics can be seen. Friendships form and are broken. Groups congregate, then change. But the need to belong remains strong in all children, with those who are not included feeling left out and unhappy.

Some children seem to make friends easily and are sought out while others find it extremely difficult. Certain social skills are necessary and may be in the formative stage during middle childhood. The first is the ability to understand that others may have different views than their own. Younger children are egocentric, believing that they are the center of the universe and that friends are there to satisfy them. "He's my friend because he plays with me" or, "He's my friend because he shares his toys with me." Older children begin to realize that others have needs and feelings too. In order to make and maintain a friendship they must make compromises to accommodate the other's needs or feelings. They may have to negotiate whether they want to go to a party or just hang out at the mall if they want to be together.

A second essential skill for making friends is the ability to recognize that others have separate identities and feelings of their own. Although children tend to choose friends who are like themselves, each has different characteristics and ways of reacting. It is a difficult lesson to learn that sometimes a best friend can be cross and want to be alone.

Finally, children have to understand that each encounter with others is part of a relationship. They tend to isolate incidents and fail to see the importance of their behavior in specific situations. If they lash out at another child in anger, they do not immediately recognize that that will have consequences for their ability to form a friendship with that person. They must learn that in order to have friends they must curb certain behaviors.

Implications for Child-Care Staff Members

Teachers and caregivers in after-school programs can have a significant impact on children's ability to make friends and be part of a group.

- Allow children opportunities to spend time with a friend without the pressure of having to engage in an activity. Let them "just hang out" in a corner of the room or an outdoor area.
- Encourage children to take another's point of view. Ask, "How do you think he feels when you call him that name?"
- Help children recognize their own psychological characteristics and that others can accept those qualities. An adult who says "Thanks for helping me understand that sometimes you just want to be alone," does that.
- Foster children's ability to examine the basis for friendships. Lead discussions about what makes a good friend and how to maintain friendships.
- Help individual children develop a plan to change behaviors that interfere with friendships. Discuss alternative ways of behaving, encourage the child to test out the behavior, and then evaluate the results. Give honest appraisal and rewards for positive outcomes. "When you asked how you could help rather than just pushing into his activity, he made a place for you."
- Discourage attempts to exclude individual children from activities. Suggest ways each can contribute.

Overview of Developmental Stages

The following summary of typical developmental characteristics of children during middle childhood should provide further help in understanding the children in your care. Each of the stages listed below covers information from the previous three chapters plus portions of this chapter. However, the list is merely a prediction of when these behaviors will occur. There will be wide variations from child to child, with some behaviors happening earlier in some children and later in others.

Five–Seven Years Old

Family Relationships
- Are more independent of parents, but still need rules
- Need assurance of being loved
- Have a sense of duty, take on family responsibilities
- Develop a conscience

Peers
- Begin to see others' point of view
- Rely upon their peer group for self-esteem
- Peer criticism of differences
- Two or three best friends
- Little interaction between boys and girls
- Learn to share and take turns
- Can participate in organized games

School
- Want approval from teacher for achievement
- Eager to learn and be successful in school
- Influenced by teacher's attitudes and values

Emotions
- Begin to inhibit aggression, resolve problems with words
- Use humor, often expressed in riddles, practical jokes, or nonsense
- Learn to postpone immediate rewards for delayed gratification

Thinking
- Usually clear about differences between fantasy and reality
- Can sustain interest for long periods of time
- Give more thought and judgment to decisions
- Good memory for concrete ideas, can remember two things for short periods of time
- Can understand and abide by rules

Language

- Learn that words and pictures represent real objects
- Can remember and relate past and present events
- Sometimes use language aggressively
- Understand more language than they use in their communication
- May tease others whose language is different from their own

Physical Development

- Girls are developing faster than boys
- Have good small-muscle and eye-hand coordination
- Are able to handle simple tools and materials
- Have a high energy level

Eight—Ten Years Old

Family Relationships

- Need parental guidance and support for school achievements
- Rely on parents for help in assuming personal and social responsibilities

Peers

- Overly concerned about conforming to peer-imposed rules
- Competition is common
- Antagonism between boys and girls often leads to teasing or quarrels
- Pronounced gender differences in interests
- Cliques of same gender are formed
- Spend a lot of energy in physical game playing

School

- Greater competition in school activities may lead to problems handling failure
- Still need teacher approval and attention

Emotions

- React to feelings of others, sensitive to criticism
- Look for friendly relationships with adults
- Make value judgments about own behavior, set standards for self
- Aware of the importance of belonging
- Strong conformation to gender role
- Independent and self-sufficient

Thinking

- Capable of sustained interest, can make plans, then carry them out
- Can begin to think logically about practical problems
- Begin to understand cause and effect
- Understand abstract concepts such as time and the value of money

Language
- Abilities to use language or to read vary widely
- Use language to communicate ideas, spend a lot of time in discussion
- Can use more abstract words
- Often resort to slang and profanity

Physical Development
- Physical skills becoming important in determining status and self-concept
- Girls are taller, stronger, and more skillful in small-muscle activities
- Have a high energy level
- Girls begin adolescent growth spurt toward end of this period
- Take responsibility for their own personal hygiene

Eleven–Thirteen Years Old

Family Relationships
- Ready to make own decision outside of the family
- Parental influence is decreasing
- Sometimes rebellious, but still need input on family values

Peers
- Peer group is a model and sets standards for behavior
- Seek information about appropriate gender roles from peers
- May conform rigidly to role assigned by peer group
- Team games become increasingly important
- Boys' and girls' interests are more divergent
- May develop crushes and hero worship
- Often self-conscious, may become boisterous to cover anxiety
- Interested in opposite gender, girls more interested than boys
- Faced with decisions regarding behavior: sex, drugs, and alcohol

School
- Worried when in a new school setting
- Begin to question adult authority, particularly in school
- School is often the focus for social experience

Emotions
- May lack self-confidence, be shy or introspective
- Worry about what others think, especially peers
- May be moody
- Physical changes heralding puberty may cause great stress
- Develop own value systems, although influenced by peers
- Seek self-identity, may result in rebellious behavior

Thinking

- Can now move from dependence on concrete thinking to abstract concepts
- Can apply logic, solve problems
- Can consider more than one solution to problems

Language

- Has a good command of spoken and written language
- Can use language to discuss feelings, thus bringing about self-understanding

Physical Development

- Boys begin adolescent growth spurt
- Adolescent growth at peak in girls, changes in body proportions
- In girls, secondary gender characteristics develop: breasts, menstruation
- Early maturing is related to positive self-image
- Boys have improved motor development and coordination, can excel at sports
- Master physical skills that are necessary for playing games

Summary

Middle childhood is an important period when children develop a sense of who they are, what they can do, and how others perceive them. Since the focus of their daily lives is school, their self esteem is closely tied to school success.

A second way children develop a sense of self is in terms of feelings of power. One source of power is their status with their peers. Another is an inner control over their own behavior.

Acceptance by their peers is a third way children refine their sense of self. School-age children can be cruel to their peers as they test their own power. Children who are often the target of teasing have a difficult time, further eroding their self-esteem.

The final standard by which school-age children evaluate themselves is in terms of good or bad behavior. Often reputations acquired during middle childhood may affect the individual's behavior into adolescence and adulthood.

Race also plays a part in how children perceive themselves and others. Children first describe themselves in terms of observable characteristics. Socialization experiences are important factors affecting children's subjective feelings about group members.

Negative encounters with persons of a different race or ethnic background can lead to a belief that all persons of that group have similar characteristics. This is the basis for stereotyping and prejudice.

Beginning in the preschool period, when children first learn the meaning of the word "friend," the need to have a friend becomes increasingly important. Young school-age children choose friends of the same gender and age who have similar interests and values. Older children rely upon friends for intimate conversations about problems, dreams, and expectations.

Children usually have one best friend and by age nine everyone knows who is best friends with whom. Later in middle childhood, children form themselves into cliques, clubs, or gangs with the main purpose of gaining independence from adults.

Cliques provide children with a sense of belonging and a feeling of power. Cliques can be limiting in that they prescribe specific ways of dressing or behaving. In the case of gangs, the purpose may be to not only operate outside the realm of adult supervision but even be antisocial. They may engage in illegal activities.

However, the need to form friendships and to belong is strong. In order to make friends certain skills are necessary: the ability to understand that others have different points of view, the ability to recognize that others have separate identities, and to understand that each encounter is part of a relationship.

References

Adler, P.A., Kless, S.J., & Adler, P. (1992). Socialization to gender roles: Popularity among elementary school boys and girls. *Sociology of Education, 65*(3), 169–187.

Edwards, C.P. (1994). Leadership in groups of school-age girls. *Developmental Psychology, 30*(6), 920–27.

Gilligan, C., Murphy, J.M., & Tappan, M.B., (1990). Moral development beyond adolescence. In Charles N. Alexander & Ellen J. Langer (Eds.). *Higher stages of human development.* New York: Oxford University Press, Inc.

Holmes, R.N. (1995). *How young children perceive race.* Thousand Oaks, CA: Sage Publications, Inc.

Opie, I., & Opie, P. (1959). *The lore and language of children.* New York: Clarendon Press.

Stipek, D.J., & MacIver, D. (1989). Developmental change in children's assessment of intellectual competence. *Child Development, 60*, 521–538.

Student Activities

1. Observe children on a school playground or in a park. Notice how they group themselves. Are there mixed-gender or single-gender groups? How many children in each group? What are they playing? Write a short paper describing

your observation, relating what you saw to the information in this chapter. Compare your findings with those of your classmates.

2. In small groups, discuss your own perceptions of the following:
   a. Asians
   b. Blacks
   c. People who do not speak English
   Describe the experiences that have led you to your perceptions. Were some of your perceptions based on prejudices? What can you do to change your beliefs?

3. Ask the children in your child-care group to draw a picture of themselves. Bring the pictures to class. Choose two to share with classmates. Show the pictures and tell what you think the pictures say about the child's self-esteem.

Review

1. Describe the changes that take place in children's assessment of their school achievement.
2. It was stated in this chapter that children derive some of their sense of self through feelings of power. What are the sources of that power?
3. Explain the importance of peers in determining children's sense of self.
4. State three ways in which child-care leaders can help children increase their self-esteem.
5. Compare the criteria for choosing friends among young school-age children with those of older children.
6. What is the primary purpose of groups, clubs, and gangs? Are there other purposes?
7. What are the positive aspects of belonging to a clique or group? What are the negatives?
8. List and explain the three skills children need in order to make friends.
9. It was suggested in this chapter that child-care staff members allow children opportunities to "just hang out" with a friend. Why is that important?
10. What would you say to a child to achieve the following:
    a. encourage him to take another's point of view
    b. help him recognize his own psychological characteristics
    c. evaluate his attempts to change behaviors that interfere with friendships

5

Families: Where Children Are Nurtured

Objectives

After studying this chapter, the student should be able to:

- State changing definitions of a family
- Describe family forms
- Discuss the effects of each family composition on children
- Review the role of caregivers in relation to parents

The Changing Family

Historically, humans have always grouped themselves together in tribes, clans, networks, or families. In her book *Families*, Howard (1978) writes, "The trouble we take to arrange ourselves in some semblance of families is one of the imperishable habits of the human race." Although we continue to group together, as society changes the definition of **family** changes. The meaning most widely used by scholars in the past signified parents and their biological children whether dwelling together or not. Legal experts have also stressed the biological relationships but broadened the definition to include any persons related by blood. This definition is becoming less meaningful in today's surrogate parenting situations. Another definition would include a group of kin and others living together day by day. Some contemporary researchers broaden the definition even further. They state that a family is an attitude, an identification with and among a group of individuals who support and nurture one another. Kevin and Elizabeth, whose family portraits appear in this chapter, even included their pets as important members of their families.

When most of us hear the word *family* we still think first of the **nuclear** (intact) family or the **extended** family. The nuclear family is made up of mother, father, and child(ren) if any. The extended family has these plus grandparents, cousins, aunts, uncles. While the extended family is more typical of traditional societies such as China or India, the nuclear family is more common in North America. Currently, even the nuclear family is declining at an alarming rate, however. Current statistics suggest that only 7 percent of American families still have this arrangement.

Many families today are headed by a *single parent* and may be indicative of changes in family composition. In 1996, 14 million children lived in a single-parent household headed by the mother and 2 million lived with their father only. The rapid rise in this type of family is partially due to the number of children born to unmarried women, many of whom are teenagers. In 1996, 45 per every 1,000 children were born to unmarried women (Statistical abstract of the United States, 1996).

Since many divorced couples remarry, many children live in *reconstituted*, or *blended*, families. Other terms used to describe these families are *recoupled, refamilied, and binuclear.* These unions may bring together children of one or both former marriages or associations as well as children born of the new marriage. They are the "his, hers, and our" children.

An increasing number of households include grandparents or are headed by a grandmother and/or grandfather. These adults provide a valuable assistance, particularly in families that have experienced a divorce. They can emotionally support children during difficult times, perhaps add some income, and provide child care. In some cases, grandmothers become the only adult in the household if both parents are deceased, incarcerated, or are on drugs.

Another family form that is becoming more visible is the **interracial family** where the parents come from different ethnic groups. In the past few decades the number of these marriages has been on the rise. Some people call them the "rainbow families" since they mix persons of two or more ethnic groups. In addition, interracial families are created when parents choose to adopt a child from a racial or ethnic group different from their own.

A fairly recent development is the **homosexual family** composed of lesbian couples, homosexual male partners, or singles of these groups. Some of the children in these relationships are the result of previous marriages to heterosexual partners. More liberal adoption laws have allowed some children to be adopted into these families. A few children have been produced through artificial insemination.

In addition to understanding family forms, it is important to note that existing families change as the members grow and develop or as their circumstances shift. The first child may have grown up in a nuclear family, but his sibling is being reared by a single parent. A child whose divorced mother remarries may suddenly find himself with several new siblings. Whatever the form, the family is the first and therefore the most important determinant in children's development.

Effect of Home Environment on Children

In the past, it was assumed that the optimum environment for children's development was the two-parent family, one in which the father went to work and the mother stayed home to care for the children. However, we need to reexamine that idea since fewer families still fit that pattern. In many households both parents are working outside the home.

According to the United States Bureau of the Census, 59 percent of children between the ages of six and seventeen have mothers who are in the workforce (Statistical Abstract of the United States, 1996). Current research still seems to favor the intact, two-parent family as providing for the optimum development of children (Dawson, 1991; Amato & Keith, 1991). Children who grow up with two loving parents who have nurtured them from birth have fewer problems, do better in school, and are less likely to use drugs or get arrested when they are teenagers. The advantages these children enjoy stem from the fact that two adults share child-rearing tasks. Each can support the other parent or even take on tasks that may be difficult for one of them. Two-parent families often have a financial advantage over other family forms. In many, both parents are wage-earners allowing them to provide better housing, health care, or education for their offspring. When the mother is proud of her work, children have a role model for making their own choices in adulthood. All of these positives for the intact family neither guarantee optimum development of children, nor eliminate the possibility that other family forms can offer many of the same benefits.

Children who attend day care have some advantages as well. They can participate in supervised activities and have new experiences. They can make friends within a wider circle than is available in their neighborhood. They learn to get along with adults other than their parents. Children who stay by themselves after school also may feel they have advantages. Many relish the freedom to come home and do what they want. They grow in independence and self-esteem as they master emergency situations or do household chores.

In spite of the advantages, there remains concern over the tremendous stress that many working parents feel. Their most frequently voiced complaint is that there is never enough time. There is not enough time for housework, time to spend with the children, or time for each other. Fatigue and stress may cause family friction or result in adults taking out their frustrations on the children. Children may feel isolated because the adults have little energy left for being parents. Children may also feel abandoned or that their parents care more about work than about them. If the children do not attend child care but stay home alone after school, they may feel lonely and sometimes frightened.

FIGURE 5–1   "Radio, Dad, me, brother, brother, Mom." *Kevin, age 5*

Single-parent families are often compared unfavorably with two-parent families. The typical view is that they are weak or somehow "broken" and therefore
bound to create troubled children. This may not be the whole story. Columnist
Ellen Goodman, writing in the *Los Angeles Times* in January 1988 said, "I have a
young friend who will tell you, if you ask, that she grew up in an 'intact single-
parent family.'" The friend told her she had invented the term when she got tired
of hearing her family described in pathological terms. It is quite likely that many
children share some of the same feelings. However, when the family structure is
the result of a divorce, children may experience feelings of loss, insecurity, or
impermanence. Children of recently divorced parents often experience a period of
adjustment during which school achievement may go down or emotional problems surface. However, if contact is maintained with both parents, and if income
and living conditions remain stable, these children do as well as those in an intact
family. The reality is that in many situations, the mother becomes the custodial
parent, and family income is often far lower than during the marriage.

Children of mothers who have never been married can raise well-adjusted children, but the odds are against fatherless children. These children are deprived of
the special kind of child-rearing fathers can provide. Kyle Pruit, a professor of psychiatry at Yale University and author of *The Nurturing Father,* says that whether
roughhousing with a five-year-old or disciplining a delinquent teen, fathers have a
different parenting style. Boys and girls both need fathers. Boys need a role model.
Girls need a father with whom they can practice heterosexual relationships.

Probably the most serious difficulty for the single-parent family, especially
when headed by the mother, is the low economic status. Women still receive lower
salaries than men, often causing these families to live at or below a poverty level.
Single parents often suffer from "role overload" as they try to nurture their children, offer sensible discipline, and provide adequate financial support. Stressors
increase with more than one child or when illness strikes.

Frequently, when the words "single parent" are used, it is assumed that they apply to mothers. However, a growing number of men are granted custody of children. According to a 1992 count by the United States Bureau of the Census, there were 1,283,000 single-father households, comprising 4 percent of families. When fathers are motivated to provide a loving, nurturing environment, both boys and girls in father-only families do as well as those living with their mother (*Ebony*, 1995). However, boys are placed more frequently with their father than girls and they seem to do even better in a father-only family than if they lived with their mother. Part of the reason may be that fathers seek custody because they want to care for their children: mothers often are given custody whether they want it or not. Another reason that children do well in a father-headed household is that they often respond well to the male as an authority figure and are less likely to get into trouble. Finally, the income level of a father-led family is more likely to be higher than of a single mother. The children benefit from a higher standard of living.

Sometimes single parents resolve some of the problems of caring for their youngsters alone by moving in with their own parents. Although there are advantages to this arrangement, there are also additional stresses on the adults and the children. One study surveying children in various family configurations found that those living with both grandparents had more behavior problems such as dependence, disobedience, and aggression. They were also found to have poorer language skills (Hawkins & Eggebeen, 1991). This is less true in cultural or ethnic groups where the extended family structure is more commonplace. The adults in these families find ways to mitigate the problems of several generations living under one roof.

When divorced adults find new spouses, the remarriage and resulting blended family are usually seen as an opportunity to start over, to resolve the difficulties of a previous union or being a single parent. For the children, the experience can be positive, negative, or mixed. If the children have been living with their mother, the economic situation improves. Boys are sometimes helped by the presence of a stepfather, especially if he takes a personal interest in them. When the father remarries, there may be a more equal sharing of household chores and routines. Children in blended families often find they have more models and choices. In addition, they may have the opportunity to live in new places and have new experiences. All these are positives.

Many adjustments are difficult, however, and vary with the ages of the children. Younger children suffer more from loss of a close relationship with both parents. Some children continue to have problems of identity and self-worth in this type of marriage. School-age children may go through a period of lower academic achievement.

While interracial families are becoming more accepted, some still face difficulties. Many children are proud of their dual heritage and feel good about themselves when they are young and their world consists mostly of the home and family. Unfortunately, when they go to school or out into the community, some are the target of discrimination. Where the family lives may be a determinant. Many mixed families choose to live in large urban areas or neighborhoods where they

FIGURE 5–2   "My family." *Tai, age 7*

will be accepted. Small towns and rural areas tend to be less tolerant of differences. The economic status and educational background of the parents may also
determine a family's comfort in a particular community. It is easier if they fit in
economically. More educated adults choose their friends to avoid people who
cause problems. There are also a growing number of magazines and books that
help parents raise children in a biracial family.

One of the biggest problems for children growing up in an interracial family
is developing their own identity. They must learn to define themselves as being
of one group or another or even a melding of the two. They may be pressured
by parents or other adults to accept their identity as one or the other ethnic
group. They are sometimes discouraged from associating with children outside of
one of their background groups. When these children are encouraged to accept
their biracial origins, they usually develop a positive self-image. It also helps
when parents teach them to appreciate the cultural richness of both sides of their
family.

Homosexual families may also be the target of discrimination. Although homo-
sexuality is no longer considered a pathological state, society still looks upon
these relationships with hostility. Children may feel something is wrong with
them when they are the targets of negative attitudes. They may also consider
themselves different from schoolmates who have a "mom and a dad." Despite
this, a number of studies show that children in these situations can and do adjust
when given adequate support by the adults. If children have an opportunity to
seek out additional role models they have an easier time developing their own
identity.

Although family composition does have an effect on children's development,
the essential ingredients for emotionally healthy children can be found in any
group. Successful families have some common characteristics.

FIGURE 5–3   "My family." *Elizabeth, age 10*

- They are affectionate. Members express their love and caring for one another.
- They have a sense of place. Either they have a stable environment or they have a commitment to their place of origin.
- They pass on their cultural heritage.
- They connect with posterity. They honor their elders.
- They promote and perpetuate family rituals. Parents pass on traditions from their own past and encourage a sense of family continuity.
- They communicate with one another.
- They respect differences among their members.

As you can see, the ingredients for an effective family can exist no matter who makes up the group. Remember that as you work with children and families in your child-care center.

Poverty

A 1996 update of census figures indicated that 13,999,000 children lived in families that were considered below the poverty line. Female-headed households are most likely to live in poverty, either totally without child support from the father or

FIGURE 5–4   *"My family and TV," Rachel, age 5½*

receiving amounts that are inadequate to bolster the family income. The impact of poverty on children can be devastating, affecting them for the rest of their lives.

Children living in substandard conditions are likely to suffer from malnutrition and disease, are subject to abuse or neglect, and are injured or die more frequently from accidents than children in better environments. Poor children frequently live in housing where they are exposed to lead poisoning due to drinking water from lead pipes or breathing lead paint dust.

In addition to health risks, children in low-income neighborhoods are behind in academic achievement because their schools are poorly equipped and maintained, class sizes are large, and teachers are poorly paid and undermotivated.

Perhaps the most devastating of all is the toll that poverty takes on children's psychosocial development. Middle childhood is a time when children become acutely aware of their circumstances compared to those they see portrayed in films or on television. When their own neighborhoods are run-down and dangerous, they develop feelings of hopelessness and depression.

Helping Children and Their Parents

Probably your most important function as a caregiver is to support the bond between parents and their children. Working parents agonize over how they can provide the best kind of upbringing for their children and still earn a living. They are sad they cannot spend as much time with their family as they would like. Many find it hard to get back to being a parent after the pressures of their job. You can help them bridge the gap between their daytime activities and their role as parents.

The key word is communicate! If you see the parents frequently, talk with them. If you seldom see the parent, you will have to rely on other means: newsletters, notes, bulletin boards, or telephone calls. Parents appreciate knowing about any changes in their children since they left them in the morning. They want to know if the children are troubled, ill, or are showing changes in behavior. You can both then work together to determine causes and bring about needed change. And communication is not one way. Ask parents to let you know when there are variations in the home situation or when they see changes in their children.

Help parents see their children's behavior realistically. Working parents often feel guilty about leaving their children in the care of others. When problems arise, they immediately think, "If I didn't have to work, these things wouldn't happen." That may or may not be so. Help them to understand that some behaviors are developmentally predictable. Children will go through those stages whether the parent works or not. Often, time alone will resolve the situation. Sometimes simple changes within the family will work miracles.

Encourage parents to use their own knowledge of their children to bring about changes. Do not be too quick to offer advice based on your own experiences. Your family and your own child may be quite different. Instead, help parents to think through the problem and come up with their own solutions. Discuss your observations of the behaviors, then ask them what happens at home. Encourage them to consider the causes. Let them suggest ways the problem might be alleviated. Obviously, if they have no suggestions, you can voice your own.

Recognize that parents sometimes express anger toward you as an outlet for their own fatigue. The anger may be a way of expressing guilt about not having more time or energy to spend with the child. In addition, the cost of child care consumes a large portion of one parent's income. Parents may be feeling "I am paying a lot of money for this care. The least you can do is to see that he gets his homework done." If you understand the reasons for the parents' frustrations you can deal with them more easily. Recognition of the fatigue helps. Most parents will respond to "It sounds like you have had a really hard day." Or "Yes, it is hard to get him to do his homework. Do you have any suggestions as to how I can be any more successful?"

Accept differences in family organizations. Examine your own prejudices about what makes a family. If you grew up in a happy, intact family, you may see that as the only alternative. Instead, be open to recognizing the strengths of each family you work with. It will help if you increase your knowledge about the changes that have taken place in the last decade by reading further in the books listed at the end of this chapter.

Encourage families to share their cultural and ethnic traditions with your center. This will be especially important to children in interracial families. Visit the children's community and talk to the residents. Learn about the cultures through books, pictures, music, and observation. Actively involve the parents by asking them to share stories, songs, drawings, and experiences that portray important aspects of their culture. One of the best times to involve parents is during holidays. Some parents may be able to spend time in the classroom showing children the way they celebrate. Others may be willing to bring you books, toys, or artifacts that are typical of their background. Still others may welcome an opportunity to get together at a workshop to make presents or decorations for the holiday.

Help all children to increase their own self-esteem. As you read earlier parts of this chapter, you learned that this is more vital for children in some families than in others. But we know that children who feel good about themselves have a better chance of getting along and of becoming happy, functioning adults. So be aware of the ways you can let children know they are liked and successful. A later chapter focuses specifically on this topic.

As a child-care worker, you share the responsibility for children's welfare and education not only with parents, but also with elementary school teachers. In a model situation, each of you would have close contact with the other. However, this does not always happen. Although you may see parents daily when they deliver or pick up the child, you seldom have contact with elementary school personnel. If your child-care center is located on a public school campus it is easier to bring about a close working relationship. If your center is outside a school, it is harder to establish a liaison with teachers. When it is impossible for you to work directly with teachers, you can monitor the child's progress in other ways. Ask parents how their children are doing in school. Make sure you know what homework children have each day and encourage them to get it done. Be aware of when report cards come out and inquire how children did.

Know when to refer parents for outside help. Find out what is available in your community so that you can suggest sources. Make referrals when the service needed is not something your center can provide. Medical or social services are examples. Make referrals when the problem with the child or within the family is acute or long-standing.

Establishing a close relationship with parents can bring about immense rewards for you and the families you work with. Parents will find they are not alone in trying to provide the best for their children. You will find that getting to know parents will add to your ability to help their children.

Summary

As society has changed, the definition of a family has evolved. Several types of families are now recognized. The nuclear family consists of mother, father, and child(ren). An extended family includes other relatives.

Single-parent families make up a growing sector. Either mother or father cares for the child or children either exclusively or for a large portion of the time.

Reconstituted or blended families are another growing phenomenon. Divorced parents remarry and combine their families, sometimes conceiving additional children.

Interracial families may combine persons from widely different races or cultures.

Homosexual couples have been able to incorporate children into their partnerships.

The family is a system that affects children's development at every age level.

The nuclear family no longer always has a stay-at-home mother who cares for the children while the father goes to work. Both parents frequently work, leaving children to care for themselves or be cared for by others.

Single-parent families are often compared unfavorably with two-parent families. More recent information indicates that children can adjust to the loss of daily contact with one parent.

Although adults see remarriage as an opportunity to start over, children in blended families may experience some difficulties.

Children of mixed-race marriages and homosexual couples may be the target of discrimination.

Close contact between parent, school, and caregivers is vital. Working parents suffer stresses and pressures. Caregivers can help by being understanding. Regular avenues of communication must be established.

Visit the children's community and talk to the residents. Learn about the cultures through books, pictures, music, and observation. Actively involve the parents by asking them to share stories, songs, drawings, and experiences that portray important aspects of their culture.

References

Amato, P.R., & Keith, B. (1991). Parental divorce and adult well-being: A meta-analysis. *Journal of Marriage and the Family, 53,* 43–58.

Dawson, D. A. (1991). Family structure and children's health and well-being: Data from the 1988 national health interview study on child health. *Journal of Marriage and the Family, 53* (4), 573–584.

Hawkins, A. J., & Eggebeen, D. J. (1991). Are fathers fungible? *Journal of Marriage and the Family, 51,* 958–972.

Howard, J. (1978). *Families.* New York: Simon and Schuster.

Single fathers: Doing it all. (1995). *Ebony, 50,* 60.

Statistical Abstract of the United States; The national data book. (1996). Washington, DC: United States Bureau of the Census.

Selected Further Reading

McLanahan, S. (1994). *Growing up with a single parent.* Cambridge, MA: Harvard University Press.

Saracho, O.N., & Spodek, B. (1983). *Understanding the multicultural experience in early childhood education.* Washington, DC: National Association for the Education of Young Children.

Thompson, R.A., Scalora, M.J., Castrianno, L., & Limber, S.P. (1992). Grandparent visitation rights: Emergent psychological and psycholegal issues. In D.K.

Kagehiro & W.S. Laufer (Eds.). *Handbook of psychology and law.* New York: Springer-Verlag.

Wallersein, J. (1993). Children after divorce. *Human Development.* Guilford, CT: The Duskin Publishing Group, Inc.

Student Activities

1. Prepare a collage depicting your own family. This can be done on a large piece of poster board, using cutout pictures, words, and phrases from magazines. Display some of these collages to your class. Ask class members to discuss the family portrayed in the collage. Verify or refute your classmates' impressions.
2. Visit a child-care center at the time parents are coming to pick up their children. Write a short paper on your impressions of parent/teacher/child relationships.
3. Bring to class an object that is meaningful to your family and representative of some aspect of your culture. It can be a picture, poem, or story, an article of clothing, or a handcrafted object. Show it to classmates and discuss its significance to you. Following the completion of all the presentations, discuss what has been learned. Have you learned something new about your own culture or about another?

Review

1. How has the definition of the word *family* changed?
2. List and describe three family forms.
3. What is the most serious difficulty for the single-parent family headed by a woman?
4. What are the advantages to children when a parent remarries?
5. What are the problems faced by children in interracial families?
6. List three characteristics of an effective family.
7. What is your most important function as a caregiver?
8. What are the advantages for children who live with a father-only household?
9. How does poverty affect children?
10. List some ways that child-care staff members can share the responsibility for children's welfare with parents and elementary school teachers.

6

Caregivers: Who Are They?

Objectives

After studying this chapter, the student should be able to:

- Describe the characteristics of an effective caregiver/teacher
- State education and experience requirements of a caregiver/teacher
- Relate children's needs to a caregiver's role

What Do Children Really Need From Adults?

If you are already working in school-age child care, you may occasionally question your choice of profession. Or if you are just considering this as a career, you may wonder if this is the right place for you. Children can be tiring, frustrating, demanding. They can also be humorous, marvelously exciting, and fun. This chapter should help you decide if you are the right person for these children and for the job.

First, try to answer the question "What do children need from adults?" Review the sections called *Implications for Child-Care Staff Members* in the first four chapters of this text. You should also remember when you were in elementary school. What did you want from the adults in your life? Children need security, a feeling they can trust adults and be trusted. They want freedom to be independent, while at the same time they like clear limits that define what they can or cannot do. They like adults who are flexible and can respond to new situations and interests with enthusiasm. They need affection, caring, and acceptance of their individual differences. They want to solve their own problems, but have an adult's help available when needed. They want to be challenged to use their skills and abilities. Probably, most of all, they want to feel competent and successful.

What Are They Called?

Many different titles are used to designate the adults who spend time with children in after-school programs. There is still no universally accepted designation that satisfies the need to indicate the importance of this type of work. Some adults prefer to be called teachers, since they certainly do teach. Others emphasize their caring role and therefore prefer to be called caregivers or guides. Those who emphasize the recreational aspect of after-school programs use recreational supervisor, or counselor. Still others use the title of leader, aide, assistant, or child-care worker. Daniel (1995) has suggested using developmentalist, while Betty Caldwell, past president of NAEYC, has coined the term educare. Until a universally accepted new word is coined reflecting the multifaceted aspect of working with school-age children, each of the above should be acceptable.

Characteristics of the Effective Caregiver/Teacher

If you want to be a caregiver or teacher of school-age children, there are certain characteristics you need. Do not be discouraged if you do not have every single quality in the following list. You will acquire some of these attributes as you gain more experience.

Someone who really likes school-age children.   Liking school-age children should certainly be the first important characteristic for a caregiver since few of us relate well to children of all ages. "Liking" school-age children means many things. It means being interested in these children, enjoying conversations with them and being with them. It means appreciating each child's unique qualities and accepting their differences.

Someone who can allow children to be independent.   School-age children are striving to be autonomous. They want to do things for themselves and to solve their own problems. Often adults want children to be compliant and obedient. They may feel threatened when children say, "I want to do it my way." Others feel frightened by what might happen when children are allowed to do what they want. It is important that children develop a sense that they can do things for themselves and that they be given the opportunity to grow in independence.

FIGURE 6–1   Caregivers should like being with school-age children.

Someone who understands child development.   You should have a good knowledge of how children develop during middle childhood. You need to know what children are like at each stage of development throughout the elementary years. What are their physical abilities? What are they capable of learning? What do these children need? How do they form their identity and acquire moral values?

It is important to be aware of the causes of behavior so you can better understand why a particular child responds the way he does. Why does one child go along willingly with the group and another wants to be alone? Why are the four ten-year-olds in your group suddenly rebelling against your ideas or directions? Why are some children easy to get along with some days, but impossible on others? To understand the "whys" of behavior you need to know the emotional stresses most children go through at various stages of childhood. When you do understand, it is easier to realize that often just the passage of time will change behavior. In other words, they are just going through an expected phase in their development. Soon it will change as they move into the next stage. Beyond that, what behaviors may create problems for children themselves? What are the things that make it difficult for them to have friends or to accomplish what they want to do? Then, and this is the hard part, how can you help each child change his behavior for more mature actions? A knowledge of development will help you find the answers.

You need a knowledge of child development to understand how to provide guidance and control in positive ways. How you control a toddler is very different from how you treat a nine-year-old. The toddler needs clear, firm limits to protect him from harm. The nine-year-old must learn to control his own behavior. Therefore, you allow as much freedom as possible while teaching him to set his own limits. It is a subtle kind of guidance that respects the child's desire to be competent.

Understanding development is basic to planning any activities in school-age child care. You need to know what children are capable of doing or learning. With that knowledge you can plan age-appropriate activities at which children are likely to succeed. Sometimes the children themselves have ideas for projects that are way beyond their capabilities. You must guide them to choose things they can do.

Someone who is a good role model.   Although parents still continue to be important, school-age children will be looking to you as a model. They watch what you do, listen to your words. They sometimes imitate you as they develop their own standards for behavior. Therefore, you should have the characteristics you want children to have. Honesty, dependability, fairness, and trustworthiness are some of the words you might consider. You could add flexibility, caring, tolerance, and patience. You could also include a happy disposition and optimistic outlook.

Whenever possible, child-care groups should have both male and female leaders. The majority of elementary school teachers are female. Boys spend a large part of their day without a male role model. When these children are being raised by single mothers, they are additionally deprived. A male leader in child care can help to fill the gap. Girls, too, need men child-care workers to help them develop their own identities in relation to males. Both girls and boys need both sexes to help them learn to trust adults outside their own home.

Someone who has lots of interests.   You should know a lot about many things. Your own curiosity and interests should have led you to seek out information you can share with children. They will be fascinated by what you know about stars, electricity, dinosaurs, or many other topics. Know, also, where to look for answers to their questions. Know how to find information in your local library. Have some ideas about what is available in your community. When you share children's excitement about learning, you will encourage rather than discourage their own desire to discover.

You should be able to do a lot of things. Any skills you have can be shared. If you are adept at woodworking, you can teach children how to use tools. If you

FIGURE 6–2   Both boys and girls need male role models.

know how to knit or crochet, children can learn as well. If you do not have many skills, find out how you can develop some. You can read how to do some of these things. There are many "how-to" books that will help you. You can also learn from someone who already has these skills.

You should be willing to learn from children. Often there is more than one way of doing things. A child may show you a way you would not have thought of yourself. But you have to be willing to consider alternatives rather than feeling there is one absolute right way. Many children have information and skills they can share with the group. Be willing to listen to children yourself and provide opportunities for others to listen as well.

Someone who allows freedom while setting limits.   School-age children are trying to move from dependence upon adults to independence. Consequently, they need the freedom to make their own decisions, set their own rules. This bolsters their self-esteem. You have to be willing to give up or share control when it is appropriate. For instance, you may want to set rules that involve safety, but allow them to write their own code of conduct in the group.

On the other hand, when limits are needed you have to be able to set them firmly and consistently. You have to be able to say "no" and mean it. That is not always as easy as it sounds. Children will test how far they can go before you will stop them, but they want to feel secure in the knowledge that you will not let them go too far. You should be clear that it is not all right to run around the pool area, as an example. Explain why the rule is necessary, then enforce it. You will gain their respect and trust.

Sometimes you have to balance individual freedoms with group rights. One child cannot be allowed to work at a noisy project alone when the group is listening to a story. If a group of children wants to play with blocks, one child cannot be allowed to take all the blocks. However, there are times when individual rights must be considered. Some children need to have exclusive use of materials or space for a period of time. Others want to be able to choose another child as a partner for an activity. You will need a great deal of sensitivity to children to decide when to meet individual or group needs.

Someone who has good communication skills.   Communication includes both the ability to convey messages and to listen. You should be able to do both well. When you give children directions they should be stated clearly. There should be no ambiguity about your meaning. "You have five minutes to finish what you are doing before snack time" is a clear statement. "It will be snack time in a few minutes" leaves room for confusion. What is a few minutes? Five? Three? Ten? You should also be able to express your feelings honestly. "I don't like it when you call me names" lets a child know exactly how you feel. In addition, good communication skills involve the ability to write in an organized, concise manner. You may need to write out information for children, for parents, or for other staff members.

The other side of communication is the willingness to listen. Children often need to talk about school, their families, or their friends. You should be willing to listen and be interested in what they have to say. Children are not the only ones who appreciate a good listener. Parents and other staff members occasionally need a "friendly ear."

One last reminder about communication. It is important when you work with children not to talk down to them. Use language that is appropriate for their level of understanding.

Someone who enjoys physical activity.   You should like to play active games and sports with children. Children who attend elementary school spend a large part of their day sitting down. When they come to child care they need to be involved in activities that allow them to move around. They want to be able to play games outdoors, climb, run, jump, skate, or whatever else is available. Both you and the children will get a great deal of pleasure doing some of these together. That takes a lot of energy and good health on your part.

Someone who cares about families.   All children you work with are part of a family. As described in Chapter 5, these families will have many characteristics. They may be like your own family or very different. It is up to you to get to know family members. Find out what they are like and what they want for their children. Try to understand their cultural values and the standards they set for their family, then be supportive and avoid criticizing them. Find ways to strengthen

FIGURE 6–3   Effective caregivers are willing to listen to children.

their role as parents. You should see child care as a family service, not just a place for children.

You should be the kind of person parents can talk to. If you are young and have not had children yourself you may find this difficult. But remember what parents probably want most is an indication that you know their children and care about them. They want to hear what their children did during the day and how their children are getting along. Sometimes they may want to talk about their children's problems. Do not feel you have to have solutions but just be willing to listen. Often it is enough to listen to a parent talk about the difficulties of working and having time for children. They do not always want advice, just understanding.

Someone who understands the role of a caregiver.   You are both a parent and a teacher when you work in a child-care center. Your job has aspects of both relationships. When children arrive at child care, they may need someone to talk to about their day. At times you have to listen to their problems. Sometimes you have to set limits or administer appropriate consequences when limits are over-stepped. You have to see that they get their homework done. These are things a parent does. At other times you become an instructor. In the course of a day's activities, you will often teach them some of the same things they learn in school. They need help with math concepts when they work on projects. They may need help reading a recipe while cooking a snack. You may encourage them to pursue their interest in astronomy, then praise their accomplishments. You explain instructions when they play a game. Your role, therefore, is a combination of teacher and parent, but is also different. Your primary role is to see that children are well cared for while their parents are at work.

Someone who is able to work as part of a team.   You should be able to get along with other adults as well as you do with children. Other staff members within your center will depend upon you or will have to coordinate their activities with yours. Therefore, you have to be willing to share responsibilities, space, and materials. Sometimes you have to be ready to do more than is expected of you. You should see working with children as a profession, not just a job. When you do you will respect fellow workers and be respected by them.

Being part of a team may also mean working with elementary school personnel. This can be difficult since caregivers often seem to be invisible, not seen as part of the school. When your center is within a school system, you are likely to be housed on the school grounds. You will have to work out the arrangements for sharing indoor and outdoor space. You may have to order materials through the school office. In order to foster a good working relationship, initiate ways to inform school personnel about your program. Let the principal know about any special activities. Offer to put up a display of children's artwork. Talk to parents at a PTA meeting. Get to know the teachers and inform them of children's activities in child care. A healthy relationship with school personnel will be worth the effort it takes to establish and maintain.

Education and Experience

Each child-care center will have its own requirements for staff members. Criteria for employment are usually based on guidelines mandated by local or state licensing regulations as well as by the funding sources that support the program. In addition, each situation will have demands based on the needs of the program or the children to be served. In general there are two broad areas of education and experience that are usually required in school-age child care.

Some center directors look for personnel who have strong backgrounds in early childhood education. Staff members must be knowledgeable in the development of young children. Directors also want people who have expertise and experience in planning a curriculum for "school-agers." Many caregivers who fit these requirements have completed courses in early childhood education and have worked in preschool programs. In addition, they may have had the opportunity to work with five- or six-year-olds. Some are able to find courses in school-age child care at colleges and universities.

FIGURE 6–4   *Caregivers can teach children new skills.*

Other directors seek personnel who have strong backgrounds in recreation. These staff members should know a lot of games suitable to this age level. Staff members should be aware of activities that are safe for young children. Caregivers with this kind of background will probably have taken courses in physical education and recreation. They may have had experience supervising playground situations or working in summer camps.

As you look at these two areas of background and experience, it probably occurs to you that a good caregiver needs both. You are absolutely right. It would certainly be ideal if that were so. In most child-care situations, however, the problem is resolved by hiring staff who have skills that complement one another. In each group there will be one person who has an early childhood education background and one who comes from recreation programs.

To further achieve an ideal staff balance in a child-care program, it would be necessary to have a staff that is comparable ethnically to the surrounding community. It also helps to have people of different age levels. A staff member over the age of thirty who has had children will bring a different perspective to the care of children than a twenty-year-old.

By now you should have a picture of the kind of person who will make a good teacher or caregiver of school-age children. Let us take one last look at the role of a caregiver in children's development.

The Caregiver's Role in Children's Development

In general terms, your role as caregiver is to foster all aspects of children's development. The ways in which you do that have been implied by the description of characteristics needed for the job. However, look at it in another way. Children have specific needs; your job is to help fulfill them.

- Children need security; you provide a secure environment.
- Children need to trust themselves and others; you show you can be trusted and that you trust them.
- Children need to be independent; you allow freedom within limits.
- Children need to develop interests; you encourage and foster those interests.
- Children need a positive self-image; you appreciate their similarities and differences.
- Children need to feel competent; you provide opportunities for them to be successful.
- Children need to acquire values; you offer a positive role model for them to imitate.
- Children need to belong to a group; you include each child and encourage friendships.
- Children need to solve their own problems; you allow them to solve their problems but help when needed.

As you can see, having a part in the development of young children is an awesome task. But should you choose this as a career you will find it is never boring for you are constantly challenged. You will find that children will force you to grow in order to keep up with their demands. It is certainly a job that will keep you learning for many years into the future.

Summary

School-age children have some specific needs. To be trusted, to be independent, to have challenges, to be accepted for who they are, and to be successful are a few.

Many different titles are used to designate the adults who spend time with children in after-school programs: teacher, caregiver, guide, recreational supervisor, counselor, leader, aide, assistant, and child-care worker. All should be acceptable.

The question of who should care for school-age children can be answered. They should be people who

- like school-age children,
- understand child development,
- are good role models,
- have a lot of interests,
- allow freedom while setting limits,
- have good communication skills,
- enjoy physical activity,
- care about families,
- understand the role of caregiver, and
- are able to work as part of a team.

Child-care programs may require personnel who have a background in either early childhood education or recreation. Both are helpful. All should have knowledge of what is developmentally appropriate for children.

In general, the role of a caregiver with school-age children is to foster all aspects of children's development.

Selected Further Reading

Bender, J., Elder, B., & Flatter, C. (1984). *Half a childhood: Time for school-age child care*. Nashville, TN: School Age Notes.

Daniel, J. (1995). Advancing the care and education paradigm: A case for developmentalists. *Young Children, 50*(2), 2.

Elicker, J. & Fortner-Wood, C. (1995). Adult-child relationships in early childhood programs. *Young Children, 51*(1), 69–78.

Gratz, R., & Boulton, P. (1996). Erikson and early childhood educators: Looking at ourselves and our profession developmentally. *Young Children, 51*(5), 74–78.

Musson, S. (1994). *School-age care, theory and practice*. Don Mills, Ontario: Addison-Wesley Publishers Limited.

Recruitment and selection of staff: A guide for managers of preschool and child care programs. (1985). Washington, DC: Department of Health and Human Services.

Stapen, C. (1988). Caring for your child-care person. *Working Woman, 13,* 148.

Whitebook, M., Howes, C. Phillips, D., & Pemberton, C. (1989). Who cares? Child care teachers and the quality of care in America. *Young Children, 45*(1), 41–45.

Student Activities

1. Visit two different kinds of child-care centers. Choose, for instance, one that is operated by a city recreation department and one that is part of a corporation.

In what ways are the children's activities the same or different in these two programs?

2. Observe several child-care teachers as they interact with children. How do their styles differ? Describe the one you would use as your own model for interactions with children.

3. Interview the director of a school-age child-care program. What are the qualities he or she looks for when hiring new staff members?

4. In class do "Quick Writes." Be prepared to share them with classmates when finished. Spend one minute responding to "One teacher was my favorite because _____." Highlight three main characteristics and then prioritize them. Finally, state why the first priority item is the most important.

Review

1. List the reasons child-care workers need a knowledge of child development.
2. Describe the qualities of a good role model for school-age children.
3. This chapter suggests a child-care teacher should have a lot of interests. Explain the reasons for that statement.
4. Effective communication has two parts. What are they?
5. Describe ways to foster your relationship with parents.
6. Why is it important that caregivers be able to work together as a team?
7. What kinds of education and experience should be required to qualify as a caregiver?

CHAPTER

7

Guiding Behavior

Objectives

After studying this chapter, the student should be able to:
- Discuss how self-esteem affects children's behavior
- Describe behaviors that create problems for individuals and the group
- Respond verbally to children in ways that will help to change behavior
- State the steps used to help children resolve conflicts

Self-Esteem and Behavior

As children move through the various stages of childhood, the things that contribute to their self-esteem change. During middle childhood self-esteem comes from being able to test their independence from adults, but they also still need strong role models and heroes to guide them in forming their own behaviors. They feel more competent physically and are mastering new skills so they can take care of themselves. Their bodies are changing and they have lots of energy. The struggles to adjust to all these changes may lead to rebellion in ways that are difficult for adults to understand or deal with. Children argue with teachers and parents, challenge their authority, question rules, or withdraw into silence and sulkiness. Even when interacting with their peers there is often a lot of aggressiveness, fighting, arguing about rules, and accusing others of cheating. All of these

FIGURE 7-1   Children who have a good self-image behave in acceptable ways.

behaviors are designed to test their own powers and refine their sense of who they are and what they can do, their self-esteem.

Self-esteem also comes from being able to be successful in achieving one's personal goals, to feel good about oneself. Each of the theorists discussed in the first chapters of this book highlighted aspects of children's development that contribute to feelings of self-esteem. Jean Piaget focused on children's growing ability to perform "operations," that is, internalize an action. He observed that as they become more social and less egocentric, they understand that others have feelings that may be different from their own. They also have better language skills and can interact more effectively with their peers. Erik Erikson emphasized children's need to master new skills in all areas of their lives. He believed children want to be successful academically and to get along with others. Both Piaget and Erikson saw that when children were successful at the tasks that were important to them their self-esteem strengthened. Chapter 4 stated that self-esteem also comes from feelings of power derived from status with their peers. When children compare themselves to others, they want to feel that they are liked and looked up to. A second source of power comes from the ability to control their own behavior. Do they behave in ways that bring approval from their parents and society? Acceptance by their peers is a third source of power. Do they have friends or are they the object of teasing and rejection? Being labeled good or nice rather than bad or not nice is a fourth source of power.

Each element of self-esteem can affect children's behavior. Persistent failure can lead to behaviors that result in further negative reactions from others. Children who fail academically may stop trying, thus setting up a pattern for failure that persists throughout their lives. Children who are rejected by their peers may become isolated and withdraw into solitary activities. Others express their feelings through negative behavior. They become aggressive or turn into bullies who tease and put others down.

On the other hand, children who are successful academically are regarded highly by their peers, can control their own behavior, and are labeled good or nice have an easier time. As a result of their enhanced self-esteem and their increased awareness of others' needs, they find it easier to do things that help others. They may be able to express sympathy for a friend who is having problems or share lunch with another whose lunch was left at home. They may even be able to be empathetic to others whom they do not know. Upon hearing about a family whose house has burned in a fire, they collect money to help them find new housing and replace their belongings. They visit older people in nursing homes or offer to help an elderly neighbor.

Changing Children's Behavior

Helping children reverse recurring cycles of behavior that interfere with reaching the goals they set for themselves is one of the most important tasks for teachers in before- and after-school programs. The task is twofold: to stop harmful or destructive behaviors, and to encourage children to act in ways that others approve of, thus enhancing their self-esteem.

Stopping destructive behavior begins with a clear understanding by both children and adults about which behaviors are acceptable and which are not. Adults must state their demands clearly, including what the child can do and cannot do, when, and how often. "You may never hit. Use words to tell him how you feel or what you want." Another example is, "I expect you to put away your materials where they belong each time you use them. Do not leave any on the floor to get stepped on or broken." A parent might say, "I want you to take out the trash and put it in the outside can without spilling any. Do it every Friday before it gets dark."

Avoid common cliché statements of expectations. "Shape up," "Try harder," and "Get a life" are examples of clichés that are often used and that have no real meaning to children. How do they shape up? What can they do to try harder? How can they get a life? Making an unspecific demand is a similar mistake adults frequently make. "I want you all to behave when we go to the museum." Children may have very different concepts of what behaving means than the adult who made the statement. It is more helpful if adults state exactly what kinds of behavior are expected. "I want you all to stay together with the group so that no one gets lost."

Expectations may also be stated in the form of rules. Both families and child-care programs have rules that children are expected to abide by. There are three kinds of rules. First, there are the things that are **mandatory,** not open for discussion or negotiation. Mandatory rules are used for actions that can be harmful to others or destructive to property. An example might be, "No hitting." Second, there are **discretionary** rules that are based on choices. The child is given the option of choosing one of a limited number of alternatives. "You can choose to do your homework now or as soon as we finish dinner and before any TV." When using this strategy it is important to be sure the child is mature enough to make the decision. If necessary, the adult can offer help in considering the possible consequences of each choice. Lastly, **optional** rules are the things that children can reasonably control themselves. An example might be that the parent wants the child to finish his homework before dinner, but the child wants to rest first and do homework later. If the child has shown responsibility in other situations, he should be allowed to choose the time for doing homework as long as it gets done before he goes to bed.

Every infraction must be dealt with every time the behavior occurs if it is to be effective. When misbehavior occurs, restate the rule or expectation firmly and in a way that shows that you mean it. "The rule is no hitting when you are mad at somebody. I expect you to use words to tell him how you feel." Sometimes it is tempting to ignore infractions because of fatigue or discouragement. However, ignoring misbehavior sends the wrong message to a child. Behaviorist theory teaches us that intermittent response to misbehavior is a positive reinforcement, increasing the possibility that the behavior will increase, or at least it will not decrease.

Timeout is a frequent response to children who exhibit unacceptable behavior, such as aggression, toward another child. The child is removed from an activity area and expected to sit by himself for a specified period of time. He is allowed to cool off and told to think about what he did. The advantage to this method is that the child is prevented from further harming another child and that he does not get attention for his behavior, thus reinforcing it. The disadvantage of this method is the fact that the child is left alone while he is experiencing strong emotions and may become more resentful toward both adults and other children. Timeout alone does nothing to help the child learn to express his emotions more effectively or to build relationship skills.

Timeout has to be followed by a discussion with the adult. The child should be asked to describe what started his behavior and to explore what he was feeling at the time. Further discussion can help him to find alternative ways of either preventing similar situations in the future or reacting to them differently should they occur.

Another method of changing children's behavior is to follow misbehavior with a **logical consequence.** This does not mean punishment. A logical consequence is intended to help the child learn, while punishment is a forceful way to stop behavior. To be an effective tool for changing behavior, this method has to be related to the specific misbehavior. If a child deliberately makes a mess while painting, it is logical to expect him to clean it up. The consequence for misbehavior should be stated in a calm but firm way that emphasizes the child's ability to be responsible for his own actions. "I expect you to clean up all that paint you have just poured onto the floor. You can get a bucket of water and a sponge in the kitchen. You might bring some paper towels, too, in case you need them."

Reinforcing positive behavior is another method of changing children's behavior. This method is based on behaviorist theory, which tells us that when behaviors are followed by a pleasant response, the behavior is likely to be repeated. Therefore, when children are observed behaving in ways that are expected by adults, they should be rewarded. The rewards can be extrinsic, coming from the environment in the form of a treat, better grades, or a special privilege. Verbal praise and positive feedback are even more effective since they enhance children's intrinsic interest. When the praise and feedback are later removed, children continue to show interest in work (Cameron & Pierce, 1994). Intrinsic rewards come from within the individual and include feeling good about oneself or feeling capable of achieving a goal.

Positive reinforcers are most effective when children are first trying out new ways of functioning. The reinforcer should immediately follow the desired behavior every time the action is observed. When the behavior seems to be fairly well established, rewards can be applied less frequently. Eventually, the reward will not be needed. An example frequently used by both parents and teachers is, "I appreciate they way you helped with the cleanup today. It really helps me to get it done more quickly."

FIGURE 7–2   "Me, when I'm mad." *Ricky, age 9*

Implications for Child-Care Staff Members

Children want to behave in acceptable ways, but often find their conflicting emotions or lack of experience cause them to act in ways that get negative responses from others. If they do not learn another way of behaving, they may be labeled as "bad, naughty, or mean." They may even take on that label themselves and wear it as a badge of importance. "I can be the baddest of the bad." Adults reverse this process by trying to understand why a child is acting in a particular way and then finding ways to help her use more acceptable ways to get what she wants or needs. Child-care staff members can:

- Try to understand the motivation behind troubling behavior. Is the child trying to get attention? Is he feeling insecure? Is he attempting to boost his self-esteem? Once the behavior is understood, appropriate measures can be taken to bring about changes. Find ways to give attention, offer support to an insecure child, find acceptable ways to boost self-esteem.
- Help children develop an honest sense of their own competence. Point out their special abilities and help them to accept the things they may not do so well.
- Help children learn to praise themselves. "You should feel proud of yourself for telling Kevin how you felt when he ruined your block building instead of hitting him."
- Allow children to express their feelings in ways that are not hurtful to others. Some children may not be able to put their feelings into words. A discussion with a caring adult sometimes helps them to find acceptable ways to relieve the feelings. Some children may need active ways to relieve feelings, particularly anger. Provide them with pillows to pound or a place to run.
- Model acceptable behavior toward other adults and toward children. Adults who are sensitive to others' needs show children how to behave in similar circumstances. Caregivers who help co-workers or express empathy when another is having difficulty demonstrate ways to interact and the positive results that follow.
- Help children devise additional ways to act on their feelings of empathy by discussing possible ways to behave. Their own limited experiences may not be enough for them to know what to do and fear of failing may prevent them from acting. "Let's think of some ways to help a friend who is having a difficult day."
- Encourage children to put their feelings into words. They may not have acquired the vocabulary to describe feelings or have not been encouraged to express emotions with words. "Tell her it makes you feel really bad when she calls you names."
- Create a nonaggressive environment. Physically, provide plenty of spaces to play and enough age-appropriate materials so that children can engage in activities with minimal conflict. Socially, adults and children should focus on supporting and respecting others, offering encouragement when needed. Wherever possible, it should be made clear that aggressive behavior gets negative results.

Behaviors That Create Problems for the Individual or the Group

Even with a knowledge of child development and good intentions, child-care staff members often find they are baffled by the behavior of one or more children in their group. These are the children who exhibit similar behaviors to other children, but what they do has increased intensity and is therefore potentially harmful. There may be a child who is not just aggressive when the situation warrants it, but who bullies other children seemingly for no reason at all. Another child may spend a good portion of his or her time alone and resists any attempts to be included in group activities. Still another may be in a perpetual whirl of motion, hardly stopping long enough to be contacted by either adults or children. Each of these children desperately needs, and probably wants, help to become a part of the group and to be accepted by others.

The Overly Aggressive Child

Nearly every group has at least one child who seems to be angry all the time and who dislikes both children and adults. Although he often complains that others are picking on him, in reality he is usually teasing other children. At times he may resort to outbursts of physical aggression or verbal attacks. This may be a child who has experienced many failures. He may be feeling powerless and only feels good when he is bullying others. He may also come from a family background that is harsh, punitive, and which provides very little nurturing. Child-care leaders can become the significant adults in this child's life, helping him to change his behavior. They can:

- Win his trust by showing him they care about him.
- Make sure he understands the rules and standards for behavior in the child-care setting.
- Be consistent with disciplinary actions. Always follow unacceptable behavior with an appropriate action such as timeout or removal of a privilege.
- Try to anticipate situations that are likely to cause his outbursts. Suggest alternative actions, activities, or situations.
- Praise and reinforce acceptable behavior whenever possible. Do not overdo, but when praise is warranted, give it. Include a description of the behavior to be repeated. "I'm happy to see that you were able to wait your turn without pushing."

The Quiet Child

The quiet or withdrawn child is often overlooked in a group because he is hardly noticed. He does not create problems, does what he is told, but stays by himself. Sometimes he may appear to be depressed or anxious. Behind this behavior the child may just be shy or he may feel he is not competent to do the things others do. He may also be afraid of rejection by other children. Child-care staff members can:

- Capitalize on his interests, initially allowing him to pursue them in seclusion. Gradually encourage him to talk about his interest with one other child, then with two children. From there, it may be possible to move him into related activities in a small group of children.
- Involve him in puppetry either alone or with a small group. He may be able to participate behind the stage or by acting through the puppet.
- Practice pretend telephone conversations. Start by engaging him in a conversation with you. Choose a topic that is likely to interest him. "I know you have a dog at home named George. I certainly like that name. Tell me about him." Encourage further conversation by additional prompting. "What are some of your favorite things you and George do together?" Encourage him to practice with another child. Suggest topics for the conversation, such as telling one another about favorite things they do on weekends or their favorite movie.
- Plan activities that will allow this child to be successful. Acknowledge his achievements by describing the behavior that allowed him to succeed. "You were really creative when you figured out how to make a curtain for the puppet theater. That was good thinking!"
- Make specific suggestions about things to say to other children or things he can do to enter into group activities. Praise his efforts when he is successful, pointing out what he did that worked.

The Overly Active Child

The overly active child creates a lot of problems for teachers and caregivers. During group times, he fidgets, talks loudly, or pokes whoever sits next to him. He never settles down to an activity, but moves randomly from one to another. His path through the room may be marked by a trail of destruction. When asked to wait his turn for a snack or during games, he gets very angry. He has a hard time making or keeping friends because he is often argumentative or manipulative. This may be acting-out behavior due to stress factors in his life such as a disrupted family life or not enough attention from his parents.

Some of these children may be classified as suffering from attention deficit hyperactive disorder (ADHD). When attempts to moderate the behavior are unsuccessful, it is important to encourage the parents to get a professional evaluation. Before referring an overly active child, however, some behavior changes can help him control his own behavior. Child-care staff members can:

- Be consistent about rules. Make sure the child understands the rules, then enforce them after every misbehavior.
- Anticipate unstructured times that are likely to create problems. Examples of these times are when the group moves from indoors to outdoors or in the transition between an activity-oriented period to snacks. Give plenty of

warning that one period is ending and another will begin. Assign this child a specific task during the time; have him help prepare the snack, then pass it out or let him hold the door while the other children go outside.

- Give this child plenty of support. Seat him nearby at group times, accompany him to an activity and help him get started.
- Help him acquire social skills. Suggest ways he might enter into others' play. Remind him of expected behavior while with other children.
- Praise him for times he is able to exercise impulse control. "I saw that you were able to stop yourself that time. You must be proud of yourself for that."
- Avoid using negative statements whenever possible. Say "You can build your buildings over here," rather than, "Don't knock down Sean's block building."
- Encourage physical exercise to use up excess energy. Physical activity also helps to stimulate beneficial hormones that bring about greater calmness.
- Simplify your environment. Consider whether there are ways you can eliminate clutter and disorder in the classroom. Are materials easily accessible without having to pull out other materials? Do materials get put back in their place so they are available the next time they are needed?

Communications That Help to Change Behavior

The ways in which adults respond verbally to children's behavior can either increase the likelihood of repetitions or bring about changes in behavior. It is normal to become exasperated with children's behavior, particularly at the end of a difficult day. The tendency then is to respond with anger, generalizations, or labeling. At one time or another most adults have made comments such as, "Jason, why are you always getting into fights?" or, "John, you're such a loudmouth." These kinds of verbal responses may momentarily relieve the adult's angry feelings but they do nothing to help the child change. In fact, they may bring about the opposite, a tendency for the child to repeat the behavior. The child knows how to irritate the adult and will take pleasure in doing it again or may feel the negative label gives him status with his peers. Child-care leaders can learn to respond in ways that are appropriate to the situation and that will help children gradually change their behavior.

Acknowledge children's feelings.   Often adults respond to children's expressions of their feelings by denying their existence or trying to change the feelings. Constant denial of feelings or a rush to change them makes children distrust their own inner senses.

Example Jennifer has been lying on the book area pillows since getting off the bus from school. Her child-care leader wants her to get involved and asks why she does not find something to do. Jennifer answers by saying: "Can't you see I'm tired?"

FIGURE 7–3   *"I am mad when my Mom spanks me." Kevin, age 5*

Inappropriate response:
Adult: "How can you be tired when you haven't done anything yet?"
An appropriate response might be:
Adult: "Yes, I know some days at school are tiring. You decide when you are rested and ready to do something."

Describe the situation.   Children are sometimes unaware of all aspects of a situation. They are concentrating on achieving their own goals and are oblivious to anything else.

Example   It is cleanup time before a field trip and there are still materials that have not been put away.
Inappropriate response:
Adult: "You guys haven't finished cleaning up so maybe you won't be ready to go on the trip. Why are you always such slobs?"
An appropriate response might be:
Adult: "I can still see some puzzles on the table and some paints that need to go into the sink. The bus will be here in five minutes so let's all be ready."

Help children recognize how their behavior affects others.   Until children reach a stage of maturity at which they are less egocentric they often fail to understand that what they do affects others.

Example   Two girls are beginning to dress up with some costumes that are kept in a large trunk. Shari pulls out a white dress and says that she wants to be a princess and wear it. Leanne looks at her and tells her she can't be a princess because she is too fat.

Inappropriate response:
Adult: "Hey, you girls. No name-calling."
An appropriate response might be:
Adult: "Shari, how did it make you feel when Leanne said you couldn't be a princess because you're too fat?"
Another appropriate response:
Adult: "Leanne, when you call Shari fat it really hurts her feelings. Did you notice how she quickly put away the dress and looked like she was about to cry?"

Conflict Resolution

Children are growing up in a world where they witness violence almost every day. They learn ways of dealing with conflict by watching the adults they see at home, in their neighborhoods, on TV, at school. Often adults behave in ways they really do not want children to imitate. Yet, children often "try on" behaviors they observe in others and only gradually learn to resolve conflicts in more effective ways. Preschool children will call upon adults to intervene in resolving disputes. School-age children gradually learn to negotiate a compromise, bargain, or use humor to lessen angry feelings. However, there are times when those strategies do not work and children resort to fighting. The fighting may escalate and children are seriously hurt or even killed. According to the Children's Defense Fund (1996), homicide is the second leading cause of death among all children and young adults and the number one cause among African-American and Latino youths.

Violence is a confrontational and harmful way of settling disputes. The act can be physical, verbal, or emotional. These methods of settling disputes are counter-productive. Violence often escalates until serious injury or death results. However, violence is only one of the styles people use to resolve conflicts. Avoidance is frequently used. When confronted with a difficult situation, the person turns away, withdraws completely, or is silent. This method does not resolve the conflict, but only internalizes the angry feelings. After repeated incidents, the anger may intensify until it erupts either in violent behavior or displays of anger out of proportion to the particular situation. The most effective way of dealing with conflicts is problem solving, yet many people, both adults and children, find it difficult to do. Child-care leaders can help children go through the steps necessary to resolve their conflicts so that each feels validated and empowered. All parties should be satisfied that they have been heard, that their feelings have been considered, and that the solution is mutually agreeable. When all parties are gathered, the adult can facilitate a discussion that takes the children through the following steps.

1. **Decide to resolve the conflict.** Each party to the dispute must agree to solve the problem. "I am willing to try to settle this argument." Set some ground rules:
   a. Each is committed to solve the problem
   b. No name-calling or put-downs
   c. Each will be truthful

FIGURE 7–4   A timeout allows tempers to cool off.

2. **Each side tells what happened.**
   a. Use I messages. "I get mad when you . . ." "I am unhappy when . . ." "I feel sad when . . ."
   b. Describe exactly what happened
   c. Relate how each felt about the incident
   d. Listen to what the other person has to say
   Example: "I was waiting for my turn at the tape player, but she grabbed it. I got mad because she does that all the time." "I had been waiting a long time and I didn't know she was too. I was surprised she got so mad at me."
3. **State what each person needs to resolve the conflict.**
   a. Be specific, use I messages
   b. Listen to other person's needs
   Example: "I just want to have a turn so that I can play the music I like." "I don't always want to hear what she likes."
4. **Explore the possible ways of solving the conflict.**
   a. Brainstorm options
   b. Evaluate the suggestions
   c. Decide which will be satisfactory to both parties

Example: "Let's think of ways to solve this problem." "Will that solution satisfy both of you?"

5. **After an interval of time evaluate whether the solution is working or whether a new approach should be considered.**
   Example: "How has it been working to have a sign-up sheet and a timer for using the tape player?" The adults in an after-school program can be powerful motivators to help children change their behavior so they can become part of a group, feel good about themselves, and achieve their personal goals. The process may be difficult along the way, but it will help to remember that change takes time and effort.

Summary

During middle childhood the things children need to feel good about themselves change. When their attempts to achieve their goals are unsuccessful, they often behave in ways that are difficult for adults to understand or deal with. Those who feel they have failed become rebellious, argue, challenge authority, question rules, or withdraw into sulkiness. They may also be aggressive and tease or put others down. Children who successfully achieve their goals, feel good about themselves, and are accepted by their peers engage in behaviors that help others.

Children's behavior can be changed when adults state their expectations clearly, including what the child can and cannot do. Expectations may also be stated as rules for a family or a care program. When misbehavior occurs, adults should respond in ways that help to change the child's actions. Timeouts, logical consequences, and positive reinforcers are ways to bring about changes in the way children act.

Some children exhibit behaviors that are similar to other children, but are more intense or potentially harmful to the individual or the group. The overly aggressive child seems angry all the time and is prone to outbursts of physical aggression or verbal attacks. The quiet, or withdrawn, child does not create problems in the group, but may appear depressed or anxious. The overly active child is often disruptive and has a hard time making friends. Child-care leaders can help these children by intervening in ways that will bring about changes.

The ways adults respond verbally to children's behavior can either increase or decrease the likelihood of repetitions and bring about changes in behavior. Adults can acknowledge children's feelings rather than denying them. They can describe situations so that children will become aware of all aspects. They can help children recognize how their behavior affects others.

Children learn to resolve conflicts by observing adults at home, in their neighborhoods, on TV, and at school. They witness the others' violent ways and imitate those actions until they acquire more effective methods. The most effective way of dealing with conflicts is problem solving, yet many adults and children find it difficult. Child-care leaders can help children resolve conflicts in ways that allow each party to feel validated. They must first all agree to resolve the conflict, then each side tells what happened. Each person relates what is needed to settle the conflict and possible solutions are generated. A solution is decided upon then evaluated after an interval of time has elapsed.

References

Cameron, J., & Pierce, W. (1994). Reinforcement, reward, and intrinsic motivation: A meta-analysis. *Review of Educational Research,* Fall 1994, *64*(3).

The State of America's Children Yearbook. (1996). Washington, DC: Children's Defense Fund.

Selected Further Reading

Bellem, D. (ND). *Discipline and conflict resolution.* San Francisco, CA: California School Age Consortium.

Curry, N., & Johnson, C. (1990). *Beyond self-esteem: Developing a genuine sense of human value.* Washington, DC: National Association for the Education of Young Children.

Dinwiddie, S. A. (1994). The saga of Sally, Sammy, and the red pen: Facilitating children's social problem solving. *Young Children, 49*(5), 13–19.

Gartrell, D. (1995). Misbehavior or mistaken behavior? *Young Children, 50*(5), 27–34.

Wittmer, D.S., & Honig, A.S. (1994). Encouraging positive social development in young children. *Young Children, 49*(5), 4–12.

Student Activities

1. Interview a caregiver. What methods does he or she use to promote cooperation? How does this person help children resolve conflicts?
2. In class, practice problem solving using the steps listed in this chapter. Work in pairs, with each member of the pair assuming one side of a controversy. Choose one of the situations below or describe one from your own experience.
   a. Two caregivers share a room. One never cleans up thoroughly when an activity is finished so that at the end of the day the room is in chaos.

b. On the playground one caregiver tends to spend a lot of time with individual children rather than supervising the group. The other adult is left to intervene when altercations occur, stimulate additional activities, and generally manage a large group of children.

Share the results with classmates. Was the process easy or difficult? Were you able to use "I" messages when telling what happened? Did each of the partners feel satisfied with the resolution?

Review

1. Describe the changes that take place when children reach middle childhood that are difficult for adults to deal with.
2. State the three kinds of rules discussed in this chapter. When should each be used?
3. List five things an adult can do to help children increase their self-esteem.
4. What are some causes for overaggressive behavior in children?
5. List three things an adult can do to help a quiet or withdrawn child.
6. Describe the behavior of an overly active child. What might be the cause of this behavior?
7. Why is it counterproductive to respond to children's behavior with anger, generalizations, or labeling?
8. Violence is not just physical, but is also _____ and _____.
9. What methods other than violence are used to settle disputes?
10. List and explain the steps in problem solving.

Section III

The Background

C H A P T E R

8

Program Planning

Objectives

After studying this chapter, the student should be able to:

- Describe developmentally appropriate practice
- Discuss reasons for planning
- List the components of an effective program
- Plan a program

Developmentally Appropriate Practice

Bredekamp (1987) first outlined the components of developmentally appropriate practice in educational programs serving children from birth through age 8 for the National Association for the Education of Young Children. Albrecht and Plantz (1993) expanded those components in Project Home Safe. Their intent was to develop guidelines specifically for school-age child-care programs. Since research on school-age care is still limited, Albrecht and Plantz sought input from school-age child care experts. They also reviewed research studies on the development of school-age children.

Developmental research leads to the conclusion that the most successful programs for young children are based on the premise that an active child in an active environment constitutes the optimum conditions for bringing about developmen-

96

tal changes. Studies done by both Piaget (1952) and Vygotsky (1978) pointed to the importance of children's interactions with their environment and the impact of the social environment on development. Piaget stressed the predictable stages of qualitative changes in a child's thinking that allow him to construct knowledge through interactions with his environment. Vygotsky believed that thinking changes as a result of instruction or support (scaffolding) from the environment and as language skills increase. Therefore, according to Albrecht and Plantz (1993), developmentally appropriate school-age child-care programs should be tailored to the developmental characteristics and needs of the children they serve. Quality programs must address the fact that children change tremendously in middle childhood and there are great variations in rate and types of change in all developmental areas. Even within an individual child there is great variation from one stage to another or within a stage of development. Bredekamp (1987) wrote of two dimensions of developmental appropriateness: **age-appropriateness** and **individual appropriateness.**

Age-appropriateness means that programs are planned according to a knowledge of the universal, predictable growth and changes that occur in children. As an example, during middle childhood children have increased gross-motor coordination, but may still have difficulty with fine-motor skills. Therefore, it is important to provide them with opportunities to further refine their motor skills, while not expecting them to be equally competent at both gross- and fine-motor coordination. Middle childhood is also a period in which children are becoming independent of parents, and increasingly want to be accepted by their peers. Program planners need to provide opportunities for children to develop friendships, learn social skills, and to function cooperatively in a group.

Individual appropriateness refers to each child's unique pattern and timing of growth. Although every child goes through predictable stages, each does so at different rates. Two children who are the same age may vary tremendously in their abilities, appearance, language, and thinking processes. Child-care programs must recognize individual differences and provide opportunities for each child to develop at his own pace and according to his own needs. As an example, one child may be tall for his age, have well-developed gross-motor skills, but finds it difficult to carry out logical processes when resolving problems. He certainly should be allowed to practice his physical aptitudes, but should also have supportive guidance to think through solutions to problems.

The guidelines listed in Figure 8–1 address all areas of an effective before- and after-school program for school-age children beginning with the role of staff. Qualifications of child-care leaders have been discussed in a previous chapter, but it should be emphasized here that they should play a supportive role to children. As young people strive for independence from their parents, they look to other adults to guide them through the process of adjusting to the outside world. Albrecht and Plantz (1993) also discuss the importance of adjusting interactions with children according to their age and stage of development. There is a difference between the needs of children who are five to seven years of age and those who are approaching adolescence. The youngest children may need more direction and motivators. The oldest children want more autonomy and adult-like responsibilities. The

Project
HOME SAFE
A Program of the American Home Economics Association

**Principles of Developmentally Appropriate Practice in
School-Age Child Care Programs**

Developmentally appropriate school-age child care programs are tailored to the developmental characteristics and needs of the children they serve. Programs are mindful that children and youth change greatly during the school-age years and that the rate and nature of change vary considerably, both among children and youth and across developmental areas within the same child or youth. Programs approach these developmental realities as opportunities, rather than as problems.

1. Developmentally appropriate school-age child care programs provide resourceful, caring staff who understand the changing role adults play in school-agers' lives.

2. Developmentally appropriate school-age child care programs recognize the increasing importance of peers to school-age children and youth.

3. In developmentally appropriate school-age child care programs, both mixed-age grouping and same-age grouping are used to facilitate the development of peer relations and social skills.

4. Self-selection, rather than staff selection, of activities and experiences predominates in developmentally appropriate school-age child care programs. Schedules allow great flexibility for children and youth. Required participation in activities and experiences is limited.

5. Developmentally appropriate school-age child care programs use positive guidance and discipline techniques to help children and youth achieve self-control and develop their consciences.

6. Environments in developmentally appropriate school-age child care programs are arranged to accommodate children and youth individually, in small groups, and in large groups, and to facilitate a wide variety of activities and experiences.

7. Activities and experiences offered in developmentally appropriate school-age child care programs contribute to all aspects of a school-ager's development.

    a. Activities and experiences foster positive self-concept and a sense of independence.

    b. Activities and experiences encourage children and youth to think, reason, question, and experiment.

    c. Activities and experiences enhance physical development and cooperation and promote a healthy view of competition.

    d. Activities and experiences encourage sound health, safety, and nutritional practices and the wise use of leisure time.

    e. Activities and experiences encourage awareness of and involvement in the community at large.

FIGURE 8–1   *Project Home Safe Guidelines*
*From "Principles of Developmentally Appropriate Practice in School-Age Child-Care Programs," by Kay M. Albrecht and
Margaret C. Plantz in Developmentally Appropriate Practice in School-Age Child Care Programs, 1993. Courtesy of
American Association of Family and Consumer Services.*

guidelines also indicate the importance of peer relationships as children move toward independence.

Both friendships with one or two others and a sense of belonging to a group are essential to children's self-esteem. Adults can facilitate peer relationships by supporting children's developing social skills. Staff members can also initiate activities that encourage children to discuss the causes of conflicts and ways to resolve them. Additionally, developmentally appropriate child-care programs use both mixed-age and same-age grouping to help children develop relationships with their peers according to their own developmental needs. Staff members should use positive guidance strategies to help children achieve inner control and self-discipline. This means that adults encourage children to resolve their own differences, that they listen to children, and encourage children to verbalize their feelings. Positive guidance also means that staff help children behave productively by describing problem situations and encouraging group problem solving.

Developmentally appropriate programs include space for a wide variety of activities for individual children or small and large groups. The program should include more self-selected activities than staff-selected activities in order to provide a balance to the child's after-school time, which follows the more structured content of their school day.

The last items on the list address the need to plan activities and experiences that meet children's desire to be competent in all aspects of their development: psychosocial, cognitive, and physical. A developmentally appropriate program will provide activities and experiences that help children develop their self-concept and need for independence. Children want to feel successful and gain control over their own actions. This can be achieved by allowing children to direct their own activities and having supportive staff who allow independence but offer guidance as needed. Children also need to be challenged to increase their cognitive abilities. There should be varied and interesting activities, that are neither too easy nor too difficult for their developmental level. The importance of physical competence and well-being should not be overlooked by those planning developmentally appropriate programs. Children should have a wide variety of activities in which they can practice skills requiring both large- and small-muscle coordination. A developmentally appropriate program will encourage children to develop sound attitudes and practices to ensure their own health and safety. There should be opportunities to learn what constitutes fitness, how to maintain health, and what to include in a healthy diet.

The last item on Albrecht and Plantz's list is a statement concerning children's awareness of and involvement in their neighborhood or community, the world beyond their families and even beyond the child-care setting. As children become more aware of others and less egocentric, they are ready to explore their community and to grapple with societal issues. This is also an opportunity to understand diversity and develop attitudes that respect differences. The youngest children can read books and experience the arts from different cultures. The oldest children may be ready to discuss global issues such as ecological conservation or social ills such as discriminatory practices. They may even become involved in activities to ameliorate these problems.

Planning for Cultural and Linguistic Diversity

The children in many school-age programs will reflect the diverse cultures and languages that exist in the nation. The challenge for adults who work with these children is to preserve their language and their cultural roots while helping them become more proficient in English and able to participate in English-based learning experiences.

To this end, the National Association for the Education of Young Children (NAEYC) (1996) has made recommendations that address issues of diversity. Their guidelines are based on the premise that every child, including those who are culturally diverse and those whose primary language is other than English, deserve a responsive learning environment. Their first recommendations focus on working with children.

> Recognize that all children are cognitively, linguistically, and emotionally connected to the language and culture of their home.

Children need to maintain a strong connection with their home environment while moving into the wider arena of school and child care.

> Acknowledge that children can demonstrate their knowledge and capabilities in many ways.

This statement recognizes that children have acquired many cognitive skills and knowledge before entering school or child care. They should be able to demonstrate those skills using their own language and then begin to build upon that base while learning a second language.

> Understand that without comprehensive input, second-language learning can be difficult.

Children may be able to learn a second language, but learning more complex cognitive skills requires an integrated approach. They need a learning environment in which to build on the skills they acquired in their first language while gaining new skills in the second. Children learn more easily when they are given instruction in their primary language.

Additional recommendations focus on families. NAEYC suggests that parents be actively involved in the early learning program, that teachers help parents become knowledgeable about the cognitive value of knowing more than one language, and that programs support the family's cultural values.

Recommendations for programs and practice in these guidelines recognize the importance of respecting and supporting children's home language.

> Recognize that children can and will acquire English even when their home language is used and respected.

Children should be able to build upon cognitive skills they already have acquired using their home language. When children have lots of opportunities to read and be read to in their home or in a group setting, they will develop literacy in a second language more easily (Krashen, 1992).

The recommendations also suggest supporting and preserving children's home language. This can be done by an adult speaking the language and also by providing many evidences of the language within the environment. Books, bulletin boards, tape recordings, labels on materials, and signs are all ways to incorporate the home language into the environment. If the caregivers do not speak the child's language, in addition to creating an environment, they can learn words and phrases from that language. If several languages are spoken by children in a group, the task may seem overwhelming. In addition to designing the environment to reflect different languages, children who speak the same language can be grouped together at times to work on specific projects. However, it is important to ensure that these children do not become isolated, and are incorporated into other groups as well.

The Importance of Planning

If you think of yourself as a spontaneous and flexible person, you may wonder if you really need to plan. Nevertheless, when you work with children, looking ahead is absolutely essential. Without it a day can lead to chaos, unhappy children, and irritable adults.

Planning ensures there will be a variety of play opportunities that will attract and stimulate children. There should be a balance between old and new activities. Some should be familiar things children like to do over and over again. Others should be new things to spark their interest.

Planning ahead allows you to gather the materials needed to carry out an activity. Knowing a day or week in advance what you will need gives you time to find, purchase, or prepare whatever will be required. When children have to wait while you collect supplies they get restless. Then, when you are ready, they may not still be receptive.

Planning lessens the number of conflicts between children. A group of children can engage in free play for periods of time, but eventually differences will arise. During the three hours or so that children are in after-school care, some free play, along with planned activities, will keep children busy and involved. Petty arguments and irritability will decrease.

Plans allow staff members to divide responsibilities. Each person should know specifically what he or she will be required to do during a period of time. Some may have responsibility for playground supervision, others for setting up activities in the classrooms. Every step of the day, including transitions, activities, snack, and free play, should be planned ahead of time.

The most important function of program planning is to ensure that both the short- and long-term goals of the program are being met. Short-term goals are those that can be achieved during a single day, a week, or even, perhaps, a month. Long-term goals are those that will not be achieved until a fairly long period of time has passed. This may cover a span of several months or even a school year. Children need to feel successful through the completion of short projects or at the end of a single activity. But they also should be learning to carry through activities that will not bring rewards until a considerable period of time has passed.

Planning also helps staff members to apply the guidelines for developmentally appropriate practices. As each day's activities are decided, they can be measured against the guidelines. Will they allow children to develop their physical skills? Are there opportunities for creative expression? Is there a balance between staff-initiated activities and time for child-initiated ones? Are there activities at different levels of difficulty so that children at diverse developmental levels can participate and feel successful?

Plans allow you to keep parents and school administration informed of program activities. Make written plans so this information is readily accessible. Post your plans on a bulletin board for parents. Provide copies for the administrative person at your school or center.

Who Should Be Involved in Planning?

The simple answer is "everyone who participates." That means all staff members, children, and parents. Staff members should have paid planning time each day. Caregivers who share responsibility for a group of children need to plan together. Before the children arrive or at the end of the day is a good time. In addition, all staff members in a school should meet periodically to coordinate their activities. Although it is often difficult to find time in a busy day with children, it is possible. Find an hour that is convenient for everyone involved. Do not rely on casual opportunities to talk about what is going to happen the next day or next week. It never works out in a satisfactory manner and the result can be a difficult day for both you and the children. Schedule a time and then stick to that schedule.

Include children in planning activities. Pay attention to their interests and ideas. Often teachers or caregivers tell children only what has already been planned. Instead, listen to what the children want to do. Even if some of their ideas are unreasonable, talking will help them to clarify their plans. It will also encourage them to think about what is important, what they find really interesting. You may be surprised to find that children often have good ideas that would not have occurred to you.

Parents can give you input to use in planning. Be sure they are aware of the daily and weekly plans you post. Ask for additional ideas. Use a suggestion box or talk to parents when you greet them at the end of the day. They often have ideas, plus materials or resources that you can use. Most parents will be grateful for this inclusion in their children's time after school.

FIGURE 8–2   Parallel bars and climbing equipment help children develop physical skills.

What Should Be Included?

Start with the routine things you and the children do every day.   Plan who will pick up children at their schools, and know what the children will do when they first arrive at day care. Decide who will take roll, when you will have the snack, who will supervise the playground, what activities will be ready. All this may seem trivial, but it is not. Children enjoy a predictable environment. Careful planning of your schedule makes the day run more smoothly for both adults and children.

Capitalize on children's interests.   Some children may want to continue themes they are working on at school, others may have some current interests unrelated to school. Holidays, too, create excitement that can generate ideas. Television or movies may also pique interests you can use. Sometimes one child has a special interest that can be shared with others. Use this child to generate enthusiasm in other children as they work together on projects.

Increase children's awareness of and respect for cultural diversity. Plan activities to help children accept the fact that we live in a society that includes peoples of many races, colors, and religions. This can be conveyed through books, holiday celebrations, art activities, toys, building projects, games, and festivals. Make these an integral part of your program, not just something you do on special occasions. Ask parents for help. Use the children as resources for customs that are representative of their culture.

Include opportunities for language-minority children to share their language with others. An example might be to have one child read or tell a story with another translating as the tale progresses. Learn and use words from the minority language during the day's activities.

Foster children's desire to become competent. Let them help with daily routine tasks that allow them to use real tools. Teach them to cut up fruit for snack time. Let them answer the telephone and take messages. Include them in the maintenance of your environment. Plan projects that use tools. Show them how to use a saw, hammer, and drill for woodworking projects. Let them measure with a T square, a tape measure, or a yardstick.

Encourage children's natural play interests. Keep a store of props that inspire music, drama, and dancing. Help them, also, to be more competent with fads that sweep through groups of children. Yo-yos, roller skates, and skateboards are not just "time wasters" but allow children to develop their skills. Use these interests to foster their physical development and greater self-esteem.

Plan a balance of activities. Include both group and individual activities. Have quiet times interspersed with more active play. Allow times for activities the children themselves initiate and conduct as well as those you choose and direct.

Have enough choices so all children can find something to do. Variety will allow for different interests and levels of capability.

Include some activities that will re-create everyday experiences. Remember that children who spend after-school hours in child care will miss these kinds of experiences. Take children with you to do the shopping for snack or for a special art project. Arrange trips to local businesses. Take walks around your community.

Allow time to meet the special needs of school-age children. Let them be alone or give them time to do what they want. Provide opportunities for them to make new friends or spend time with existing friends. Some children may even need time to rest or just do nothing.

Plan how transitions will be accomplished. Will the children go from one activity to another in a whole group or individually? Will one adult stay on the playground to receive children as they leave the classroom? Will everyone have snack at the same time or as they get hungry?

Now that you know what goes into planning the daily activities for an after-school program, a few more guidelines should be helpful.

FIGURE 8–3   Encourage children to try all kinds of activities.

Be sure that any activities are developmentally appropriate. Know what children are capable of doing. Plan activities that allow success, but also offer a challenge.

Vary the settings for activities. Try painting outdoors or put on a play under a tree.

Be flexible. If your plans are not working, change them. Or allow children to decide they want to do something different from what you had planned.

Encourage adult/child and child/child interactions. Sometimes, set up activities so you can be involved with children. At other times, encourage children to work together.

Help children change their attitudes about male/female stereotyping. Beware of falling into the trap of unconsciously planning different activities for boys and for girls. Encourage them, instead, to try all activities.

Organizing the Program

There are several approaches to organizing the program for your after-school group. The following are types that have proved successful in different situations. No one is more effective than the other. The appropriateness of each will depend upon many factors: your goals, the children involved, your physical layout, the materials available to you, and the ratio of children to adults. You may even use several types for greater variety, so try what works for you.

Independent Projects

Many children have abundant ideas about what they want to do. Their own enthusiasms lead them to be involved in reading, making maps, constructing models, collecting. These children will work diligently by themselves. Some children want to continue alone on a project they began with a group. They may follow a group project to grow crystals with a study of how crystals are used in tools, industrial equipment, or even in jewelry.

Often, you will initiate an idea for a project based on the interests or needs of a particular child. A child may talk about a visit to a local planetarium with his grandparents. You can suggest a variety of activities about stars and the solar system. Another child may need encouragement to use language. Begin with making simple puppets, then a puppet theater. Few children will be able to resist staging their own plays.

It is important to allow as much freedom to pursue individual interests as possible. Children should feel they can still do the kinds of things they might do if they were home. All you have to do is allow enough time, provide the materials, and offer guidance when needed.

Group Activities

In order to foster group unity, there will be times when you want all the children to engage in the same activity. A group may work on a single project that has many parts. Each part will be completed by small groups of children. An example might be preparation for a drama to be presented at a parent meeting. Some children can write the script, some make costumes, some the scenery. Then new groups can be formed to delegate acting parts, rehearse, change scenes, and arrange lighting. This is a typical example of a long-term project that might be many months in the making.

Sometimes limitations on space or equipment may dictate your decision to have all children doing the same thing at the same time. If you have limited space indoors for extensive projects, you may have to divide your group with some children on the playground while others work in the classroom. There are some child-care facilities that have one room set aside for a specific activity such as arts and crafts. In this case, children may have to sign up to use the room or groups are scheduled for designated times.

FIGURE 8–4   Most school-age children have the skills needed to play soccer.

Groups may have a variety of configurations. Some may consist of children who are close to one another in age or in abilities. Others may have a mixture of ages and proficiencies. When there are wide differences in ages such as from five to twelve in a class, it is workable to plan some things for the younger children and others for those approaching adolescence. Each age level has different developmental needs and interests. At other times, a mixed group allows opportunities for the older children to help the younger ones. This can add to the older children's self-esteem.

Whatever the reason for grouping children together for an activity, make sure these activities build on previous skills or interests. Also make certain these experiences further the goals of your program.

Interest Centers

An interest center is a space carefully arranged to accommodate the activity for which it will be used. A variety of interest centers throughout the room environment allow children to move freely from one to another. This encourages exploration in different areas of the curriculum. Typical interest centers found in child-care environments are block building, science, art, reading, music, cooking, computers, and drama. Within each of these areas, basic materials are always available to the children. Some materials are changed from time to time to add new interest and stimulation. A block area might contain a selection of standard wooden blocks, animals, cars, signs. At times you might add people, trees, boats, airplanes, or colored blocks. Styrofoam sheets, flat wood pieces, or metal forms also invite new kinds of play. Stock an art area with paper, crayons, marking pens, scissors, and paste. For variety add different colors, sizes, or shapes of paper. Consider using paper punches, staplers, templates.

FIGURE 8–5   "Me doing a magic trick." *Vince, age 7*

Field Trips

Field trips can be a simple walk around the block or an all-day trip to the beach. Both should be planned carefully, although obviously, a walk takes less planning than an all-day excursion. Start by deciding the purpose of the trip. A walk can reinforce a project to map your neighborhood or collect material for a nature collage. A trip to the beach can include collecting shells or studying wave patterns as the tide changes. As with all other activities, fit this into the overall pattern of activities.

Plan each detail so both you and the children know what to expect. Obtain permission slips from parents for car or bus trips. Arrange for lunch and transportation. Make sure there are enough adults to properly supervise the children. Discuss the arrangements with your administrator and other staff members. Tell the children where they are going, what they will do, what the rules will be. (Make sure you visit the site ahead of time so you will know what to expect and can plan appropriately.)

Plan further with the children so they will get maximum benefit from the trip. For instance, if they will be going to the beach to gather shells for a collection, prepare ahead. Read books, look at pictures, talk about the different kinds of shells they might find.

Clubs

Clubs are ongoing groups organized around common interests of the participants. When they belong to a club, children have an opportunity to pursue a topic or an interest in depth. They learn to set goals for themselves, solve problems, and to cooperate with others on common goals. Some club activities may require them to do extensive research and then to communicate their findings to others, thus developing skills that are part of scientific endeavors. Typical topics are: photography, calligraphy, cooking, magic, collecting (shells, rocks, stamps), stitchery, space, drama, or sports. Within any group of children there are likely to be other ideas as well. A leader for the group is appointed, either a staff member or an outside volunteer. Sometimes you can find a parent, community resident, or senior citizen with a special interest who will be willing to share information with the club. Decide how many the group can accommodate and ask the children to sign up.

Clubs can provide children with the experience of making a long-term commitment. When they sign up for a club, they state they are willing to spend a specified period of time with the group. This may be as short as one month or as long as four to six months.

Clubs also give children the chance to be a part of a small unit within the larger day-care group. This can foster friendships built on a mutual interest. In addition, club participation helps children learn to govern themselves as they set rules and elect officers for their organization.

At the end of the period, encourage children to share what they have learned with others. This can be in the form of an exhibit, a presentation, or demonstration. Whenever possible, invite parents to participate in these events. Schedule a presentation for a parent meeting. Draw their attention to a display when they come to pick up their children. The children can also write about the club's activities for your center's newsletter.

Spontaneous Activities

You should have a store of activities ready that can be used for unexpected situations. One of your aides calls in sick, the weather turns cold and rainy, another group stays too long on the playground, the record player breaks down. All of these and many other emergencies will happen, so it helps to be well prepared.

Know some games you can use to keep a group occupied. Twenty questions is an old standby that everyone enjoys. Learn some others as well. Every caregiver should have a store of songs children like to sing. They often want the same ones over and over again, but occasionally introduce a new one. You might consider learning some stories or making up your own. Tell these with appropriate dramatics.

Have some materials you can bring out for rainy or snowy days when you have to be indoors. These should be a selection of things you do not put out every day. A new game, special books, or unusual art materials are some of the possibilities. Indoor days could also allow children to spontaneously organize activities such as dramatizing a familiar story or dancing to music.

Some spontaneous activities will be child initiated. In order for child-initiated activities to occur, adults have to be willing to follow children's lead and the environment must have a variety of easily accessible materials. This kind of play is most often seen in the dramatic play center, where children engage in elaborate imaginary or real-life scenarios. A wide selection of costumes and accessories will afford children the opportunity to work through troublesome feelings, learn social skills, and increase their ability to communicate clearly. Dramatic play also takes place with blocks, with additions such as animals, human figures, cars, airplanes,

FIGURE 8–6   Some children may need help with their homework.

and rockets. Children also engage in spontaneous activities outdoors, but here too, they need time and materials to allow them to fully explore their fantasies. The adventure playgrounds seen in some public parks capitalize on this idea by providing boards, boxes, hammers and nails, and pipes. Children can use these to construct objects that are needed for their play.

Community Involvement

You can use community resources to provide children with a wider range of activities. Instead of duplicating classes or facilities that are available elsewhere, use these to enrich your program. This kind of reaching out will also give children less of a feeling of isolation from the kinds of experiences their school friends might be having.

Some of the possible situations are the following:

A girl or boy scout troop could meet at your site so your children could attend.

A local swimming pool might offer reduced rates for children when they are supervised by their own teachers or caregivers.

A nearby volunteer nature center might offer to sponsor activities your children could attend.

Have resources come to the center. For example, organizations that train dogs for the blind will come and talk and bring a dog.

Your children could attend community classes sponsored by the local school district or recreation department in return for having an extra adult to supervise.

Join other sites within your day-care organization for some activities.

Community activities might also include participation in the community in other ways. For instance, your children could get involved in beautifying their neighborhood. They can grow plants from seeds, make them available to residents, and even offer to plant them if needed. Recycling is also a popular cause.

Children can set up bins for receiving materials and then take them to a redemption center. A local rest home for elderly patients may appreciate visits from the children. They can collect toys for less fortunate children to be distributed at Christmas time. Do not forget the possibility of children lobbying their governmental representatives over issues affecting children. They can write letters, make posters, distribute flyers, or appear at hearings.

Community involvement is a valuable participation experience for children and should not be missed just because they are in child care.

Making a Schedule

A good program is more than just a series of activities. The structure of those activities within the context of the day allows children to enjoy their time in child care. There should be plenty of time for each activity, but not so much that children get bored.

From reading the previous pages you know what goes into a typical day with children. Start by writing down the specifics for your program. Include everything you do each day, then add things that have to be done less frequently. Next, estimate how much time to allow for each activity. As you put your schedule into effect, you will probably revise it a few times.

A typical schedule for a before- and after-school program may look like the following:

6:00 A.M. Children arrive individually.
Breakfast is available for children who are hungry. Some children may want to finish homework, others finish a project from a previous day. Still others may want to work quietly at an art center or read. A few may be wide-awake and need to run off energy outdoors.

8:15 A.M. Children complete whatever they are doing and prepare to go to school.

8:30 A.M. Children board the bus for their elementary schools.

When children return to the center at the end of the day, they may follow this schedule.

3:00 P.M. Children arrive in a group on the bus.
Some may be hungry and need a snack. Others may want to rest a bit before joining activities. Still others may need to spend time with their caregiver to talk about what happened at school.

3:15 P.M. Most children want to be outdoors after a day of sitting in school. Schedule outdoor free play, exercises, organized games, or sports.

4:15 P.M. Indoors for a variety of activities: homework, clubs, individual projects, reading, cooking, talking with friends.

5:30 P.M. Finish activities, straighten environment, collect belongings. Children may read alone or in a group until parents arrive.

Your job as a teacher or child-care worker should be enjoyable and exciting. Planning will help to avoid many of the frustrations that make that difficult to achieve.

Summary

Developmentally appropriate practices are those that are tailored to the developmental characteristics and needs of the children and youth they serve. Age-appropriateness means that programs are planned according to a knowledge of the universal, predictable growth and changes that occur in children. Individual appropriateness refers to each child's unique pattern and timing of growth.

Guidelines for developmentally appropriate practices address all areas of an effective child-care program for school-age children. They include the role of staff members, provision for the development of peer relationships, the use of positive guidance, an environment that accommodates small and large groups, and activities that are geared to the developmental level of the children.

The National Association for the Education of Young Children has made recommendations for working with children whose home language is other than English. Adults should recognize the importance of children's home language and acknowledge that children can demonstrate their knowledge and capabilities in many ways. Learning a second language can be difficult and children need to be able to build upon their cognitive skills using their home language. They will then be able to move on and gain new skills in the second language.

NAEYC recommends that programs and practice support children's home language by providing evidences of the language in the environment. Books, bulletin boards, tape recordings, labels on materials, and signs are all ways to incorporate the home language into the child-care environment. Adults should also learn some words and phrases from the children's home language. When several languages are spoken by children in a group, it helps if they can work together at times.

Planning is essential to a good child-care program. It will ensure there will be a variety of activities that interest children and needed materials will be ready. Conflicts between children will be less frequent. Staff members can share responsibilities. You can implement both short- and long-term goals. Parents and administrative personnel can be kept informed.

Everyone who is involved should be included in planning: all staff members, children, and parents.

When planning activities for your child-care group, capitalize on children's interests. Increase their awareness of cultural differences. Foster children's desire to be competent by teaching them how to do real jobs using real tools. Encourage their play interest and provide enough choices of things for them to do. Try to balance activities between group and individual, quiet and active, child initiated and adult initiated. Include everyday experiences such as a trip to the grocery store or a walk around the block. Allow time to meet each child's needs. Do not forget to plan for transition times.

There are several ways to present activities: independent projects, group activities, interest centers, field trips, clubs, spontaneous activities, and community projects.

Draw up a schedule by first listing everything you do each day. Allow adequate time for each activity, but not so much that children get bored.

References

Albrecht, K.M., & Plantz, M.C. (1993). *Developmentally appropriate practice in school-age child care programs* (2nd ed.). Dubuque, IO: Kendall/Hunt Publishing Company.

Bredekamp, S. (Ed.). (1987). *Developmentally appropriate practice in early childhood programs serving children from birth through age 8.* Washington, DC: National Association for the Education of Young Children.

Krashen, S. (1992). *Fundamentals of language education.* Torrence, CA: Laredo Publishing.

NAEYC position statement: Responding to linguistic and cultural diversity—Recommendations for effective early childhood education. (1996) *Young Children, 51*(2), 4–12.

Piaget, J. (1952). *The origin of intelligence in children.* M. Cook (Trans.) New York: International Universities Press.

Vygotsky, L. (1978). *Mind in society: the development of higher psychological processes.* Cambridge, MA: Harvard University Press.

Selected Further Reading

Bergstrom, J.M. (1990). *School's out.* Berkeley, CA: Ten Speed Press.

Boutte, G., Van Scoy, I., & Hendley, S. (1996). Multicultural and nonsexist prop boxes. *Young Children, 52*(1), 34–39.

Cech, M. (1991). *Globalchild—Multicultural resources for young children.* New York: Addison-Wesley.

Katz, L. G., Evangelou, D., & Hartman, J.A. (1990). *The case for mixed-age grouping in early education.* Washington, DC: National Association for the Education of Young Children.

Lewis, B. (1995). *Kid's guide to service programs.* Minneapolis, MN: Free Spirit Press.

Student Activities

1. Talk to a group of school-age children. Find out what they are interested in by asking what they do after school, what they read, or what they watch on television. Is there a difference between boys' interests and girls' interests? Are there age-level differences?
2. Write a short paragraph about what you liked to do when you were between six and ten years old. How did you get started with these interests? Did your parents encourage them, did your friends?
3. Survey your community to find out what resources are available that might be used by a school-age child-care group. Is there a wide variety or limited choices?
4. Set up a schedule for an all-day child-care program. Include as many of the suggestions from this chapter as possible.

Review

1. Define developmentally appropriate practice. What is the difference between age-appropriateness and individual appropriateness?
2. What is the primary role of staff members in a child-care program? How should they adjust their interactions to the youngest children and then to the oldest?
3. State five reasons for careful planning when you work with school-age children.
4. Defend the statement "Staff members should have paid planning time each day."
5. How can you include children in your planning?
6. In what ways can parents help you to plan a good program?
7. Suggest three activities you can include to increase children's desire to become competent.
8. List three approaches to presenting activities.
9. In what ways can field trips be used to enhance a child-care program?
10. How can children who attend child care be more involved in their community?

CHAPTER

9

Creating an Environment

Objectives

After completing this chapter, the student should be able to:
- Describe ways in which the physical environment enhances development
- State general guidelines for planning indoor and outdoor space
- Draw a plan for a child-care room with an adjoining playground
- Discuss ways to adapt the environment when space must be shared

How the Environment Enhances Development

The physical environment is the basic component of a child-care program, the foundation for everything that happens there. The very best program activities, materials, or equipment will be less effective if the physical setting does not meet the needs of the children for whom it is designed. This means that the physical setting should be developmentally appropriate, supporting and enhancing all areas of children's development: physical, cognitive, emotional, and social. The environment should encourage children to participate in activities that will further their development, not discourage them.

Earlier chapters indicated that children's physical development is proceeding rapidly during middle childhood, although fine-motor control lags slightly behind gross-motor control. Indoor areas can be planned to provide children opportunities to increase both these skills. To develop fine-motor control they need space where they can work puzzles, do art projects, build with small blocks, or construct models. There should also be space for dancing or active games that will increase gross-motor control and eye-hand coordination. Outdoor areas provide many opportunities for gross-motor activities such as running, jumping, and throwing, but care should be taken to see that there is a variety of activities that progressively enhance physical development. As children become more adept at using their large muscles, they should have a place where they can play hopscotch, baseball or soccer, and swim, bike, or roller blade. Space can also be provided for some activities that increase small-muscle control. Planting seeds in a garden bed, doing nature collages, and modeling with clay are some examples.

A developmentally appropriate child-care environment will provide many places where children can enhance their cognitive abilities. In Chapter 2, you read that Piaget and Vygotsky believed that children need to be active participants in the development of their own intelligence. In order to do that, the environment must invite participation and offer a wide variety of choices. Children must be free to explore and discover, to hypothesize and experiment, in order to increase their knowledge about the world around them. Each area must include space for children to work comfortably and to have their materials close at hand.

There should also be storage space to keep ongoing projects safe or to display their work. Social skills and language are also components of cognitive development. Work areas should be conducive to verbal interactions among the children. Round tables for some activities and enclosed spaces for others encourage children to talk to one another. Comfortable places for reading also encourage children to increase language skills.

During middle childhood, peer relationships and a sense of belonging to a group become extremely important. Children will usually find places where they can get together, but an effective child-care environment will structure places that foster both a group rapport and friendships between children. This means that the setting needs to have a space where all of the children can gather at one time for activities or discussions. There also should be places where two friends can just "hang out" and talk. Spaces for clubs also allow children to form relationships and share interests within a small group.

Developing the Plan

The originators of child-care centers seldom have the luxury of choosing or building a facility that fits the program they envision. Most often after-school programs are housed in extra classrooms, multipurpose rooms, cafeterias, or gyms. However, within any physical space it is possible to create an environment that welcomes children and makes them feel safe and secure and enhances their development. It just takes more thought and ingenuity in some situations than in others.

FIGURE 9–1   This reading area is partially enclosed by book racks.

If you are not sure where to start, get a feel for how children play. Watch them playing in your neighborhood, at a park, or on a school playground. Note how the children group themselves. Do they all play in one large group or do two or three children do something together? You probably will see that the groups are small and that children tend to stake out their own territory. They meet in specific places each day, then continue play activities together. Watch, also, how they change their space whenever they can. Many will use boxes for forts, some will build tree houses from scrap lumber while others pitch tents so they can be alone. Some children add materials to already existing structures to suit their own needs. They place a wide board on the jungle gym to make a platform for their space ship or enclose a climbing structure with large packing boxes for a clubhouse.

Consider the characteristics of your particular group of children. Their diversity should be reflected in your environment. Look at their age level. Are they all about the same age or is there a wide variation? What skills and abilities do they have in common? What are their interests? Is there a predominant ethnic group? Do some children have special needs? Each of these should be considered when planning your environment.

Think next of the goals of your program. Your space should allow children to do the things stated in your goals. If you want children to be able to work independently, you have to provide a place where they can do that. If you want to encourage a group feeling, there have to be places where the whole group can gather or do something together. If your goal is for children to develop their physical skills, you must provide space and equipment where that can happen.

When you have followed the above suggestions, you should have a fairly good idea of your constituents—the children who will use your environment. In addition, your goals tell you what you want these children to be able to do. It is up to you to set the stage where children and activities can mesh. There are some general considerations that may guide you in planning both indoor and outdoor space.

Overall Design of Indoor Space

Make the indoor space attractive and homelike. Add color. Place flowers on a shelf or table, hang artwork done by the children on the walls. Paint some of the furniture an interesting color. Put a colorful rug in a corner to set off that space with a touch of brightness. Try changing the lighting. A harsh light is somewhat jarring and distracting. A softer light might create a more relaxed atmosphere.

Set up boundaries for activities. A corner of the room invites privacy. Make it more secluded with a free-standing rack for books. A table and shelves can define space where individual projects are to take place. A rug tells children this is a place for floor activities. A large space that is left open can accommodate group meetings.

Areas should be used consistently for the same purpose. The block area should be used for block building, not active games; the quiet area for reading or quiet talking, not loud music activities. That is not to say these can never be changed. Change them when the need arises. If a space is not working as planned, discuss it with the children, then be open to their suggestions as to how the area can be rearranged.

Leave pathways for easy access to all activities and to entrances and exits. Look at the most likely traffic patterns children might use to move around the room or from indoors to outdoors. Arrange work areas so they are undisturbed by children tramping through them.

Make each area readily identifiable by children, staff members, and parents. The kinds of materials you place there, the furniture, or the arrangement should inform everyone of the purpose. Some programs go so far as to place signs at these areas. A good idea, perhaps, but purpose can be conveyed just as effectively by the materials and equipment.

Remember that some activities go well together and can be placed next to one another. Others clash and diminish the usefulness of each. Dramatic play may be incorporated into block building; these two activity areas can be in close proximity. On the other hand, children trying to read quietly in a corner will be disturbed by noisy construction projects. These two areas should be some distance from one another.

Minimize crowding in activity areas by allowing enough space for large group functions and limiting the number of children who can work comfortably at other areas. An open area where the entire group can meet should be spacious enough so that children are not pushing right up next to one another. In the activity areas, avoid crowding by making it clear that only a specified number can participate at an activity at any one time. Four chairs at a table indicate that four people can sit there. The children may attempt to add chairs, but can be reminded of the limitation, then directed to another area.

What Should Be Included?

There should be enough space so children can move about safely. Check the licensing regulations in your state to determine the number of square feet per child you will need. Add enough tables, chairs, shelves, and cabinets to accommodate your program. Leave enough room so children do not bump into furniture or trip on equipment.

Include places where children can work on individual or group projects. They will probably need a table, some chairs, and a place to keep their work until it is completed. This area may also include a place where they can display their completed work.

Have a place where each child can keep his belongings.   Children will be coming to you from school carrying backpacks, lunch pails, and jackets. Everyone should have a cubby, shelf, or box in which to deposit these articles until they are ready to go home.

Make room for messy activities near a water supply.   Many art projects such as clay, painting, or papier-mâché will require a ready supply of water. Cooking projects, too, tend to be messy. These two areas can be right next to each other and share a sink for water.

Set aside an area for quiet reading, resting, or just talking with friends. An enclosed corner as described above will serve this purpose. Furnish it with a low sofa, beanbag chairs, large pillows, and a soft rug. Add books and magazines.

Leave an open area where your whole group can be together at times. Many schools leave the center of a room for this purpose. This space can also be used for large-muscle activities indoors when you cannot go outside. You can dance, do exercises, or gymnastics when the space is unobstructed.

Remember to arrange a place where children can complete their homework.   Have computers and printers available for homework. Provide access to the Internet. A table and chairs in a quiet area of the room is needed. Make sure the lighting is adequate so children can see well. Some children will be able to work together at one table, others may need their own work place. You may have to set up a small individual table for the child who needs to work alone.

If you can, provide high spaces and low spaces.   Many centers with limited floor space resort to a double-decker approach. Imagine a climbing structure that could serve as a dramatic play area in the upper level with a quiet hideaway underneath. The upper level might even become a stage for dramatic productions.

FIGURE 9–2   Mats or large pillows invite children to relax, read together, or just talk.

Designate places to hang artwork, display photographs, or feature news items.   This can be a bulletin board near the entrance so parents can also enjoy it. If you do not have a bulletin board, use picture gum or masking tape to attach items to the wall.

Provide adequate storage.   This should include both closed cupboards and some that are accessible to the children. Use closed cupboards for the things you do not use all the time. Examples are special art or project supplies, games, table activities, or books. Some materials should be on open shelves or cupboards so children can use them as they wish. Always keep a basic assortment of art materials readily available. Change these periodically with those you have stored away.

If your curriculum includes club activities, arrange a place for children to meet.   Let the children decorate the space and add a sign with the club name. Furnish the club area with whatever is needed for their particular activity. A collector's club will need a table and chairs. A drama club could use a stage and a place to store props.

If your group includes some older children (children between the ages of ten and thirteen) design a special place for them.   A separate room would be best, but if you cannot provide that, set up a corner for them. Make it their special place in which younger children are not allowed. The equipment might include a tape recorder/radio, model kits and games, beanbag chairs or large pillows. If the room size permits, add a ping-pong table, air hockey, or a pool table.

Do not forget the adults when you design your indoor space.   Arrange a place where you can prepare materials and keep any records that are required by the program administrators. In addition, there should be a cupboard or drawer where you can keep your personal belongings.

Parents, too, must be considered.   There should be a place for sign-in/sign-out sheets and mailboxes for notes to individual families. In addition, you might install a bulletin board where you can post schedules, pictures of the children, reminders of upcoming events, or any other items of interest to all the parents. Designate a space for lost and found articles.

Now that you know what must be included, you can conceptualize the placement of activity areas. Try using a scale drawing of your room. Mark the doors and windows, then designate areas. Check that you have included an area for each activity in your program plan. Try to imagine yourself and the children living in the space. When you actually place furniture and storage cabinets in the environment, walk through it again, thinking about how it will function. If you are satisfied, try it with your group of children. After a period of time evaluate your arrangement and get input from the children. Do not be afraid to change it, however. As long as everything is movable and not built-in, you can reorganize it. Be flexible.

When You Have to Share Indoor Space

You may not have the luxury of a space that can be set up and left intact at the end of each day. It can be overwhelming to have to arrange your environment at the beginning of each day, but with a bit of preplanning and some imagination it can be done. If you use adaptable materials and have movable cabinets, your task can be managed. The following are some suggestions that have worked for other programs, but each space may require you to devise your own strategies.

Set up interest centers each day. This will be easier if you plan ahead by having all the materials you will need in a basket, a large box, ice-cream cartons, or shoe boxes. Carry them to the table or area where children will use them.

Install large casters or wheels on cupboards, bulletin boards, or dividers used to designate areas. Sometimes it helps to label these to specify their use. Put locks on the cupboards.

Design furniture that can be taken apart when it must be put away at the end of the day. Buy or construct modular furniture made from sturdy, lightweight building material such as tri-wall. Add large vinyl pillows and vinyl beanbag chairs to be used in reading or listening areas.

A large pegboard on wheels is adaptable for many uses. It can be a convenient place to hang woodworking tools or art supplies. It can also divide one work area from another. (You can divide spaces with folding screens, sheets, or blankets, as well.) Have some shelves that are also equipped with casters. Use these for art materials, games, block accessories, science materials.

Use plastic stackable containers for the children's belongings.

Carpet squares can be used to define an activity area if there is no rug. This will make the floor more comfortable as well as designate a space. Carpet pieces can often be obtained inexpensively from carpet stores or from carpet installers.

Allow children to rearrange the indoor environment. They may be able to see possibilities that adults have not considered. Before starting, however, discuss with them the kinds of activities that must be provided for, then have them offer suggestions. Compile their suggestions, then let them vote on the ones to be implemented. Draw up a plan and execute the changes. Evaluate how the plan is working after a trial period.

Work together with other occupants of your space so that everyone has an understanding of what can be done and what cannot. Meet with the principal or building administrator on a regular basis to reinforce mutual commitments to serving children and their families and to resolve any problems that arise. Maintain contact with teachers to determine ways in which the goals of the child-care center can complement those of the school. Set up an agreement with school secretaries about use of office equipment and the telephone. Have an explicit understanding with the janitors about who has responsibility for cleaning, taking out the trash, and who will clean up when others use the space.

Overall Design of Outdoor Space

It is rare that child-care staff members are able to design a new playground. Most have to adapt an existing facility to suit the needs of their program and the children they serve. Whether starting from scratch or adapting an existing playground, it helps to visit other child-care centers, parks, or schools to see how others have planned play spaces for children. Note how the children use both the open spaces and any permanent equipment. Are some not used at all? What kinds of equipment attract the greatest number of children or hold their interest the longest? What kinds of play occur? What do children do in the open spaces? This valuable information will be useful when planning child-care outdoor areas.

The next step is to take an inventory of everything in the outdoor space that will be available to the center. Map out areas that cannot be changed and indicate the places that are open. Brainstorm ideas for the space with other staff members. If children are already enrolled in the center, get their input. They may have wonderful suggestions for what they would like to have. Make a priority list of what will be needed and figure the cost of each item. If financial resources are limited, plan to purchase first items that are likely to be used the most or that have the greatest capability for multiple uses. Are there things that staff members or parents can build or install, thus decreasing the cost?

Clarify program goals that will be supported by the outdoor environment. What is it you want children to be able to do as a result of using the space?

FIGURE 9–3   *Children like to test their skills on outdoor climbing equipment.*

Remember that outdoor space is not just for helping children to develop physical skills, but can help them grow cognitively and socially as well. Outdoor play can involve problem solving, investigating, observing, listening, matching/naming objects, and predicting, to name just a few cognitive skills. Socially, outdoor play can help children learn to cooperate, share, develop friendships, engage in group fantasy play, and foster a group cohesiveness.

A playground should be based on a knowledge of child development. Review the chapters on development at the beginning of this text to remind you of what school-age children are like. They are extremely active and like to have lots of space to run, jump, and throw. They want to be competent at any activities that require physical agility and need places where they can practice their skills. They want to have places where they can be with their peers, either one-on-one or with a group.

Most important of all, the outdoor area should be safe for children, while offering some challenges. They need to be able to use the equipment without undue possibility of injury, but they also want to test their skills at doing hard things. Provide some equipment that all children can use successfully, then add one or two things that will challenge them to increase their dexterity. Be prepared to add new equipment when children reach higher levels of skill. All school-age children will be able to swing, climb a jungle gym, go up a ladder, and slide down a slide. They may need additional adroitness before they can tackle a swinging bridge strung between two structures or traverse a horizontal ladder.

Design your space with children's special needs in mind. If the group includes children with physical limitations, include spaces to which they will have access. Some possibilities are to include paved pathways that are wide enough for a wheelchair, a raised sandbox or a sand table, wheelchair accessible areas for throwing balls, and climbing equipment with a transfer station, allowing a child to go from chair to climber. Many playground equipment companies will offer advice on how to adapt their pieces to fit the needs of children with disabilities.

What Should Be Included?

Include both single-purpose and multipurpose equipment.   Most children love the old standbys: swings, jungle gyms, climbing rope, a sandbox. Swings are single purpose: they can only be used for swinging. A climbing structure can be multipurpose, having many different kinds of play possibilities. A sandbox seems to be single purpose on first glance. You immediately think that it is just for digging, but children can find almost endless ways to incorporate other kinds of play into this area. They will build dams, cook elaborate foods, and search for dinosaur bones, to name just a few.

Add some materials so children can construct their own equipment. Large blocks, boards, cartons, cable spools, and sawhorses present interesting possibilities. Consider using tires, inner tubes, logs, sheets of wood or cardboard. These are materials for "adventure playgrounds" that are actually available in some parts of the country. Children can be marvelously inventive in what they can devise.

As needed, bring out equipment to stimulate new play ideas.   Balls, racquets, hoops, hockey sticks, jump ropes, tumbling mats, and horseshoes are just a few choices. (Do not forget a pump for rejuvenating deflated balls.) Chalk for sidewalk games, yo-yos, and batons might be added depending upon the interests of the children. In different kinds of weather there are additional items to use. When it is hot, bring out a hose, buckets, sprinklers, a small pool, and boats. For areas that get snow, provide shovels, sleds, and snow saucers.

Include areas where children can have some privacy.   A playhouse, park bench, treehouse, or even a secluded corner under a tree can be a place where children can gather to chat with a friend or just be alone.

Allow spaces for special activities, some protected from inclement weather.   Some games need a hard surface, others dirt. Set aside a safe place away from pathways where children can practice skateboarding or roller-skating. Use a covered area for art or table activities that can be enjoyed when the sun is hot or even when it rains.

Have a variety of surfaces on your playground.   Include grass, dirt, cement or asphalt, sand or wood chip areas for added interest. In addition to these surfaces it is nice to leave some planted areas in the yard. Trees, flowers, shrubs, or a garden area add a pleasing touch to any yard.

Provide an opportunity for children to learn about and gain respect for their natural environment.   Growing urban areas have almost obliterated any wild and natural places for children to play. As a result, many children today have little contact with the outdoors and many even express fears of insects, snakes, and plants (Bixler et al, 1994). The playground of a child-care center can allow children to explore the outdoors within a relatively safe setting. Create an area that contains unmanicured grass, bushes, plants, some rocks, a small hill, some trees, and a birdbath and feeder. Add a garden where children can grow vegetables or flowers, plant flowers that will attract butterflies or hummingbirds, and include wild grasses or plants native to the area. In addition, allow children to construct their own play spaces or private hideaways with tree limbs, boards, boxes, and large tires. Children will strengthen their appreciation of the outdoors if they share responsibility for maintaining the area.

Remember to have a water outlet in the yard, both a drinking fountain and hose faucet.   Active children get thirsty and water is needed for many art projects. If hoses are added children will be able to build dams in the sandbox, learn how water sculptures any area where it runs freely, maintain a garden, or observe how sunlight shining through sprinkler spray makes a rainbow.

The outdoor area of a child-care center may be the only opportunity some of today's children have to engage in free, active play. Many live in apartments or areas where they cannot play outside their houses because it is not safe. In addition, many will get home after dark. Therefore, you should put as much thought into the kinds of activities you provide for children outdoors as you do for inside time. Play outdoors is not just a chance to run around and let off steam, but an opportunity for additional learning and the acquisition of skills.

When You Have to Share Outdoor Space

If you have to share outdoor space with other programs or with neighborhood children, you have an additional challenge. You probably will not be able to change the environment, but you can add your own movable play equipment. Bring out easels and painting materials, a box of balls or other sports equipment, digging tools in a crate, or games to play on the grass. You will have to look at the possibilities of the space available and add whatever you can.

Allow your children to mingle with others using the space. It would be difficult if your children felt different from neighborhood youngsters in a park just because they were in day care. Establish clear rules about where they can go and what they can do, but allow as much freedom of movement as you safely can.

Environment affects us all in subtle ways. A good atmosphere will encourage children to be relaxed and engage in productive play. Poor conditions may result in upset children who cannot settle down to sustained activities. Design your child-care space with thought and be willing to change it as needed. You and your children will be glad you did.

FIGURE 9–4   "Me on the bars." Mariah, age 10

Summary

The physical environment is the basic component of a child-care program, the foundation for everything that happens there. A developmentally appropriate environment will support and enhance all areas of children's development: physical, cognitive, and social. Few child-care staff members have the luxury of designing a facility that exactly fits the program they envision. Most have to adapt space in unused or dual-use spaces within another facility. With thought and ingenuity it can be done, however.

There are some overall guidelines to help you plan indoor space. Make it homelike, adding such things as color or soft lighting. Delineate boundaries for activities and use these spaces consistently for the same purpose. Leave pathways to doorways as well as to all classroom areas. Each area should be easily identifiable as well as exist comfortably with adjacent spaces.

Include in your indoor environment the following:

- enough space to meet licensing requirements
- a place for individual or group projects
- a cubby for each child to keep his belongings
- water supply for messy activities
- an area for reading, resting, or talking
- an open area for large gatherings or active games
- a place for children to do homework
- high places and low places
- a bulletin board for art, notices, and parent information
- adequate storage
- club area

- special place for older children
- a place for caregivers and for parents

When you have to share indoor space you can organize materials in easy-to-carry boxes or crates, install casters on all furniture, use shelves or pegboards to divide work areas, use carpet pieces to delineate a space, allow children to set up the environment, and work with other occupants to avoid misunderstandings.

Before you begin to draft a design for a playground, visit a variety of places where children play: other day care centers, school playgrounds, or parks. Your playground should reflect what you know about children. All outdoor areas should be safe, but also offer some challenges to children. If you have children with special needs in your group, you will have to do additional research to know how to meet their needs.

Include in your playground the following:

- both single-purpose and multipurpose equipment
- some materials children can use to construct their own equipment
- add new play ideas as needed: balls, hockey sticks, jump ropes, etc.
- space for special activities
- a variety of surfaces
- a water outlet
- a natural, unstructured space

When you have to share outdoor space with other programs, add movable equipment, allow children to mingle with others using the area, establish clear rules about what children can and cannot do.

Selected Further Reading

Bixler, R.D., Carlisle, C.L., Hammitt, W.E., & Floyd, M.F. (1994). Observed fears and discomforts among urban students on field trips to wildland areas. *Journal of Environmental Education, 26*(1), 24–33.

Clemens, J.B. (1996). Gardening with children. *Young Children, 51*(4), 22–27.

Haas-Foletta, K., & Cogley, M. (1990). *School-age ideas and activities for after school programs.* Nashville, TN: School-Age Notes.

Herman, M.L., Passineau, J.F., Schimpf, A.L., Treuer, P. (1991). *Teaching kids to love the earth.* Duluth, MN: Pfeifer-Hamilton Publishers.

Kritchevsky, S., & Prescott, E., with Walling, L. (1977). *Planning environments for young children: Physical space.* Washington, DC: National Association for the Education of Young Children.

Morris, L., & Schultz, L. (1989). *Creative play activities for children with disabilities: A resources book for teachers and parents.* Champaign, IL: Human Kinetics Books.

Nabhan, G.P., & Trimble, S. (1994). *The geography of childhood: Why children need wild places.* Boston: Beacon Press.

Rivkin, Mary S. (1995). *The great outdoors, restoring children's right to play outside.* Washington, DC: National Association for the Education of Young Children.

Wilson, R.A., Kilmer, S.J., & Knauerhase, V. (1996). Developing an environmental outdoor play space. *Young Children, 51*(6), 56–61.

Student Activities

1. Obtain several catalogues from companies that supply playground equipment. Select a climbing apparatus and three other articles for a school-age playground. In class, defend your choice in a group of two other students. Compile the list of choices from each group member, then negotiate and agree on buying only three items.
2. Visit three child-care sites that are under different auspices: church, recreation program, school district, community organization, or privately owned. Record the kinds of furniture and equipment available in their indoor space. Share your findings with your classmates.
3. Draw a floor plan of an ideal indoor space for a group of twenty children from the age of six to eleven.
4. Use the list of things to include in an indoor environment discussed in this chapter. How might you have to adapt your plan to accommodate a child in a wheelchair?

Review

1. List five general guidelines to remember when planning indoor space.
2. Indicate which of the following activities can be placed next to one another: block building, music, art, science, cooking, karate club, homework, drama practice, woodworking, wood sculpting, reading, table games.
3. State five things to be included in indoor space.
4. List three possible storage containers for children's belongings. Can you suggest any others?
5. Describe the arrangement of an art area.
6. What are the requirements for a space where children can do their homework?
7. What is meant by single-purpose and multipurpose equipment? Give examples of each.
8. Why is it important to provide wild spaces for children in an outdoor play area?
9. List some equipment you might take outside to stimulate new play ideas.
10. In what ways can you adapt both indoor and outdoor equipment when you have to share space with other programs?

Section IV

The Curriculum

C H A P T E R

10

Games and Other Fun Things to Do

Objectives

After studying this chapter, the student should be able to:

- Discuss why games should be part of a child-care curriculum
- Plan and implement a variety of games for outdoor and indoor play
- List some guidelines for making games fun

How Games Can Enhance Development

Games offer children a change of pace after a day in school. Their choice of activity in the after-school hours, though, will depend on their energy level and personality. Some have a lot of energy after sitting down all day and need to be active. Others are tired and want to rest. Some children are gregarious and ready for playing in groups. Others want to be by themselves and choose activities they can do alone. Fortunately, games offer a wide variety of options. They can be intensely vigorous or played quietly. Participants can be in large groups, small groups, or one child can play alone.

Games provide many opportunities for children to practice their physical skills. Although boys and girls have just about equal motor skills, boys have greater forearm strength and girls greater overall flexibility. Their body size, coordination, and inherited talent will also affect their agility. As a result, they often select games at which they can excel; boys often prefer basketball or volleyball and girls choose gymnastics. Encourage them to try new activities by emphasizing the fun of participating, not the degree to which they are successful.

Children learn to work together when they play games. By middle childhood, most understand that rules are for everyone and that they must abide by the rules to be a part of a group. Typically, they often spend more time discussing and negotiating the rules of a game than they do actually playing. In the process, however, they learn about fairness, how to take turns, and to accept that each person can be a leader or a follower. In addition, they experience the fun of a group effort.

Games reinforce and extend children's cognitive skills. They are using logic when they have to plan the next move in checkers or a series of strategies in chess. "If I do this . . . then next I do that . . . this will happen." Many games involve problem solving as well. A marvelous example is a game called Jenga®. The game begins with a completed tower, eighteen levels with three blocks at each level. Each player removes one block and places it on the top of the tower without toppling the structure. It takes a great deal of looking, thinking, and predicting before deciding which block can be safely removed. Trivial Pursuit® encourages children to remember facts. Dice games or Yahtzee® require math skills.

Children can gain an appreciation for their own or other cultures by playing the games of different countries. They learn that games often are played as part of celebrations, for holidays, or to bring groups of people together in a common activity. They will also find that in some cultures, games teach children skills they need for survival. Figure 10–1 on page 135 and Figure 10–3 on page 143 are two examples of ethnic games. *The Multicultural Game Book,* by Louise Orlando (1993), lists many more.

There will probably always be some children who will view games as an opportunity to win or to be the best in order to enhance their self-esteem. You may not be able to entirely eliminate this tendency toward competitiveness since it is so much a part of their environment at school, on television, in the news. However, you can minimize this tendency by including games that are non-competitive and that encourage creativity. Also, reinforce children for their efforts and their skills, rather than being best or first. A poem by Mat Zwerling, published in the January 1991 issue of *Young Children* addresses the matter of competition. He wrote:

Child's Play
I watched the relay races today,
First grade recess
Filled with teachers' whistles and students' squeals,
with shouts and seeming delight.
The winning team screamed and jumped,
Gave high-fives and handslaps just like on t.v.
One winner clenched his fists and put on a game face,
Almost grim, Will Clark in the Series
Giving high-fists and raising arms in triumph.
The other team slowly walked away;
And I thought this really is the beginning.
Surely, surely, there is a better way.
How can there be losers in children's play?

Games and Safety

Safety should be a top priority in child care. During middle childhood, children's motor abilities are developing rapidly. Most are able to succeed at many tasks they were unable to do during the preschool period. However, they often overestimate their competence and attempt feats that are beyond their capabilities. At this age, they are also comparing themselves to their peers and they want to be best at whatever they do. These characteristics cause this age level to have a very high incidence of playground accidents. A study done by the National Electronic Surveillance System in 1988 for the U.S. Consumer Product Safety Commission found a high incidence of injuries on playground equipment among children ages five to fourteen years. Monkey bars had the highest incident of accidents, followed by seesaws, swings, and slides. In order to make the outdoor time as safe as possible, there are some guidelines to remember.

Set clear rules for using all equipment and make sure the children know the rules. See that rules are consistently enforced. Never allow children to use equipment in inappropriate or unsafe ways or engage in an activity that is potentially injurious.

Make certain all equipment meets standards or laws that apply to child-care facilities. These may involve the height of equipment, type of cushioning under climbing structures, or the size of openings in railings.

Have enough adults to supervise the outdoor areas and maintain the required ratio of adults to children. Train staff members to position themselves where they can see the widest area under their supervision and to be vigilant at all times.

Before planning any vigorous activity, consider all the ways children might get hurt and eliminate the most dangerous hazards. Never plan an activity that is potentially harmful. When an activity is introduced, make children aware of the possible hazards, ask them to suggest ways to prevent injury, and add additional cautionary measures, if necessary.

Every staff member should know the center's policies and procedures for managing accidents. There should be a written statement easily accessible to every classroom that should include: procedures for dealing with an accident, telephone numbers for nearby emergency services, and information regarding notification of parents.

All staff members should know first-aid procedures. They should know how to treat minor injuries and to recognize when an injury requires medical attention. Staff members should carry out a follow-up after an accident, reviewing the causes, and making suggestions for preventing a similar mishap in the future.

Sometimes it is also important to do a follow-up with the children. Children may be upset by the accident and need to be comforted. They may want to know what happened and why. Make sure discussions with children are low-key but factual and honest, focusing on ways to prevent the same kind of injury in the future.

Outdoor Games

Many outdoor games have been played by generations of children. If you look at pictures painted several centuries ago, you are likely to find children playing some of the same games they still play today. Pieter Bruegel's paintings done in the sixteenth century, for instance, include children playing blindman's buff, hide-and-seek, and drop the handkerchief. The street games played on the sidewalks of New York and other large cities have been passed down from parent to child, with each generation adding its own variations. Most of these games are noncompetitive but are designed to test the player's skills. This section will remind you of some of the old favorites as well as provide you with some new ideas.

Activities

Jump Rope

Purposes: Develop physical coordination

Promote cooperation to maintain rhythm

Enhance language development, especially for children learning a second language

Jumping rope is often done to a rhythmical song or chants. The beat sets the timing for jumps and counts the number of times the individual jumps before he makes an error.

In other chants, words direct the individual to perform different motions while continuing to jump.

> Cinderella, dressed in yellow,
> Went upstairs to kiss a fellow,
> By mistake, she kissed a snake,
> How many doctors did it take?
> 1,2,3, . . .

> Teddy bear, teddy bear, touch the ground,
> Teddy bear, teddy bear, turn around,
> Teddy bear, teddy bear, jump real high,
> Teddy bear, teddy bear pat your thigh.

Hopscotch

Purposes: Develop balance and large-muscle strength

Encourage play by traditional rules

Increase eye-hand coordination necessary for aiming

A hopscotch board can be seen on the floor of the Forum in Rome, indicating that generations of children have played the game. Paintings by the sixteenth-century artist Pieter Brueghel show children playing hopscotch. In Italy, the game is called "Heaven and Earth," earth being the starting point, and heaven the finish.

Draw the traditional pattern for hopscotch. Vary the rules by hopping with the stone held on the back of the hand. Or, hop without the stone, but with the eyes closed.

Instead of the usual rules for hopscotch, try some variations. Set up a set of six squares, three on each side. Number them from one to six. Have children jump through the squares in sequence with a stone held between their shoes. They must jump with both feet together like a kangaroo. If the stone is dropped, that player's turn is lost.

Hopscotch   **Hopscotch variation**

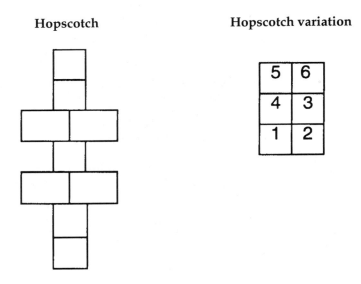

Sock Ball

Purposes: Develop eye-hand coordination

            Reinforce playing by rules

Push a tennis ball or sponge ball into the toe end of a tube sock. Tie a knot close to the ball. Children can toss this ball back and forth holding the open end. Vary the throws: twirl the sock before throwing, toss it underhand. To make catching more difficult, especially for older children, rule that they can only catch the ball by the tail.

Stalker

Skills:	Large motor and listening skills	
Ages:	7 and older	
Players:	7 or more	
Materials:	Two scarves for blindfolds	
	Watch or timer	

PLACE OF ORIGIN

Botswana

About the Game

The *springbok* is an animal similar to a gazelle, but is found only in southern Africa. Like many games from this region, this one is about a real-life skill: hunting. For centuries children have played this game imitating adult Bushmen stalking a springbok.

Through play, children learn the life-long skills of good hunters: patience, concentration, hand-eye coordination.

Playing the Game

1. Have all the players form a circle. Choose two players to start the game: one will be the HUNTER, the other the SPRINGBOK. Blindfold them both and then spin them around. Have one player announce for the hunt to begin.
2. Moving quietly within the circle, the HUNTER tries to catch the SPRINGBOK, while the SPRINGBOK tries to avoid the HUNTER. Players forming the circle can either remain silent or make animal noises to distract the HUNTER and SPRINGBOK. No one is allowed to touch the HUNTER and SPRINGBOK.

Ending the Game

After a set period of time, if the HUNTER fails to catch the SPRINGBOK, the "animal" wins and a new HUNTER is brought out. If the SPRINGBOK is caught, two new players take over.

FIGURE 10–1   *Stalker Game*
From The Multicultural Game Book by Louise Orlando. Copyright © 1993 by Scholastic Inc. Reproduced by permission.

Leapfrog Race

Purposes: Foster trust in others and group cohesiveness

             Develop large-muscle coordination

Have the children line up single file in two separate lines. When the starting signal is given, the first player in each line crouches down on hands and knees. The next player jumps over his back and then becomes a second back. The third player then must leap over two backs before becoming the third back. This continues until all players have had a turn. When the first player has jumped over all his teammates' backs and is at the head of the line again, he stands up. Each player at the end of the line follows the same procedure until all players are standing. The first team to have all players standing is the winner.

Catch the Dragon's Tail

Purposes: Promote group cooperation

             Practice being leaders and followers

             Increase gross-motor skills

Eight or ten children line up, one behind the other. The last person in the line tucks a handkerchief in the back of his belt. At the start signal, the dragon begins chasing its own tail. The object is for the person at the head of the line to snatch the handkerchief. When the head finally gets the handkerchief, he becomes the tail. The second in line then becomes the new head.

A version of this game is played in China, where the dragon is a symbol of good fortune. The game is often played at Chinese New Year celebrations.

In the Chinese version, the children line up, putting their hands on the shoulders of the person in front. The first person is the head and the last one the tail. The tail calls out: "1, 2, 3, dragon." The head leads, running and twisting trying to catch its tail. If the body of the dragon breaks, the dragon dies. The head then moves to the end of the line and becomes the tail. The game continues with a new head leading until everyone is too tired to play.

PomPom Paddle Ball

Purposes: Develop eye-hand coordination

             Provide practice in pair cooperation

Make paddles using five-inch lengths of broom handle or dowel. Drill a hole in one end of the handle. (Do this with the wood securely held in a vise.) Using wire cutters, cut the hook off a wire coat hanger just below the twisted part. Shape remaining wire into a triangle. Pull a knee-high nylon stocking over the triangle. Secure the end with a bit of tape. Push the two ends of the wire into the handle.

Make a pompom by looping yarn around a six-inch piece of cardboard. Use enough yarn to make a small ball. Slip the yarn off the cardboard, then secure the middle with a piece of yarn. Clip all the ends and shape into a ball.

FIGURE 10–2   Tires can be used to set up one station of an obstacle course.

Children can play in pairs, tossing the pompom back and forth. Vary the game by having children form into two lines facing each other. A group of six children works best. Have them toss the pompom back and forth between one team and the other.

Obstacle Course

Purposes: Develop large muscles

                Foster self-confidence by presenting increasingly difficult tasks

Set up an obstacle course using whatever equipment you have available. Place a sign showing the number at each station so children can proceed in sequence. Start with easy tasks and make them increasingly difficult. However, be sure that all activities are safe and that all the children can complete most of the tasks. Some suggestions are:

- walk through a ladder that is lying flat on the ground
- crawl through a tunnel made of tables or large cardboard cartons
- balance on a balance beam or walk on the edging of a sandbox

- jump in and out of a staggered series of tires lying flat on the ground
- jump from wooden packing boxes of several heights
- swing from a knotted rope
- climb a rope net
- shinny down the fireman's pole of a jungle gym

Snake

This game is played by children in Ghana, where there are many different kinds of snakes.

Purposes: Develop coordination

Provide practice in cooperating with others

Increase gross-motor skills

One person is chosen to be the snake. The snake goes to his home, an area that is large enough to fit several children.

When given a signal (blow a whistle) the snake comes out of his home and tries to tag other players. Anyone who is caught holds hands and tries to catch others.

The original snake is the head and determines who is to be tagged next. The end person, or "tail," can also tag players.

If the snake's body breaks, the group must return to its home and start again. Free players can try to break the snake's body, forcing the snake to return home.

The game ends when all the players have been caught or when everyone is totally out of breath.

Tug of War

At one time, Tug of War was a portrayal of the battle between the forces of good and evil. In Burma, the battle represents the natural occurrences of rain or drought. The custom is to allow rain to win.

In Korea, villagers play the game to determine which village will have the best harvest.

This version is played in Afghanistan.

Purposes: Develop gross-motor skills

Increase coordination

Provide practice in balancing

Increase the ability to plan strategies

Provide the players with a baseball bat or a wooden board about 3 feet long (sand all edges so they are smooth).

The players draw a line on the ground and stand on opposite sides. Each player clutches the board. The object of the game is to pull the other person across the line.

Active Games That Can Be Played Indoors

You should know a few active indoor games children can play when the weather prohibits outdoor play. Even on warm days, children sometimes need to be moving around while inside. The following are some games that can be played indoors, but you can set them up outdoors if you wish.

Activities

Beanbag Bowling

Purposes: Practice in taking turns

Cooperation needed to set up pins after each turn

You will need one or two beanbags and four to ten tall, slim cans. Pringles® cans work best but you also can use tennis ball cans. In addition, you need a smooth, shiny floor or a long piece of plastic carpet cover. Place the cans in one of the configurations shown below. Each child sits at the end of the "alley," then slides the bean bag toward the pins. Children can keep score, adding the number of pins knocked down at each turn.

For a variation of this game, use cylindrical floor blocks for the pins and a soft ball. Players roll the ball, knocking over as many pins as possible.

String Ball Bowling

Purposes: Increase eye-hand coordination

Increase ability to reproduce a pattern when resetting the pins

Increase math skills

Develop teamwork and cooperation

A version of this game was played in France many years ago. It was brought to the United States by Dutch settlers and developed into the modern game of bowling.

Bowling

Bowling variation

Use a hollow ball, either a tennis or racquet ball. In addition, you will need duct tape, string, and cans or plastic bottles. Cut a small slit in the ball. Have children knot one end of a six-foot length of string, then push the knot into the slit. Tape the string to the top of a doorway, letting the ball clear the floor by about three inches. Find ten plastic bottles of the same size. Spray paint them all the same color. Pour 1½ inches of water into each. Replace their caps securely. Set the bottles in a triangle, leaving space on either side of the doorway. Players swing the ball around the pins on either side and hit them from the back.

Beanbag Shuffleboard

Purposes: Practice motor skills of throwing, pushing

            Improve math skills: writing numbers, adding

            Taking turns, scorekeeper and player

Use masking tape or chalk to mark off a court on an area of smooth floor. The court should be a large triangle, sectioned into six segments. Number each segment, giving the smallest segment the highest score. Children sit on the floor at the large end of the triangle and slide their beanbag along the floor. Each has two turns. Each can keep his own score or a scorekeeper can be appointed. After a set number of turns, the scores are totaled.

    In a variation of this game, a broomstick or long dowel can be used as a shuffleboard stick. Instead of sitting, children stand, then push the beanbag with the stick.

Shuffleboard

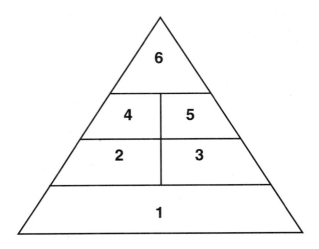

Ping-Pong Jai Alai

Purposes: Refine eye-hand coordination

Encourage cooperation when working in pairs

Provide a ping-pong ball and tall can for each child. A Pringles® can, tennis ball, or large frozen juice can is suitable. Children drop or toss the ball with one hand, then try to catch it in the can. You can vary the game by suggesting they let the ball bounce twice or three times before catching.

Children also might work in pairs, with one child releasing the ball while the other catches. The catcher then puts the ball in play for his partner.

Indoor Basketball

Purposes: Strengthen eye-hand coordination

Rehearse turn-taking

You will need the inner ring of an eight-inch embroidery hoop, heavy tape, and a Nerf® ball. Have children tape the hoop to the wall as high as their arms can reach. To play the game, each player gets three chances per turn to make a basket.

Box Marble Shoot

Purposes: Develop small muscles of hand and fingers

Increase math skills: number recognition and addition

For this game you need a shoe box, felt marking pens, scissors, and marbles. Draw five arches on one side of the box. Make one large arch, two medium, and two short. Mark number values above each arch. Cut out the arches. Each player gets three marbles and several turns to complete the game. Players shoot their marbles, trying to get them through the slots. At the end of a set number of turns, each player totals his score.

Kulit K'rang

Children in Indonesia play this game with small shells.

Purposes: Develop eye-hand coordination

Increase reaction time

Predict where pieces will fall

The players sit in a circle around a bowl. Each player is given an equal (10–15) number of playing pieces (dried beans, peanuts, pebbles, seashells). Leave about twenty pieces in the bowl. Each player places his pieces on the floor in front of him.

The first player puts a piece on the back of his hand, then tosses it in the air. He must grab another piece from his pile, then catch the falling piece.

If he has successfully caught the falling piece, he takes one piece from the bowl. If unsuccessful, he must put one piece in the bowl.

Play continues until the bowl is empty or all the players are out of pieces. The player who then has the most pieces wins the game.

Indoor Games

There are many commercial games you can use in child care. Ask the children what they like to play at home. Remember the games you enjoyed when you were a child. Visit toy or game stores to find games that are appropriate for school-age children. In addition to the commercial board games, there are some that you and the children can make. Also, encourage the children to think of their own ideas for games. Once you begin, new ideas will be generated.

Introduce children to simple card games; they are inexpensive because they require only a deck of cards. Some are described below, but you can find others in the books suggested at the end of this chapter.

Activities

Three-dimensional Tic-Tac-Toe

Purposes: Develop ability to recognize spatial relationships

Use deduction; predict results when moves are made

Mark off a 9×9-inch square on a piece of tagboard. Leave a small border around the edges. Divide the square into nine 3-inch squares. Cut a toilet paper tube into five ¾-inch rings. Cut the heads off ten wooden matches. Glue or tie pairs of matches together in the shape of an X. Children can use felt markers to color the tube circles one color and the match X's another. Players take turns, one using the X's and the other the O's. Each places his token on a square. The purpose is to get three of his tokens in a row down, across, or diagonally.

Memory Game

Purposes: Practice the ability to match like symbols

Develop the ability to remember placement of objects in space

Find twenty pairs of pictures. You can use playing cards from two decks or secure your own matching pictures. They should all be the same size and with no identifiable marks, patterns, or colors on the back. Two to four children can play this game.

Mix the cards, then place them facedown on a table. Players take turns selecting two cards at a time. The cards are shown to the other players. If the cards are a matching pair, the player keeps them. If not, they are placed back in their original spot. The next player then has a turn. The game ends when all the pictures have been picked up. The player with the most pairs is the winner.

Old Maid

Purposes: Practice ability to match like pairs

Accept that it is all right to lose

This game can be played by three or more and requires a pack of fifty-two cards. Remove one queen from the deck, then deal the remainder to the players. The

Nim

PLACE OF ORIGIN

China

Skills:	Counting, creative thinking and planning skills
Ages:	8 and older
Players	2
Materials:	21 toothpicks, beans, or other small markers

About the Game

This is the thousand-year-old Chinese game of *Nim*. It doesn't have any set patterns or rules. Here, however, is one way it might be played.

Playing the Game

1. Players will need 21 toothpicks or other small game pieces. Arrange the sticks in one row as shown in the picture.

2. Taking turns, the players pick up 1, 2, or 3 sticks at a time.

Winning the Game

The player to pick up the last stick, loses.

FIGURE 10–3   Nim Game

From The Multicultural Game Book *by Louise Orlando. Copyright © 1993 by Scholastic Inc. Reproduced by permission.*

goal of the game is to get rid of one's cards by getting matched pairs and laying them on the table.

Each player picks up and examines his cards. He can discard any matching pairs by placing them facedown on the table. If he has three cards of the same value, he can only discard two of them.

To begin the game, the player to the left of the dealer fans out his cards and offers them facedown to the next player on his left. That player takes one card and incorporates it into his hand. If he now has a pair, he places it facedown on the table. He, in turn, offers his cards to the next player. The procedure continues around the table until all the players have managed to pair and discard their cards. One person is left holding the odd queen, the "old maid."

Rotation Dice

Purposes: Practice in taking turns

Enhance math skills: set recognition, adding

Two or more players can play the game and all you need is a pair of dice.

Each player takes turns trying to get a specified number on each throw. There are eleven rounds to the game.

In the first round each player tries for a two. In the second, each tries for a three. In the third round, each tries for a four. Succeeding rounds follow the sequence to the last round when the sum of both dice must be twelve.

If a player succeeds in throwing the number he is trying for, he gets that number of points. For instance, if he is trying for a five and succeeds, he can add five points to his score. If he does not succeed in throwing the number he needs, he ends that turn with no points. At the end of the eleventh round, the scores are totaled and the player with the most points wins.

Tic-Tac-Toe Dice

Purposes: Strengthen math concepts:

writing numbers

number recognition

adding

Two or more players can play. You need two dice, a score card and pencil for each child. (The score grid can be drawn on a piece of paper or a 3 × 5-inch card.) Have each player make a score grid with twelve squares.

In each of the spaces write the numbers from one to twelve. Start with the upper-left square with one proceeding down the first column. Put five at the top of the second column, go down to eight. Write nine at the top of the last column with twelve at the bottom-right corner.

Each player throws the dice only once each turn. On each play players cross out a number or numbers on the score card. They can cross out a total or each of the two numbers. Players also can cross out any combination of numbers that equals the total on the dice. As an example, if a five and a two are thrown, the following combinations can be crossed out: six and one, or five and two, four and three, or one, two, and four. The first person to cross out all the numbers is the winner.

Tic-Tac-Toe

1	5	9
2	6	10
3	7	11
4	8	12

Solitaire

Card games that are played alone in the United States are called "solitaire." In England, these games are called "patience."

Purposes: Increase ability to concentrate

Reinforce ability to count accurately

Practice recognition of symbols for suits

Shuffle a deck of cards. Deal out seven cards in a line, with the first card faceup and the others facedown. Deal out the line again with the second card faceup and the others facedown. Follow this pattern starting consecutively with the third, fourth, fifth, sixth, and seventh card.

If an ace is showing, remove it and put it above the line of cards. Turn over the card under it or if it was the first card, replace it with one from the deck. The object of the game is to fill each of the suits from the ace to the king in a line above the game line.

Remove three cards at a time from the remainder of the deck, looking only at the top card. Play a black card on a red card, sequencing the numbers from largest to smallest. Cards can be removed from one pile to place on another, thus freeing the bottom card. The game ends when all four suits have been filled or no more plays can be made from the remaining deck cards.

Ajaqaq

During the dark winters Canadian Eskimos play a variety of games to pass the time. At one time they believed that playing this game would make the sun return earlier.

Purposes: Develop fine-motor skills

Increase eye-hand coordination

Give each player a curtain ring or similar weight ring about two inches in diameter, an eight-inch stick, and twenty inches of string. Tie one end of the string to the ring and the other around the end of the stick. Hold the stick in one hand. Flip the ring in the air, then try to catch it on the end of the stick.

All Ears

Purposes: Develop listening skills

Associate sound with familiar objects

Discriminate similar sounds from one another

This is a game for a group of children. All you need are several objects that make a sound.

Sit where you cannot be seen by the children (behind a shelf or a hanging bedsheet.) Make a sound with each of the objects. Players guess what the object is or what action made the sound.

Some ideas for objects that make a sound:

- shake a rattle
- bounce a ball
- pour water
- dial a telephone
- cut a piece of paper with scissors
- staple two pieces of paper together
- open a can of soda that has a pull tab
- snap your fingers
- crumple up a piece of cellophane
- blow up a balloon until it pops
- rub two pieces of sandpaper together
- saw a piece of wood
- pound a nail into a piece of wood
- bite an apple
- unwrap a candy bar
- rotate a hand eggbeater
- jingle some coins together

At the end of the game, ask the children to think of other objects that can make a sound. Add some of those to your next game.

Guidelines for Having Fun With Games

Before introducing any game to children, play it yourself. Know how the game is started and how the first player is determined. Although you want children to read the rules of a game, you should be familiar with them.

Introduce new games periodically. Although children like to play the same games over and over, they also need to keep extending themselves. Once they master a game, there may be little challenge. Therefore, look for new games. Talk to other caregivers to get ideas.

FIGURE 10–4   *Children enjoy the challenge of new games.*

Encourage children to invent their own games. All games start with an idea of something that would be fun. Let them make their own board games, develop new ways to play outdoor games, think of new ways to use available materials.

Help children feel competent when they gain new skills. Provide authentic feedback by describing their real accomplishments. Praise their efforts to improve their own performance, for being able to solve a problem, or for being a committed team player.

Encourage children to share their own favorite games with the group. Suggest that they bring games that are part of their cultural background.

Encourage youngsters to try increasingly difficult tasks. Once they have mastered one task, they are often more willing to try harder ones. Encourage them to do so, but do not pressure them. Praise them for their efforts.

Stress cooperation rather than competition. You cannot avoid having a winner and a loser when playing some games. Children need to learn they do not win all the time. Some of the challenge in playing certain games is to see who can be first or fastest. However, you do not want children to have winning as the primary focus of games. Therefore, do not set up contests or give prizes. Instead, praise all children for their participation, their sportsmanship, and their efforts.

Be flexible about rules. Many games have an accompanying set of rules. However, young children like to change rules or develop their own. Allow them to do so when all the players agree.

Enjoy physical activity yourself. Feel the joy children experience when they run, catch balls, or shoot baskets.

Remember the games you especially enjoyed in childhood. Teach the children how to play them. Your enthusiasm will be contagious.

Enjoy the challenge of indoor games. Sit down and play solitaire. Try Trivial Pursuit® with some friends. Test out some of the other games described in this chapter. Above all, have fun.

Summary

Children need a change of pace after long hours at school. Some like to be active while others need to rest. Some are ready for socializing, but others want to be alone.

Games allow children to practice motor skills and to work together. Games also reinforce and extend cognitive skills.

Some children will view games as an opportunity to win, but you can minimize this tendency by including noncompetitive games.

Always be aware of safety. Know the laws and guidelines governing child-care settings. Set clear rules and enforce them consistently. Have enough adult supervision. Staff members should have first-aid training.

Many popular outdoor games have been played by generations of children.

Active games that can be played indoors allow children to work off energy.

Although there are many commercial games children like to play, there are others you can make.

Games should be fun. Guidelines for enjoying games with the children in your child-care center are:

- Introduce new games periodically.
- Help children feel good about themselves when they acquire new skills.
- Encourage children to try increasingly difficult tasks.
- Stress cooperation rather than competition.
- Be flexible about rules.
- Enjoy physical activity yourself.
- Remember the games you played as a child and teach them to the children.
- Enjoy the challenge of indoor games.
- Have fun.

Selected Further Reading

Brandeth, G. (1981). *The world's best indoor games.* New York: Pantheon Books.

Chipman, G., & Chipman J. (1983). *Games! Games! Games!* Salt Lake City, UT: Shadow Mountain Press.

Collis, L. (1989). *Card games for children.* Hauppauge, NY: Barron's Educational Series, Inc.

Johnstone, M. (1988). *Card games.* London: Ward Lock, Ltd.

Orlando, L. (1993). *The multicultural game book.* New York: Scholastic Professional Books.

Sackson, S. (1992). *A gamut of games.* Mineola, New York: Dover Publications, Inc.

Stassevich, V., Stemmler, P., Shotwell, R., & Wirth, M. (1989). *Ready-to-use activities for before and after school programs.* West Nyack, NY: The Center for Applied Research in Education, Inc.

Student Activities

1. Visit an after-school program. Ask the children to fill out a questionnaire on their favorite games. Ask them the following questions:

   - What is your favorite game?
   - What do you like best about that game?
   - What do you dislike about it?
   - Summarize your findings.
     Were there any games mentioned by several children?
     Why do you think those games were popular?
   - Share your findings with the class.

2. Choose one of the indoor or outdoor games listed in this chapter. Teach the game to a group of school-age children. Was it successful? If not, why not?

3. Make one of the games described in this chapter. Try it out with a group of adults and children together. Did both adults and children enjoy the game? How do you think the participants benefited from playing the game?

Review

1. What are the factors that affect children's choice of active games?
2. Which pieces of playground equipment cause the greatest number of accidents?
3. What should be done to ensure the safety of children when they engage in vigorous outdoor play?
4. Name three academic skills that are reinforced when children play table games.
5. List four outdoor games.
6. Name three indoor games that allow children to move around.
7. Briefly describe how Old Maid is played.
8. List eight guidelines for having fun with games.

CHAPTER 11

Imagination and the Arts

Objectives

After studying this chapter, the student should be able to:
- Discuss the importance of art, music, and drama to children
- Plan and implement appropriate activities for art, music, and drama

Role of the Arts in Supporting Development

Watch a group of children as they paint at easels, dance with scarves, or listen to music. Notice their expressions of concentration, joy, or relaxation. You cannot help but conclude that creative activities satisfy children in a way few other experiences can. Children enjoy the arts because everyone can be successful. There is no right or wrong answer or just one way of doing things. They also find it is a way to communicate things they might not be able to put into words. They can use bright colors when they are happy or subdued colors to show sadness. They often feel more relaxed after they pound, roll, or cut clay to release pent-up emotions. They learn what their bodies can do when they dance to music. They relive and remake their own experiences with puppets or in plays.

Art can be shared with others or experienced privately. Painting alone lets a child express feelings or ideas that might not be easy to put into words. Group painting on a mural entails planning, compromise, sharing, and cooperation—all of which are important social skills. Listening to music by oneself can be a way to release tension and achieve a sense of inner peace, experience emotions vicariously, or to just enjoy the sounds and rhythms. Even dancing can be enjoyed by oneself and offers opportunities to increase physical abilities such as large-muscle control and coordination. Group dancing can be a social activity requiring sensitivity to one's partner or to the group. Patterned dances necessitate remembering sequences, an important cognitive skill.

Art, music, and drama can help children from diverse cultural and ethnic backgrounds gain a greater appreciation for their own culture as well as share their heritage with others. Children can view art done by prominent artists from different countries or they can use the same materials. Some cultures use sand for painting, others paint with brilliant colors, while still others use only black on white paper. Music can tell stories about a people, convey values or ideas, use a rhythm that can be identified with a way of life. Children can dramatize a folk tale, write their own plays, or use puppets from different countries. Through each of these media, children learn how others live their lives. The result should be a greater tolerance for differences and a greater appreciation of similarities from one country to another.

Very young children use art experiences simply to try out materials. In preschool, children use all their senses to investigate the properties of art materials. They want to find out how colors mix together, how a paint brush works, and how clay feels. They seldom know ahead of time what they are going to create. In kindergarten, children still enjoy just trying out materials for the pleasure of the experience, but they are beginning to realize they can express feelings and past occurrences as well. They sometimes decide to portray something specific, as Ryan did in his drawing shown in Figure 11–1. "I'm going to draw a picture of me

FIGURE 11–1   *"I'm getting in trouble 'cause I'm jumping on my mom's bed." Ryan, age 7*

when I get in trouble for jumping on my mom's water bed." By the end of the elementary years, they can set goals for themselves and want recognition for their accomplishments. "I want to learn how to paint with oil paints."

The arts can provide children with a lifelong interest in all creative media. When children view others' creations they are introduced to new ways to express ideas and feelings. When they study paintings or sculpture, they appreciate how artists use color and form to create something beautiful. While they listen to music, they hear how other people express emotions. When they watch a play, they share in others' experiences.

Most important of all, art is a perfect medium for helping children develop divergent thinking, their ability to think creatively. When they work on a project, problems often arise. Since there are no right or wrong answers, no single way to accomplish a creative task, they are forced to consider alternatives. "What if I used a different kind of paper for my picture?" "I wonder if this would sound better in a different key or on another instrument?" "How can I make this sculpture stand up straight?" Each time children are encouraged to weigh the possibilities and find which suits their particular project, they are practicing creative thinking.

When you plan any creative activities, start first with children's interests. Capitalize on these to formulate your program. Allow them to expand their interests or find new ways to express them. Find out also what they are learning in history or social studies at school. Plan activities that complement these school experiences. For some children, the creative activities they experience in child care will be all they have. Cutbacks in school districts' money or personnel are often felt first in school art programs. For these children your program will become an even more important part of their lives. Let them enjoy one or more of the arts every single day.

The most effective art program will meet the needs of both the youngest children and the older ones. Younger children want plenty of opportunities to freely explore what they can do with materials. They should have lots of materials available at all times and time to use them in any way they want. The end product of their efforts should be less important than the experience. As children get a little older, approaching the end of the elementary years, they become more critical of what they produce. They want to learn how to use real tools to enhance their efforts. They appreciate the opportunity to learn techniques from real artists or people who have special skills.

Visual Arts

There are so many art activities youngsters enjoy that this chapter can give you ideas for just a few. Read the books listed at the end of this chapter, investigate what is available at your local library, and talk to other teachers or caregivers. Attend workshops sponsored by NAEYC or other professional organizations. Look around you at all the possible materials children can use to construct, paint, or draw. Throw nothing away for it might become part of your art program!

Activities

Clay and Other Kinds of Modeling Media

Purposes: Develop fine-motor coordination

Enhance understanding of spatial relationships

Transform an idea into a three-dimensional object—from symbolic to concrete

Gray or terra cotta clay.   Easy to use, can be dried in a kiln. Provide plastic forks or knives, small combs, garlic presses, and small pieces of sponge for varying the texture of sculptures. Add real sculpting tools for further interest.

Display pictures of native American pottery. Tell children pottery bowls can be made using long coils of clay. Demonstrate how to roll the clay into a long coil, then start winding a tight circle for the bottom. Continue winding, building upon the base circle. Keep the bowl shape. When the desired height has been reached, the outside of the bowl can be smoothed with a sponge dipped in water. Allow the bowls to dry, then provide glazes so the children can paint on designs. Fire the bowls. Display the bowls.

Plasticene.   Readily available, but tends to be difficult to soften and work with. It comes in a variety of colors. Will not harden for a permanent sculpture.

Dough.   Fairly inexpensive, you can vary the texture. (See Figure 11–2 for recipes.)

Papier-mâché.   Paper strips or pieces plus liquid starch. Use a balloon for a base. Dip the paper in the starch, then lay it on the surface of the balloon. Overlap the pieces and make at least two layers. Let it dry thoroughly, then prick the balloon. You should have a fairly solid round sphere. (Finished product can become the head or body of an animal. Use paper towel tubes as the legs and neck. This can also be used as a puppet head.)

For added interest, bring a Mexican piñata to class. Show the children that it has been made of a papier-mâché sphere similar to the ones they have made. Encourage them to make their own piñatas with balloons and papier-mâché. When the papier-mâché is dry, prick the balloon. Help the children cut a slit at the top of the sphere so that the piñata can be filled with candy if desired. Pull out the balloon. Provide tissue paper in a variety of colors, scissors, a small brush, and liquid glue. Show the children how to cut fringed strips from the tissue paper. Brush the sphere with the glue. Tell them to lay the strips evenly on the sphere, each strip slightly overlapping the previous one. Remember to leave the slit visible if the piñata is to be filled.

Flour and Salt
   4 cups flour
   1 cup salt
   Food coloring
   Water to moisten
   Mix the dry ingredients together. Add food coloring to water. Add water to dry mixture to achieve the desired texture. This dough will dry hard in the air and then can be painted. If a reusable dough is desired, add two tablespoons of cooking oil.

Sawdust Dough
   2 cups sawdust
   Liquid starch
   1 cup flour or wheat paste
   1 tablespoon glue (if flour is used)
   Mix until the dough has a pliable consistency. Can be air-dried and then painted.

Cornstarch Clay
   1 cup cornstarch
   ⅓ cup vegetagle oil
   ⅔ cup flour
   Put cornstarch in a bowl and add oil. Mix well until starch has been absorbed. Gradually add flour until the mixture is thick and the desired consistency. Knead well for several minutes. Store in an airtight container.

Cooked Dough
   1 cup flour
   ½ cup salt
   2 teaspoons cream of tarter
   1 cup water
   1 tablespoon oil
   1 teaspoon food coloring
   Combine dry ingredients in a saucepan. Mix liquids and gradually add to dry ingredients. Cook over medium heat, stirring constantly until a ball forms. Remove from the heat and knead until the dough is smooth. (This is a very pliable dough that lasts for a long time.)

FIGURE 11–2   *Variations of Play Dough*

Construction

Purposes: Reinforce divergent thinking through exploring possibilities in found objects

Enhance understanding of spatial relationships

Develop fine-motor coordination

Styrofoam and pipe cleaners.   Use styrofoam meat trays or packing pieces, heavy cardboard, or cork board as a base. Cut pipe cleaners into different lengths.

Add additional peanut-shaped, round, or square styrofoam package fillers for further interest.

Toothpicks, natural or colored.   Combine with small corks, drinking straws cut in different lengths, or small wooden beads. Lengths of copper or colored wire can be added. This sculpture can be free-standing or pushed into a base of styrofoam.

Wood.   Use a flat piece of wood or heavy cardboard as a base. Add lumber scraps cut into interesting shapes, wooden beads, wooden buttons, tongue depressors, wood stir sticks, wood lathe scraps. (Many interesting shapes can be obtained from a furniture manufacturer or a high-school woodworking class.) Furnish white glue. For a variation, add pieces of tree bark, small twigs, seed pods.

Recyclable cans.   Create "can creatures" using clean soda or juice cans. Provide construction paper in assorted colors, fluorescent paper, markers, scissors, white glue, and assorted objects (yarn, buttons, beads, feathers, etc.). Encourage children to imagine a "creature" with the can as the body. They can cut out feet or arms from the paper. Make hair from fringed pieces of paper or yarn. Buttons or beads can become eyes or clothing decorations. Display the "creatures" when they are finished.

A variation of this type of construction uses chopsticks. Explain to the children that people in Asia use chopsticks instead of forks. (This activity might follow preparation of a Chinese or Japanese meal.) Give each child a chopstick and a piece of plasticene for a base. Provide feathers, yarn, construction paper, scraps of fabric, small movable plastic eyes, felt-tipped markers, scissors, and white glue. Encourage the children to use their imaginations to create interesting "people."

Sand casting.   Use a flat cardboard box filled with slightly damp sand for a mold. Mix a batch of plaster of Paris in a bucket. Children can make a free-form depression in the sand. Pour in plaster of Paris and let it set. For a variation, let them press shells or other objects into the sand. Remove the objects to leave an imprint before pouring the plaster.

Collage

Purposes: Increase appreciation of the natural environment

Enhance sensitivity to differences in color, texture, and appearance of different materials

Develop fine-motor skills

Nature collage.   Have children collect natural objects outdoors or on a walk: leaves, twigs, bark, dried grass, seed pods, acorns, pinecones, feathers, rocks. Give each child base of heavy paper, tagboard, styrofoam, or wood. Provide white glue.

Paper collage.   Small pieces of paper: wallpaper, gift wrap, greeting cards, paper doilies, construction paper, aluminum foil, cellophane. Give each child a base of cardboard, heavy textured paper, or thin box top (from stationary or shoe box). Provide white glue.

Fabric.   Small pieces of fabric: felt, lace, ribbon, yarn, buttons, colored beads, small silk flowers, and dried or paper flowers. Give each child a base of colored tagboard, construction paper, or a thin box top. Provide white glue.

Shapes.   Provide children with a piece of drawing paper on which has been drawn one of the following shapes: squares, triangles, rectangles, circles, ovals parallelograms, etc. cut from construction or other kinds of paper. Challenge the children to create a picture with the shape as the base. Provide marking pens, paints, an assortment of paper and fabric pieces, scissors, and white glue.

Seeds.   Provide an assortment of seeds in different colors and shapes. Give each child a piece of heavy paper, cardboard, tagboard, or wood for a base. Provide white glue and a small brush. Encourage them to create a picture using the seeds.

To stimulate interest in seed collage, display pictures of the New Year's Day parade floats in Pasadena, California. Explain that many of the colors that are seen on the floats are made from millions of seeds that are glued on to the base.

African Kente Cloth

Kente cloth is used for shirts, ties, and hats in many African countries. Display pictures of the cloth or obtain samples. Point out that the cloth is made up of simple geometric patterns on square or rectangular shapes.

Supplies needed: construction paper of assorted colors, rulers, scissors, crayons or marking pens. Display the cloths when they are finished along with pictures of Kente cloth.

Large Masks

Masks have been used for ceremonies to bring power and spiritual forces to the people who wear them. They often have intricate designs or carvings. Display pictures of ceremonial masks or visit a museum that displays them.

Supplies needed: large pieces of tree bark or palm frond bases (large pieces of corrugated cardboard can also be used), scissors, white glue, construction paper in assorted colors, found objects. Remind the children they can build up parts of their masks with construction paper pieces or add found objects to make the masks scarier.

Painting and Drawing

Purposes: Increase language—new words relating to artistic endeavors

Provide opportunity to move from one intellectual level to another in a nonthreatening environment (scaffolding)

Increase awareness of cultural differences and similarities through appreciation for ethnic art

Crayon rubbings.   Use any thin white paper over flat stones, leaves, sandpaper, corrugated paper, cardboard shapes. Use the flat side of a crayon to cover the entire sheet of paper, picking up the design underneath.

Chalk painting.   Cover a sheet of paper with a thin layer of liquid starch. Provide several colors of chalk, either sharpened to a point for a thin line or blunted for a thick line. Use a rag, piece of paper towel, or fingers to mute or brush colors together.

Melted crayons.   Use pieces of crayons without paper coverings. Allow children to smash crayons in a heavy bag with a mallet. They can then sprinkle crayon bits onto a piece of paper, cover it with a second sheet. Let them press the paper with a warm iron. Peel off the top sheet. A variation can be achieved by sprinkling crayon bits on paper, then set it in the hot sun to melt.

Tempera paint.   Provide a variety of colors so children can choose their own palette. Give them a choice of brushes: thin, fat, stiff, or soft. Provide a variety of textures of paper: rice paper, grocery bags, parchment, newsprint, wallpaper. Try changing the shape of paper: long, thin rectangle; large or small oval; large or small square; triangle, hexagon. For added interest, let them paint outdoors, on the floor, at table easels.

Textile paint.   Provide a variety of colors of textile paint (obtain from a fabric store). Give children a choice of fabrics of different colors, textures, and sizes.

Crepe paper paint.   Use paper with a slick finish (finger paint or butcher paper). Provide each child with lengths of crepe paper streamers. Give each a squirt bottle of water. They can tear the crepe paper, lay it on the paper, then spray it with water. The colors will fade onto the paper, running together. If the paper is tilted, the colors will run down the paper.

Paint with different tools.   Provide toothbrushes, feathers, roll-on deodorant bottles, small sponges, cotton balls, sponge-top bottles, Q-tips, foam swabs (used for cleaning audio and video equipment), flexible spreaders (used in cake decorating), squeeze bottles.

Oillike paint.   Mix one part powdered tempera with two parts liquid dishwashing detergent. Mix well until the mixture becomes thick and creamy. Use a small palette knife or popsicle stick to spread the paint on paper.

Field trip.   Visit an artist's studio. Ask the artist to demonstrate some techniques to the children. Point out the safety precautions used by the artist.

Museum visit.   Visit a museum. Request a tour with a docent who can tell the children about the exhibits. Children will enjoy seeing how artists painted people, landscape, or abstract designs. As a variation, visit an art gallery to see special exhibits.

Display ethnic and cultural arts.   Obtain paintings, sculptures, folk art, and illustrated books from different cultures. In conjunction with the displays, provide children with art materials that use the same colors or materials. Encourage them to produce their own ethnic art.

Example 1: Display Asian landscape paintings. Provide the children with long sheets of white paper and the subtle colors typical of these paintings: pale greens, tans, black, creamy beige, white, and orange or red for accents. Supply brushes with slim bristles. Encourage children to make their own landscapes of an imaginary view or of a place they have been to. (To add interest to this activity, play some Asian music while the children paint.) When they are finished, mount the pictures with a piece of bamboo at the top. Tie a black string to the bamboo and display the pictures.

FIGURE 11–3   *"Prince, ballerina, and the kids. They're at a dance." Stephanie, age 5*

Example 2: Display pictures of Native American sand paintings. Tell children to look at the designs that were used. Supply them with square pieces of cardboard, colored sand (obtain from pet stores or make your own by mixing powdered tempera with the sand), white glue, and small brushes. Instruct the children to draw a design on the paper, then paint glue on a part of the design that will be one color. Sprinkle the sand on that portion, let it dry briefly before painting another section. Continue in this manner until the painting is complete. Display the paintings when they are completely dry.

Example 3: Show children paintings done by Mexican artists. Tell them to observe the vibrant colors and color mixes that these artists used. Provide some bright paint: orange, red, yellow, pink, purple, black. Tell children to create their own picture, perhaps portraying an experience from their own lives. Display the pictures.

Equipment to Have Available

- Aprons
- Brushes—various sizes and shapes
- Boards for clay—Masonite, plastic, or wood
- Drying racks
- Easels—floor and table
- Matting knife
- Paper cutters—for single sheets and for large rolls of paper
- Popsicle sticks, palette knives
- Rags and towels for cleanup
- Reproductions of fine art
- Rulers, measuring tape
- Scissors—assorted sizes, left- and right-handed

- Sculpting tools, garlic press
- Sponges— large and small, natural and manufactured
- Staplers

NOTE: For a good source of inexpensive and interesting material to use in your art program contact:

Creative Educational Surplus
9801 James Circle, Suite C
Bloomington, MN 55431
(612) 884–6427

Discussion

Enhance children's experience by helping them learn more about art. Discuss the following topics with them:

- How things look: light, texture, color, position
- Effect of using contrasting colors: light and dark, bright and dull
- Two-dimensional surfaces: forms, variations in size and shape
- Drawing techniques: line drawings, imaginative and decorative styles
- Painting techniques: dry or wet brush, stippling, finger painting, color mixing
- New words: colors—ivory, crimson, burnt sienna, hot or cold, primary
- Professions: painter, sculptor, ceramist, illustrator, cartoonist, designer, museum director

Music and Movement

When children enter kindergarten, most are able to sing simple songs, although they may not always be on pitch. They have favorite songs and seem especially attuned to music with a pronounced rhythm. Given a few simple instruments, they will imitate rhythms they have heard or create their own. They also like to move to music, using their whole bodies or just their hands or feet. By the end of elementary school, most children have developed a good sense of rhythm and beat. They can remember and sing a large selection of songs and have added the new skill of being able to sing in harmony. Some are able to play instruments and a few will be able to write down simple musical patterns or songs.

Music should be a part of every day. It does not have to be a formal music time but can be integrated into the daily routine. Start the day with a few songs, then have instruments available for children to use when they wish. Take instruments outdoors on occasion so children can play or dance in a different environment. Occasionally play records or tapes during activity times.

FIGURE 11–4   *"Me dancing." Rachel, age 5*

Activities

Purposes: Increase physical coordination

Develop listening skills

Provide an outlet for expression of feelings

Enhance appreciation of ethnic contributions to the arts

Musical styles.   Play different kinds of music: lullaby, folk music, marches, gospel, rock, jazz. Have the children identify each style, then ask them to compare two styles. How are they alike or different? Provide many opportunities to hear music, encouraging the children to really listen to how the music is formed. Place tapes or CDs in a listening corner for children to enjoy at leisure.

As an added interest, play selections of music from different countries and cultures. Select reggae from Jamaica, opera from Italy, a mariachi band from Mexico, sitar music from India, balalaika music from Russia, flute music from the Andes, or Native American drum music. Ask the children to compare the sounds of the music. Why do they think the music is representative of the country?

Paint to music.   Play different kinds of music as children paint. Suggest they paint what they hear. Include ethnic music.

Dancing with props.   Add props to enhance movement: scarves, balloons, hoops, colored rope, streamers, dress-up clothes.

Mirroring.   Provide a scarf for each child. Group them in pairs. Have one child act as leader, making movements using the scarf. A second child mirrors those movements. After a short period, change places.

FIGURE 11–5   *Children can make their own music with an electronic keyboard.*

Instruments.   Provide a variety of simple instruments: autoharp, drums, rhythm sticks, shakers, castanets, tambourines, bells. Allow children to experiment with the sounds.

Provide the materials for children to make their own instruments. (See Anders, *Making Musical Instruments,* listed at the end of this chapter.)

Listening corner.   Set up a listening corner with a tape recorder or CD player and earphones. Provide a selection of tapes. Change them periodically.

Musical statues.   Play a tape or CD while children dance. Instruct them to "freeze" in whatever position they are in when the music stops. Stop and start the record several times.

Shadow dancing.   On a sunny day, take the tape or CD player outdoors. Encourage children to dance, watching their own shadows as they move.

Video.   Let children view a video of dance segments. (Check your library or watch for television shows you can tape.) Discuss the kind of dance portrayed, then encourage children to dance to the video.

Visitor.   Invite a musician to your center to demonstrate techniques. If possible, allow children to try out the instrument. Include musicians who play instruments that are typical of a particular ethnic group or are representative of a country.

Equipment to Have Available

- Autoharp(s)
- Banjo
- Blank tapes for recording
- Books—song, poetry
- Dance props—tap shoes, tutus, scarves, streamers, canes, hoops, ropes
- Earphones for listening center
- Ethnic musical instruments—maracas, bongo drums, Chinese temple blocks
- Guitar
- Piano
- Tape or CD player—assortment of tapes or CDs. Select all kinds of music including ethnic and holiday pieces
- Recorders
- Selection of percussion instruments—drums, rhythm sticks, shakers, castanets, tambourines, bells
- Television monitor and videotape player

Discussion

Some concepts to discuss with children to enhance their learning:

- Musical terms: tempo, pitch, dynamics (loud/soft)
- Movement: walking, running, swaying, balance
- Dance forms: ballet, folk, tap, interpretive, jazz
- Instruments: names, how they produce sound, care of instruments
- Listening: differentiating sounds, following musical directions or beat

Drama

From a very early age children engage in dramatic play. Toddlers charm their parents by imitating actions or situations they observe around them. Preschoolers use dramatic play to try out what it feels like to be a grown-up. They play at being mom or dad, doctors, firefighters, teacher. As they get a little older, dramatic play becomes a way to conquer feelings of being scared or helpless. Four-year-olds and young "school-agers" play at being monsters, Superman, or the current popular TV figure. During the middle childhood years, youngsters use dramatic play to consolidate and understand what they are learning in school and at home. Although they may still dress up and act out situations, they also use small toys, blocks, or other materials to replay a trip to the fire station or other community facilities. They may also reenact what they see happening on television news or familiar shows. Older children take a more organized approach to dramatic play. They want to write their own scripts, assign parts, make costumes, and stage plays. This activity provides a variety of opportunities to practice skills that youngsters are trying to develop during this period of their childhood. Writing a script entails

FIGURE 11–6   *Children use puppets to relive past experiences or express feelings.*

listening to how people talk during conversations, writing words, and organizing a story line. Negotiations and compromise are necessary to be certain that all participants have an opportunity to contribute according to their own skills or interests.

The best kinds of dramatic play occur when children can play whatever they wish. Allow children many different opportunities to use their imaginations in both spontaneous and organized activities. Make materials available as their interests dictate.

Activities

Purposes: Provide practice in negotiating and compromising during a group effort

Enhance the ability to set long-term goals and to postpone gratification

Increase the ability to portray ideas, feelings, and experiences through drama or using blocks

Puppets.   Design and make different kinds of puppets. Try shadow, finger, stick, papier-mâché, or sock puppets. Read about how puppets are constructed and used in other countries. (See Figure 11–7 for ideas.)

Papier-mâché Puppet
   Materials needed:
      dried papier-mâché sphere made on a balloon
      length of cardboard tubing from paper towel roll
      felt and cloth scraps
      yarn, ribbons, buttons
      marking pens
      tempera or acrylic paint, small brushes
      scissors, glue
   Directions:
      Cut a small opening in one side of the sphere. Gently push the cardboard tubing into the opening. Paint the face with flesh tones. Let the face dry overnight before adding features. Use yarn for making hair. Cut fabric or felt scraps for clothing, making it large enough to cover the child's hand. Decorate clothing with ribbons or buttons.

Sock Puppet
   Materials needed:
      clean sock, can be white or colored
      buttons
      eyes (you will find these in a hobby shop)
      felt, fabric scraps
      yarn, pipe cleaners, ribbons
      scissors, glue
   Directions:
      Show children how to fit the sock over their hand and then make a moving mouth with thumb and fingers. Let them glue scrap materials onto puppet to create a face.

Shadow Puppets
   Materials needed:
      cardboard strips or popsicle sticks
      construction paper
      scissors
      marking pens
      staple gun
   Directions:
      Have children draw a figure on the construction paper, then cut it out. Staple the figure to the cardboard strip or popsicle stick.

FIGURE 11–7   Puppets

Puppet theater.   Permanent or impromptu. Older children can make a permanent theater using carpentry tools and plywood. Make a theater from a large appliance box. An impromptu stage can also be as simple as a table covered with a blanket or a wall of large blocks.

Produce a puppet play.   Have children write a simple script or use a favorite story. Let them make the puppets, plan the production.

Drama kits.   Collect a variety of props children can use for dramatic play. Store them in related sets for different jobs: beautician, doctor, mechanic, astronaut. (Listen for children's interests, then provide additional props for play.)

Makeup.   Provide makeup (theatrical makeup, if possible) and mirrors. Allow children to try out ways to use makeup. Have tissues and cold cream for cleaning up when they are finished.

Blocks.   Provide both small and large blocks. Add accessories as children's interests dictate: cars, airplanes, boats, people, animals, trees, signs. Add additional materials: cardboard packing forms, styrofoam pieces, plywood, cardboard tubes.

Play.   Have children write and produce a play. They can also adapt a book or use a published play. (Check the library for suitable plays.)

Tell stories.   Encourage the children to tell their own stories that have a beginning, a middle, and an end. During group time, have one child start a story with a few sentences. The next child takes up the story line and continues with a few more sentences. Each child must listen to all the previous story tellers in order to remember the gist of the story before continuing. The last child has the most difficult part because he or she must bring closure to the story. As a variation, tape the story as the children tell it. Place the tape in the listening corner so that children can hear it again.

Read folktales.   Folktales are stories that once were told by parents, grandparents, or community storytellers. Originally they were not written down, but passed on from generation to generation. Read folktales at group times or encourage small groups or pairs of children to read to one another.

Invite an adult storyteller to visit.   Ask the adult to tell the children a story that was a favorite when he or she was a child. Encourage stories that have been part of a family tradition or culture.

Field trip.   View a puppet play or children's drama. Look for professional performances at theaters or amateur performances at schools, community centers, or libraries.

Discussion

Some concepts to discuss with children:

- Imagination: new ways to tell a story or express feelings
- Props: how to make props and costumes for their productions
- Scripts: books, poems, films, TV shows
- Skills: skills needed to produce a drama
- Puppets or marionettes: which fits a particular character
- Manipulating puppets to create a story

Equipment to Have Available

- Blocks—wooden floor blocks, large hollow blocks, small colored blocks
- Block accessories—cars, boats, airplanes, people, animals, trees, signs

- Boxes, shelves, racks for storing props
- Carpentry tools—saw, measuring tape, yardstick, hammer, sander, nails
- Dress-up clothes—skirts, dresses, capes, shoes, hats, wigs, scarves
- Floor lights—standing lamps, spotlights
- Mirrors—individual makeup mirrors, full-length mirrors
- Puppet theater or materials for construction
- Sewing tools—needles, thread, pins, scissors
- Tape recorder
- Window shade or curtains

Not all children are going to grow up to be painters, sculptors, actors, musicians, or playwrights. However, you want them to learn that when they go out into the sometimes harried world of adulthood, the arts will provide continuing pleasure and relaxation. By having a variety of art activities available, all children can find one that suits their own individual needs and abilities. So, make art of all kinds an integral part of your day. Both you and the children will reap boundless benefits.

Summary

Creative activities satisfy children in a way no other experiences can. This is because they all can be successful. They can communicate nonverbally and release emotions. They learn about themselves and can relive or remake their own experiences.

An additional bonus is that art can be shared with others or experienced alone.

Creative activities should be based on children's interests. Some form of art activity should be part of every day.

Very young children use all their senses to explore the properties of art materials. By kindergarten age, they learn that their feelings and experiences can be portrayed symbolically. Art activities provide the media for doing so. By the end of middle childhood, children set goals for themselves and want recognition for their accomplishments.

The most effective art program will meet the needs of both the youngest children and the older ones.

Kindergarten children can sing simple songs and like to imitate rhythms they have heard or create their own. By the end of elementary school, most children have a good sense of rhythm and beat. They can remember many songs and even sing in harmony. Some can play instruments or compose music.

From an early age, children engage in dramatic play. Toddlers imitate what they see. Preschoolers try out adult roles. During middle childhood, youngsters use dramatic play to consolidate learning. Older children want to write their own scripts and produce their own plays.

The arts will provide continuing pleasure for children into their adult years. Art of all kinds should be an integral part of the child-care day.

Selected Further Reading

Anders, R. (1975). *Making musical instruments*. Minneapolis: Lerner Publications Company.

Bernstein, B., & Blair, L. (1982). *Native American crafts workshop*. Belmont, CA: David S. Lake Publishers.

Bruchac, J. (1991). *Native American stories*. Golden, CO: Fulcrum.

Carlson, L. (1993) *EcoArt*. Charlotte, VT: Williamson Publishing.

Carlson, L. (1990) *Kids create!* Charlotte, VT: Williamson Publishing.

Cherry, C. (1990). *Creative art for the developing child* (2nd ed.). Belmont, CA: David S. Lake Publishers.

Corwin, J. (1990). *African crafts*. New York: Franklin Watts.

Gutwirth, V. (1997). A multicultural family study project for primary. *Young Children, 52*(2), 72–78.

Haas, C., & Friedman, A. (1990) *My own fun—Activities for kids ages 7–12*. Chicago: Chicago Review Press. (Available from School-Age Notes, Nashville, TN).

Kohl, M., & Potter, J. (1993). *Science arts, Discovering science through art experiences*. Bellingham, WA: Bright Ring Publishing.

Milford, S. (1990). *Adventures in art, art and craft experiences for 7- to 14-year-olds*. Charlotte, VT: Williamson Publishing.

Ryder, W. (1995). *Celebrating diversity with art, thematic projects for every month of the year*. Glenview, IL: Scott Foresman.

Sierra, J. (1991). *Fantastic theater, puppets and plays for young performers and young audiences*. New York: The H.W. Wilson Co.

Computer Software/Video

Children's Songs Around the World (Laserdic VHS). Baldwin, NY: Education Activities. Primary.

Let's Visit Mexico (Mac IBM CD-ROM). Fairfield, CT: Queue. Advanced.

Meiko: A Story of Japanese Culture (MPC CD-ROM). Novato: CA: Broderbund/ Digital Productions.

China: Home of the Dragon (Mac Windows CD-ROM). Orange Cherry/ New Media Schoolhouse. Intermediate, Advanced

Thinkin' Things Collection 1 (Mac IBM Windows MPC CD-ROM). Redmond, WA: Edmark. Primary, Intermediate.

Thinkin' Things Collection 2 (Mac IBM Windows MPC CD-ROM). Redmond WA: Edmark. Primary, Intermediate, Advanced.

Thinkin' Things Collection 3 (Mac MPC CD-ROM). Redmond, WA: Edmark. Intermediate, Advanced.

Student Activities

1. Visit a library, museum, community center, and a theater in your community. Ask about programs or resources they might have that would interest school-age children. Prepare a list to share with your classmates.
2. Plan and implement one of the activities suggested in this chapter. Write an evaluation of the experience. Were there things you could have done differently? If so, how?
3. Talk to teachers/caregivers in three different child care groups. Ask which creative activities their children most enjoy. Find out why they think those activities are so popular.

Review

1. This chapter stated that "creative experiences satisfy children in a way few other experiences can." Give three reasons why that statement was made.
2. In what way does a preschooler's use of art materials differ from that of a child approaching adolescence?
3. Give five examples of art activities appropriate for school-age children.
4. List three musical concepts to discuss with children in order to enhance their learning.
5. You want to encourage children in your child-care group to enjoy more music. What kinds of equipment should you have available?
6. Relate the developmental steps in children's dramatic play from toddlerhood to older middle childhood.
7. List some accessories children might use with blocks for dramatic play.

CHAPTER 12

Science and Math

Fostering Curiosity Through Science

Children are incredibly curious about the world around them. They constantly want to know why events happen. Why do seeds sprout? Why is there a rainbow when it is still raining? Why does a magnet pick up some objects and not others? Whenever possible children take objects apart to find out what is inside. What makes the hands on a clock move? What is inside a radio? They also try to gain mastery over objects in their environment. They are delighted when they can operate a pulley to pick up an object or attach a lightbulb to a battery and make it light. Computers and video games provide a whole new array of things to master.

During middle childhood, children's ability to understand scientific phenomena and principles is limited because the shift from concrete thinking to abstract occurs very gradually. They do not begin to think logically until about age eight or nine. This means they have difficulty grasping concepts that are part of scientific explorations. Children cannot always predict that a liquid that becomes a solid (gelatin) when cooled will become liquid again when heated. They also do not always understand cause and effect. They know popcorn pops when you heat it, but do not know why. In addition, children often puzzle over alternative solutions to everyday problems. They have learned one way to resolve the problem and cannot think of other possibilities.

Science activities allow children freedom to explore materials and carry through experiments in a nonthreatening atmosphere. Through fun activities, they not only acquire the skills necessary for scientific inquiries, but also gain confidence to seek solutions to problems in other situations. First, they learn to observe carefully and objectively when watching changes taking place slowly in plants or animals during a life cycle, or instantaneously during some chemical reactions. Observation is the most basic scientific skill and fosters curiosity for further investigation. Second, children learn classification when they sort objects into groups with common characteristics or arrange them in order from smallest to largest. Classification is a useful skill that helps children order information according to similarities, differences, and interrelationships and is crucial to concept formation. Third, they can predict and even run the risk of being wrong when guessing outcomes in situations they have not encountered before. Predicting is the ability to consider alternatives as they answer questions about consequences of different actions. Measuring is a fourth skill that can be acquired when they chart the growth of plants over a period of time or when they attempt to quantify results. Measuring facilitates classifying and comparing. A fifth skill, inferring, occurs when they predict outcomes based on what they already know from previous experiences. Children observe cause-and-effect patterns and expect similar results in similar circumstances. Last, through sharing information with one another they practice communicating information to others. Scientific information must be communicated in ways that are clear, concise, and unambiguous. These skills are needed for effective problem solving.

Activities

Biological Science

Purposes: Develop an understanding of the natural environment

           Acquire the ability to nurture and care for living creatures

           Observe the life cycles of plants and animals

           Cultivate awareness of endangered species and the need to preserve them

Let children care for live animals: a bird, gerbil, guinea pig, hamster, kitten, rabbit, snake, fish, salamander, lizard, tortoise. Ask children to help choose the animal to be added to their classroom. Before introducing the animal, have children research what the animal eats or drinks, what kind of environment it needs, and how to care for the animal. Consult with a local pet store and check with a veterinarian. Construct a habitat appropriate for that animal.

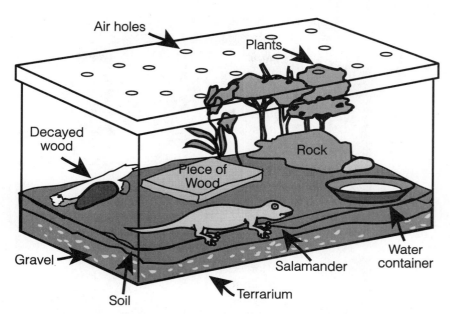

FIGURE 12–1   *Salamander Habitat. From Wheeler, R. (1997). Creative Resources for Elementary Classrooms and School-Age Programs. Albany, NY: Delmar Publishers*

To stimulate scientific inquiry, encourage children to observe the animal. For instance, a hamster can generate questions about what kinds of vegetables the animal will eat. Let them predict, then test out various choices by offering a selection of lettuce, carrots, celery, and spinach. Note which the hamster prefers. Which will it not eat?

Older children can add to this activity by creating imaginary animals. Stimulate their imaginations by reading aloud Dr. Seuss' *If I Ran the Zoo* (Random House, 1950). Set up a display of the animals when they are finished.

Let children observe the life cycle of frogs.   Get some frog eggs or tadpoles from a stream, pond, or lake. Put them in an aquarium with plenty of pond water and a few pond plants. Feed the tadpoles extra food: boiled spinach or other leafy green vegetables. Observe the growth.

Encourage children to predict how long it will take the tadpoles to turn into frogs. Let them chart the growth, noting the decrease in size of the tadpoles' tails and the appearance of legs. How close were they in their predictions?

Cultivate a garden outdoors.   Involve the children in a discussion of whether they want a vegetable or flower garden. Provide seed catalogues, books on plants, or magazines that have a gardening section. Take a trip to a local nursery.

Have children measure the amount of space that can be allotted to the garden and research the type of plants that can be grown at different seasons of the year. Have them draw a plot plan spacing the various plants according to what they have learned about plant requirements. Plant the garden.

Invite further inquiry by asking the children to keep track of which plants come up first. If they have planted vegetables, which are ready for harvesting the earliest?

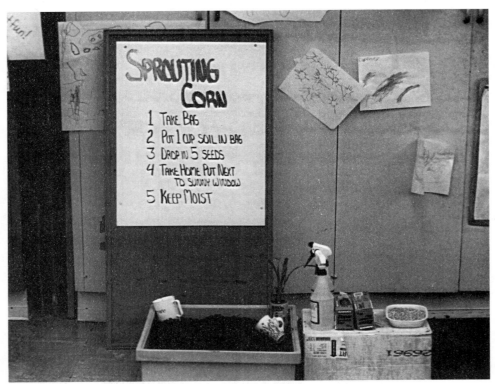

FIGURE 12–2   A bulletin board shows children the steps needed to sprout corn.

Play Twenty Questions to encourage children to use their senses in identifying fruits, vegetables, or parts of aromatic plants. Choose five or more examples that have distinctive odors. Punch holes in the sides of a corresponding number of paper bags. Place each item in a separate bag and fasten it shut. Code each bag with a number on the outside. Prepare a card with the code numbers and a space for naming the contents. Allow each child to smell the bags and write down what they think it is. When every child has had a turn, open the bags and let them check their answers.

Keep potted plants in the classroom.   Include a variety of plants: those grown from seeds, from cuttings of mature plants, from pits or tubers (avocado pits or sweet potatoes). Research plant requirements for growth. How much water do different kinds of plants need? What kind of food do plants require? Why do some plants grow better in shade than in bright sunlight? Ask children to prepare a bulletin board showing different plants that grow in the shade and those that require a lot of sunshine. Suggest that they draw pictures of the plants, use seed packets, or cut out pictures from magazines to show the plants.

To further encourage scientific inquiry, tell the students they can perform an experiment to determine how much sunlight a plant needs. Have them plant a bean seed in each of ten plastic cups filled with sterile potting soil. Place half of the cups at various distances from a window light source but not in direct sunlight.

Cover the other cups or place them in complete darkness. Keep the soil in all the containers wet, but be careful not to overwater. Compare the growth of the two sets of plants once a week and chart their progress. Record the height and condition of the plants in each container. As a conclusion to the experiment, discuss what they have learned about plant requirements for sunlight.

Grow plants from "invisible seeds."   Pour a thin layer of canned soup into a flat dish. Have children place bits of dirt, bread crumbs, or floor dust onto the soup. Cover with a plastic wrap and put in a warm place. Within a few days mold spores will begin to grow. Provide a magnifying glass or microscope so children can examine the different "plants."

To stimulate further inquiry, do a second experiment to observe molds growing on other materials. Rub a piece of bread on the kitchen floor, sprinkle it with a little water, and place it in a sealed jar. Place a piece of cheese in another jar, and a fruit peel in a third jar. Seal the jars and place all three in a dark location. Observe the changes periodically, noting the different times it takes molds to grow on the three media. Provide a microscope or magnifying glass so children can see the molds. Are the molds that grow on bread, cheese, and peels the same or different than those on the soup?

Learn about endangered species and what can be done to prevent total extinction of these plants and animals.   Contact National Geographic, Greenpeace, or the Sierra Club to find out if they have videotapes, magazines, speakers, or other sources of information about endangered species. *The Sierra Club Book of Weather*, by Vicki McVey (1993), published by the Sierra Club of San Francisco is listed in the Selected Further Reading section under Biological Science. Children can also obtain additional information from:

The Nature Conservancy
P.O. Box 17056
Baltimore, MD 21298

The Sierra Club
85 2nd Street, Second Floor
San Francisco, CA 94105
(415) 977-5653

If there is a wildlife preservation area in your vicinity, schedule a field trip. Observe and record the plants and/or animals found at the preserve. Follow the visit with a discussion of why it is important to save these plants and animals from extinction.

Older children can explore what is happening to the rain forests throughout the world. They can write to:

RainForest Action Network
300 Broadway, Suite 28
San Francisco, CA 94113

Provide books for children to read on their own. Some excellent sources are: *Vanishing Rain Forest* by Diane Willow and Laura Jacques (1991); *The Rainforest* by

Billy Goodman (1991); *What's in the Rainforest?* by Suzanne Ross (1991). Place the books in the reading corner and allow time during the day for the children to read. Place a map of the world on a bulletin board and ask children to color in rain forest areas as they discover them in their reading.

Physical Science

Purposes: Foster a questioning attitude

Observe physical phenomena—electrical, magnetic, optical, chemical

Predict outcomes—opposing magnetic forces, chemical changes

Understand basic scientific principles

Experiment with electricity.   You can purchase inexpensive electrical kits at stores that carry radio and video parts. These ordinarily use 1.5 volt storage batteries and flashlight bulbs. Set up simple circuits. See Figure 12–3 for a diagram.

To determine how a flashlight uses an electrical current, provide: a flashlight that holds two size D batteries, a 16-inch strip of aluminum foil, duct tape, two D batteries. Unscrew the top from the flashlight. Wrap one end of the foil around the base of the bulb holder. Remove the batteries from the base of the flashlight. Use the duct tape to fasten the batteries together, with the negative end of one on top of the positive end of the other. Stand the negative terminal of the bottom battery on the foil strip. Press the base of the bulb holder to the positive tip of the top battery. The bulb will light because an electrical current has been created.

Demonstrate magnetic force.   Provide a horseshoe magnet plus some iron filings in the lid of a stationary box. The box can be supported on blocks or a pile of books. Let children pass the magnet under the box and see the pattern the filings form. They will observe the two opposing forces emerging from the two sides of the horseshoe magnet.

For additional exploration of the opposing forces of magnets, provide a variety of shapes and sizes of magnets. Encourage children to try linking several magnets together or moving other magnets by using one.

Demonstrate refraction of light through concave or convex lenses.   Provide old eyeglasses from which the ear-pieces have been removed, a prism, magnifying glass, and flashlights. Cover a table with a blanket. Let children work in the dark under the table to experiment with the ways light is refracted through the different objects. Ask children to compare what happens when the light passes through the different objects.

Another way to demonstrate how an object can refract light is with a lamp and cotton handkerchief. Remove the shade from a lighted lamp. Have children stand about 6 feet away from the lamp and hold the handkerchief up to their eyes. When they stretch the cloth, the light is separated into a starburst of light with dim bands of yellow and orange.

Make a prism to explore what happens when light passes through. For this experiment, supply transparent tape, three microscope slides or three strips of clear plastic (same size as the slide), modeling clay, and water. Tape the three slides together to form a triangle. Press one end into a wad of clay. Fill the prism

Simple Electricity Experiments

Simple Circuit

Equipment: Two pieces of electrical wire, with stripped ends
D battery
Small torch bulb
Single bulb socket

Directions:
Screw bulb into socket. Attach one end of each wire to screw poles of the socket.

Touch one free end of the wire to the top of the battery and the other to the bottom.

Discover where the wires have to make contact in order to light the bulb.

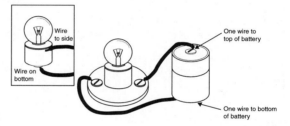

Circuit Variations

Equipment: Battery
Three bulb sockets, three bulbs
Six pieces of electrical wire, with stripped ends

Directions:
Attach wire from battery to the sockets in the configuration shown below at left. This is a series circuit. What happens if you unscrew one of the bulbs?

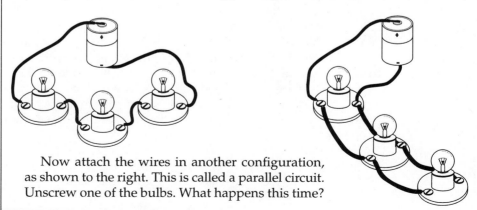

Now attach the wires in another configuration, as shown to the right. This is called a parallel circuit. Unscrew one of the bulbs. What happens this time?

FIGURE 12–3   Simple Electrical Circuits

Materials:
  Chunks of coal or charcoal briquettes
  Glass pie pan or low or clear glass bowl
  Tablespoon
  Pint glass jar for mixing

Mix:
  4 tablespoons plain salt (uniodized salt)
  4 tablespoons water
  2 tablespoons clear household ammonia
  4 tablespoons laundry bluing
  Food coloring in squeeze bottles or eyedroppers

Spread newspapers on work area. Heap coal in pie pan. Let children measure salt and water into jar. Warn children to hold their noses while you measure and pour the ammonia into the jar. Add the bluing. Cap the jar, then mix the contents until the salt is dissolved. Slowly pour the mixture over the coal. Children can drip food coloring in separate places on the coal. Put the dish in a place where children can watch the crystal formation, but do not move the dish. (The crystals are somewhat fragile and will collapse easily.)
Caution: The ammonia and bluing should be handled by an adult, not the children. Warn children not to touch the coal and its surrounding liquid while they are dripping on the food coloring.

FIGURE 12–4   *Crystal Garden*

with water then hold it up to a brightly lighted window or shine a flashlight through it. What happens to the light?

Observe crystal formation in a crystal garden.   Supply materials as described in Figure 12–4. Provide a magnifying glass so that children can closely view the crystals that form.

A crystal formation demonstration can also be done with salt. Children may want to make their own individual crystal experiment. If so, for each child supply: a pipe cleaner, clear cup, ½ cup hot water, ⅓ cup salt, a spoon, a pencil. (Some children may need help when handling the hot water.) Bend the pipe cleaner around the pencil, leaving the two ends hanging down. Pour the hot water into the cup and add the salt a spoonful at a time. Stir after each addition so the salt dissolves thoroughly. Place the pencil across the top of the cup so the ends of the pipe cleaner are in the water. Place the cup in a place where it will not be disturbed. Crystals should begin forming after only a few hours, but they will change each day. When all the water has been crystallized, the pencil can be removed and hung on a string where it can be enjoyed. For a variation, add food coloring to the water before adding the salt.

Experiment with simple machines.   Use everyday materials to allow children to explore simple machines such as levers, incline planes, pulleys, and wheels. Add PVC pipe lengths, rain gutters, wood planks, and blocks to provide a multitude of physical science activities. Let the children explore freely.

Earth Science

Purposes: Cultivate curiosity about the Earth and the solar system

Encourage scientific inquiry

Provide practice in predicting outcomes

Increase knowledge of the principles of earth sciences

Explore the solar system.   Obtain posters or photos taken during space explorations. The National Aeronautics and Space Administration (NASA) should have views of Earth taken from outer space, pictures of astronauts at work, and photos from space probes of Mars, Venus, Mercury, and Jupiter. The Jet Propulsion Laboratory in Pasadena, California, and the Smithsonian Air and Space Museum in Washington, DC are also sources of materials. Your local library may have books, cassette tapes, or videos as well. Set up a bulletin board display. Obtain books on space that children can read or browse through in the book corner. Provide a tape recorder and earphones if tapes are available. To stimulate children's interest in space and space travel, ask them to draw or paint a picture of what they would find if they were actually on one of the planets. They might do another picture of things they would take with them on their trip to the planet. Display the pictures and ask children to discuss their choices and to explain why certain items would be necessary or desired.

Help students understand the principle that allows a rocket ship to enter space by explaining that it is based on Isaac Newton's third law of motion (for every action there is an opposite and equal reaction). Provide each child with a balloon. Tell them to blow up the balloon and hold their fingers tightly around the neck to keep air from escaping. Let the children release their balloons, one at a time. Do they know what happens? How does Newton's law apply? (The balloon pushes air backwards as it is released through the neck. The escaping air pushes the balloon forward.) The children can also consider which balloons went the farthest and why? Is there any way they might control where the balloon-rocket goes?

Visit a planetarium, if possible. Your community may have one, but also find out if a nearby college or university has one.

Chart the weather for a month.   Provide a calendar form for each child or a large one for a bulletin board. Obtain a thermometer that records both temperature and barometer reading that can be placed outdoors. Have children record daily temperatures, barometer reading, and weather conditions. Ask them to bring weather reports and predictions from daily newspapers. Have them keep track of how many times the predictions are correct. Can they predict the weather based on a given day for the following day?

Have children write for more information about weather predicting and tracking. Good sources are:

American Meteorological Society
1701 K Street NW, Suite 300
Washington, DC 20006

National Climate Data Center
Federal Building
Asheville, NC 28801

National Weather Service Public Affairs Office
1325 East-West Highway
Silver Spring, MD 20910

There is also a bimonthly magazine:

Weatherwise
Heldref Publications
1319 18th Street NW
Washington, DC 20036

Have children make a rain gauge.   You will need a clear plastic tube that is sealed at one end (jewelry beads often come in this kind of tube.), a ruler, masking tape, a pencil, and a piece of clay. Attach the tape along the entire length of the tube. Calibrate by placing the ruler against the tape, then (starting from the bottom) mark off one inch, two inches, etc. to the top of the tube. Set the tube into the clay, making sure it stands straight. Place the gauge outdoors where it will collect rain. Add rainfall records to the weather charts.

Tell children they can make "lightning." Provide each child with a balloon. Inflate the balloons, then darken the room. Tell children to rub their balloon on the carpet or on their wool clothing. Have pairs of children hold their balloons end-to-end, almost touching. If the room is dark enough, they will see an electrical spark jump between the balloons.

Demonstrate the force of gravity with a pendulum.   Tie a string to a plumb bob or fish weight. Have children attach it to the center of a camera tripod, then position the tripod over a tray that contains a thin layer of sand. Have them adjust the length of the string so the weight can swing freely, but barely touches the top of the sand. When the pendulum is gently started, it will trace a pattern in the sand.

For a variation, use a tray with sand that is deep enough to hold golf tees upright. Have the children place the tees in a circle in the center of the tripod. Have them predict which tees will be knocked over first. Which one will be last?

Equipment to Have Available

- Animal habitats, an incubator for hatching eggs
- Ant farm with a supply of ants
- Aquarium with books on tropical fish
- Binoculars and bird identification books
- Bug house, bug-capturing containers, butterfly net
- Calculators, computers, software programs
- Collections of shells, rocks, and fossils

FIGURE 12–5   A globe can help children understand world weather changes.

- Filmstrip projector and filmstrips
- Flashlights
- Hair dryer, small vacuum, bicycle pump
- Household scales or simple balance with weights
- Levers, incline planes, pulleys, wheels
- Magnets: bar and horseshoe, assorted sizes
- Magnifying glasses, insect collections
- Measuring cups
- Microscope with prepared and blank slides
- Mirrors, plain and ground
- Prisms, eyeglasses, gyroscopes, color wheels
- PVC pipe lengths, rain gutters, wood planks, wood blocks
- Rock polishing equipment, jewelry tools
- Rulers, meter stick, T-squares, tapes, and protractor
- Tripod
- Sun-sensitive papers and outlines
- Telescope, and books on astronomy, a globe and compass
- Terrarium, seeds, potting soil, small pots
- Typewriter with plenty of inexpensive paper
- VCR, selected cassettes, tape player, earphones

FIGURE 12–6   An incubator lets children watch eggs
hatching.

Math in Child Care

A before- and after-school program can provide children with many opportunities
to use and reinforce math concepts they are learning in school. This can be done
with either spontaneous or planned activities. Spontaneous activities occur when
children need to add up scores during indoor or outdoor games. They must use
math to measure ingredients while preparing snacks or when deciding portion
size. They may have to calculate materials needed for a project or the cost of buying the materials.

Planned math activities can be designed to further children's cognitive development, helping them progress to the stage Piaget called concrete operations.
When they manipulate, count, and measure real objects they develop concepts

that eventually can be linked to the symbols for the objects. When they hold objects in their hands, weigh, or count them the concepts of size and number are evident. These concepts can later be recalled when they are confronted with new situations requiring math.

Activities

Purposes: Increase vocabulary and understanding of math concepts

Strengthen ability to count and carry out mathematical calculations

Classify objects according to common characteristics

Increase ability to use math concepts in new situations

Recognize how math is used in everyday life

Weigh a variety of objects.   Set up a center with different types of scales: balance, electronic, and spring. Include many different objects the children can weigh or balance. Ask children to weigh the objects and record their weights. Are the weights the same on different scales? Which objects are the heaviest? Are the heaviest objects also the largest? Encourage them to experiment with the balance scale. How many objects of one kind on one side of the balance does it take to counterweight objects on the other side? After a few experiments with this activity, provide different objects and ask the children to estimate their weight before putting the object on the scale. How accurate were they?

Provide a bathroom scale so children can weigh themselves. Include a basket of large stones. After determining their own weight, how many stones does it take to equal that amount? Make a wall chart of children's weights and the equivalent number of stones. Ask children to sort objects according to their weight. Let children weigh a collection of rocks, then sort them into groups. To simplify the activity, tell them to put together those that weigh one pound or less, then between two and three pounds, etc.

Measure in feet and inches.   Secure a measuring tape to the floor or use two yardsticks, end to end. Tell children to look at the divisions on the tape, pointing out the inch and feet marks. Have children lie down next to the tape. Ask one child to record each child's height in feet and inches.

The youngest children can reinforce the concepts of feet and inches by making a string showing their own height. Use colored yarn, Cheerios for the inches, and colored beads to signify feet markings. Older children could make a chart of all the group members to add to the weight chart described above.

Tell children they can measure a friend with a different kind of "feet." Supply each child with a piece of white construction paper and ask them to trace a friend's foot. Cut out the foot shape. Have children take turns lying down while another child uses the foot pattern to measure how many it takes. Show them how to turn the pattern end over end each time so that they start from the correct place each time the foot is moved. Record the number of "feet" it takes to go from foot to head.

Classify objects according to common characteristics.   Collect a variety of objects and scraps that are made of either natural or man-made materials.

FIGURE 12–7   Nuts and bolts help children match objects by their size.

Include: cotton balls and synthetic sponges, wool and synthetic fabrics, wood and vinyl flooring materials, plastic and wood toys, paper and plastic office supplies, newspaper and cellophane. Tell children to decide what each material is made of and sort into piles for natural or man-made.

In autumn, collect an assortment of leaves to be sorted according to colors and shape. Provide an assortment of small objects with a variety of tools to pick them up. Include: beads, buttons, seeds, tiny Easter eggs, small animals, beans. Have children use tweezers, tongs, strawberry hullers, or needle-nose pliers to pick up the objects and place them in small boxes, egg cartons, or partitioned boxes. Tell them to match the objects according to color, size, or category of the objects. Can some objects be placed in more than one category? How do you decide where to place each object?

Collect pictures of a variety of foodstuffs. Divide a large piece of poster board into four columns with a marking pen. Label each column with a food group: dairy, fruits/vegetables, grain, protein. Ask the children to place the pictures in the appropriate columns.

Prepare a snack that requires math skills.   To help children practice the skill of re-creating a pattern, have them prepare kabobs. Older children can use serrated knives to cut fruits and cheese into equal sized chunks. (Younger children may require help from an adult or an adult can do this part.) Supply one bamboo skewer per child. The adult makes a pattern using alternating pieces of different fruits interspersed with cheese. Ask the children to form like kabobs for themselves.

Provide several large pizza shells. (These can be found in the frozen food section of the market.) Supply the necessary toppings: mozzarella cheese, parmesan cheese, pepperoni, sliced mushrooms, etc. When the pizzas have been baked, ask the children to count the number of children in the group and decide how many pieces to cut each pizza into.

Estimate numbers by guessing how many objects in a jar.   Obtain a large (16 oz.) clear glass or plastic jar. Fill the jar with marshmallows, jelly beans, or other small food items. Place the jar in front of a chart labeled "Weekly Food Estimates." Provide small cards or slips of paper near the jar and a marking pen. Ask children to write down their name and an estimate of how many objects there are in the jar. Thumbtack the cards to the bulletin board. At the end of the week, ask several children to open the jar and count the items. You can also have the group count the items together. Who guessed the closest to the actual number? Have the children write the actual count on their own card. Place the cards in an envelope and save them. After repeating this activity over several weeks, are they getting better at estimating?

Play table games that require counting.   Any game in which children have to count the number of squares to move their pieces will help them develop counting skills. Monopoly® remains a favorite of many children. Look for others suitable for the ages your center serves.

Equipment to Have Available

Baskets, boxes, egg cartons

Collections of small objects: beads, buttons, seeds, eggs, animals, beans

Cooking equipment

Rulers, tape measures, calculators

Scales: balance, spring, electronic

Table games

Tweezers, tongs, needle-nose pliers

Guidelines for Child-Care Staff Members

There are some guidelines to help you plan activities that allow children the maximum opportunity for learning. They are:

- Give children many chances to explore and experiment on their own. Set up learning centers or have materials easily available for children to use when they wish.

- Provide enticing materials that will encourage them to want to participate. Listen to the children to find out what they are interested in and then supply them with the means to pursue those interests. In addition, stimulate them to want to explore new interests.
- Do not give answers too readily. Ask questions that stimulate children to hypothesize, predict, or think of other possibilities. "What would happen if you . . . ?" "What can you do differently next time?"
- Listen to the children to find out what they already know or what they are thinking. Help them to correct any misinformation or add to the knowledge they already have. Design appropriate activities that will lead them to a higher level of understanding.
- Make a special effort to encourage girls to enjoy science. Many young women believed at an early age that science was not for them. Girls need to hear about successful female scientists and to experience the joy of discovery themselves.
- Maintain a questioning attitude and a sense of wonder yourself. Be alert to any possibilities for exploration and you will probably learn along with the children.

Summary

Children are incredibly curious about the world around them. They want to know why things happen and how things work. They are also trying to master their environment. Science can help them achieve these goals. School-age children have limited ability to understand scientific principles. They cannot always think logically and this affects their ability to predict processes that can be reversed. They are just beginning to understand cause and effect and have difficulty considering alternative solutions to problems. Science activities let children explore materials and carry out experiments in a nonthreatening environment. Participation in the activities helps children acquire some basic scientific skills that are transferable to other situations. They learn to observe, classify, predict, measure, infer, and communicate information to others.

Suggested activities begin with the biological sciences since these are usually the easiest for children to understand. Experiences in physical and earth science are also included in this chapter. You do not need to spend huge amounts of money for science equipment. Many items can be found in most households.

A before- and after-school program can provide children with many opportunities to use and reinforce math concepts they are learning in school. This can be done with both spontaneous and planned activities. Spontaneous activities occur when children play games or prepare snacks. Planned activities can be designed so children manipulate, count, and measure real objects. In this way they develop concepts that can be linked to the symbols for the objects in new situations where math is needed.

Guidelines for staff members to help in planning activities that allow children maximum opportunities for learning are:

- Give children lots of opportunities to explore freely.
- Provide enticing materials.
- Do not give answers too readily, but encourage children to find answers to their questions.
- Listen to children to find out what they already know, then help them to correct any misconceptions.
- Maintain a questioning attitude and a sense of wonder yourself.

Selected Further Reading

General Science Books

Blaw, L. (1994). *Super science.* Bellevue, WA: One From the Heart Educational Research.

Churchill, E.R. (1991). *Amazing science experiments with everyday materials.* New York: Sterling Publishing Company, Inc.

Friedhoffer, R. (1990). *Magic tricks, science facts.* New York: Franklin Watts.

Van Cleave, J. (1996). *202 oozing, bubbling, dripping and bouncing experiments.* New York: John Wiley & Sons, Inc.

Wheeler, R. (1997). *Creative Resources for elementary classrooms and school-age programs.* Albany, NY: Delmar Publishers.

Biological Science

Alan, G. (1992). *Jack and the beanstalk.* New York: Doubleday Books for Young Readers.

Challand, H.J. (1986). *Plants without seeds.* Chicago: Children's Press. Primary.

Dr. Seuss. (1950). *If I ran the zoo.* New York: Random House. Primary.

Goldenberg, J. (1994). *Weird things you can grow.* New York, NY: Random House. Intermediate, Advanced.

Goodman, B. (1991). *The rainforest.* New York: Tern Enterprise. Intermediate.

McVey, V. (1993). *Sierra Club guide to planet care and repair.* San Francisco: Sierra Club.

Ross, S. (1991). *What's in the rainforest? 106 Answers from a to z.* Los Angeles: Enchanted Rainforest Press. Intermediate.

Willow, D., & Jacques L. (1991). *At home in the rain forest.* Watertown, MA: Charlesbridge Publishing, Inc. Primary.

Zike, D. (1993). *The earth science book, activities for kids.* New York: John Wiley & Sons, Inc.

Physical Science

Ardley, N. (1991). *The science book of electricity.* Orlando, FL: Harcourt Brace Jovanovich Publishers.

Cash, T., & Taylor, B. (1989). *Electricity and magnets.* New York: Warwick Press.
Friedhoffer, R. (1992). *Magnetism and electricity.* New York: Franklin Watts.
Glover, D. (1993). *Batteries, bulbs, and wires: Science facts and experiments.* New York: Kingfisher Books.

Earth Science

McVey, V. (1991). *The Sierra Club book of weather wisdom.* New York: Sierra Club/Little Brown.
Parsons, A. (1993). *Earth: A creative hands-on approach to science.* New York: Macmillan Publishing Company.
Van Cleave, J. (1996). *Ecology for every kid: Easy activities that make learning science fun.* New York: John Wiley & Sons.
Williams, J. (1992). *The weather book.* New York: Vintage Books.
Zike, D. (1993). *The earth science book: Activities for kids.* New York: John Wiley & Sons, Inc.

Math

Challoner, J. (1992). *The science book of numbers.* Orlando, FL: Harcourt Brace Jovanovich Publishers.
Kurth, M. (1996). *Math in my world: Over 130 child-centered math activities.* Cypress, CA: Creative Teaching Press, Inc.

Computer Software

Biological Science

Mammals: A Multimedia Encyclopedia (Mac IBM CD-ROM) Washington, DC: National Geographic Primary, Intermediate, Advanced.
The San Diego Zoo Presents: The Animals! (2.0) (Mac MPC CD-ROM) Novato, CA: Mindscape Educational Software. Primary, Intermediate, Advanced.
Wonders of Science CD-ROM Library: A World of Plants (Mac MPC CD-ROM). Washington, DC: National Geographic. Primary, Intermediate.
Eco-Adventures in the Rainforest (Mac IBM) San Diego: Chariot Software Group. Intermediate, Advanced.
Rain Forest: Imagination Express (Mac MPC CD-ROM). Redmond, WA: Edmark. Primary, Intermediate, Advanced.

Physical Science

Learning About Electricity (Laserdisk VHS). Chatsworth, CA: AIMS. Primary, Intermediate, Advanced.

New A+ Science (Mac IBM Windows) Oklahoma City: American Education Corporations. Primary, Intermediate, Advanced.

All About Science I (Mac IBM CD-ROM) Fairfield, CT: Queue. Advanced.

Earth Science

Stars and Planets (GS IBM). Mill Valley, CA: Advanced Ideas. Primary

Exploring Our Solar System (Mac Windows CD-ROM). Chatsworth, CA: AIMS. Advanced.

Space Shuttle (Mac MPC CD-ROM). Novato, CA: Mindscape Educational Software. Intermediate, Advanced.

Weather: Air in Action Series (Mac Windows CD-ROM). Chatsworth, CA: AIMS. Advanced.

Everything Weather (Mac MPC CD-ROM). Princeton, NJ: Bureau of Electronic Publishing (Thynx). Advanced.

Math

Hands-On Math (Apple II Mac IBM) Grover Beach, CA: Ventura Education Systems. Primary, Intermediate, Advanced.

Millie's Math House (Mac IBM Windows CD-ROM) Redmond, WA: Edmark. Primary.

Student Activities

1. Find out if your city sponsors contests or fairs for student science projects. Enter some of your children's work. If you cannot find a local event, have one at your center. Ask high-school or college science teachers to be judges.
2. Plan one of the activities described in this chapter and implement it at your school. Record your observations of the children as they participated in the activity. What did they do and say? Bring the materials and your observations to class and share them with your fellow students.
3. Plan a field trip to a local site of scientific interest. The power-generating station, the beach, an observatory, a museum, a radio or television station all provide insights into how science is basic to our civilization. Follow the trip with discussions about what the children learned. Describe the trip to your classmates. Were there things you would do differently next time?

Review

1. Science is a curriculum area that can help children achieve mastery over their environment. Explain that statement.
2. School-age children have limited ability to understand scientific principles. Why?
3. What are the skills necessary for scientific inquiries?
4. Describe several ways you can help children learn about plants.
5. Briefly describe three physical science activities.
6. List five inexpensive items of equipment that can be used for science experiments.
7. Name three unplanned or spontaneous situations in which children must use math.
8. Planned math activities can be designed to help children progress to the stage that Piaget called concrete operations. Explain what is meant by that statement.
9. Describe two math activities.
10. The text presents guidelines for staff members when planning and implementing math activities. What are they?

13

Planning for the Future

Objectives

After studying this chapter, the student should be able to:

- Explain the importance of preparing children for future adult roles
- List skills future workers will need
- Plan and implement experiences that help children explore a variety of jobs and workplaces

Importance of Preparing Children for the Future

There is a revolution taking place in the workplace, says Toffler (1990) in his book *POWERSHIFT: Knowledge, Wealth, and Violence on the Edge of the 21st Century.* Most people accept Toffler's premise that tomorrow's workers will have to master new techniques in order to manage complex technology. In addition, Toffler says the whole character of the workplace will have to change in order to take advantage of the new tools. Workers will be expected to take a more active role in decision making. They will need to resolve problems and challenge preconceived assumptions. He predicts there will be few places for uneducated people or those without the required characteristics and skills.

High school or college is too late to begin preparing young people for their future employment. It is a process that begins in early childhood and continues

FIGURE 13–1   *"When I grow up I want to be a baby-sitter." Tai, age 7*

throughout the school years. We do not know what kinds of jobs will be developed in the future. We do know, however, that many future career opportunities will involve literate, educated workers. In order to achieve this, we must begin in early childhood to encourage children to be motivated learners who retain and use what they have studied. They must have meaning-based experiences that emphasize thinking, cooperative problem solving, decision making, and an opportunity to challenge preconceived ideas. Many of the activities throughout this book stress just those skills.

In addition to acquiring skills for the future, children should have an opportunity to experience the real world of work. At each stage of development children differ in their ability to think about the future and their own role as adults. As they grow and have more experience, their ideas change. Tai, whose drawing is shown in Figure 13–1, wants to be a baby-sitter. At age seven, being grown-up may mean being a teenager who can take care of younger children as her sister does. Ten-year-old Elizabeth, whose drawing appears in Figure 13–5 on page 201, already knows she is going to be a zoologist. She has developed an engrossing interest in animals and has a large collection of pets. She may very well continue this focus, but she could also branch out into other areas as she learns more about the adult world.

The school-age period is a good time to introduce children to adult jobs and workplaces. Although you may not have the equipment or resources to introduce children to advanced technology, you can help them experience a variety of jobs. Start with their interests. Listen to their conversations, watch their play, and observe what they draw. Implement their ideas through the use of theme units or special-interest clubs. Plan visits to local workplaces.

Exploring the Options

The following activities are only a small sample of areas that might interest children. Use them as a starting point from which to develop experiences that will catch the enthusiasm of your particular group of youngsters.

Activities

Map Maker (Cartographer)

Purposes: Provide practice in portraying concrete objects as symbols on a map

Encourage cooperative problem solving

Increase awareness of spatial relationships

Reinforce math concepts of area, distance

Set up an interest center with a globe, an atlas, and maps of the area surrounding your school. Prepare activity cards asking the children to find specific places on the globe or map. Sample directions might include:

- Find the country we live in.
- Outline the state where our city is situated.
- Find our school on the map.
- Find your street on the map.
- Mark a route from your home to school.
- How many blocks is it from your house to school? How many miles?
- How long does it take to drive from home to school? How long would it take if you were to walk?
- Where do your grandparents live? How many miles?
- How long would it take to get to your grandparents' house in a car? By airplane?

Map your neighborhood. Provide children with notepads and a pencil. Take them on a walk around the school neighborhood. Instruct them to write down distances in blocks. Tell them to note where buildings are located. When you return to school, have the children draw a map of your neighborhood on a large piece of paper.

Construct models of the buildings in your neighborhood to place on the map. Provide paper, light cardboard, scissors, glue, tape, and marking pens.

Place the neighborhood map in the block area. Encourage children to use blocks to construct the buildings.

Obtain a plot plan of the area around your center. (Call the planning office at your city hall.) Discuss the kinds of information shown on the print and how it is used.

Provide map puzzles. There are wooden and jigsaw puzzles of the United States. Look for them in toy stores or contact your local museum of history.

Construction Worker

Purposes: Increase vocabulary to include words related to construction projects

Practice ability to translate an idea into a concrete object

Strengthen decision-making skills

Provide opportunities to work together cooperatively

Learn to use a variety of tools safely

Let children plan and organize a workshop area.   Discuss common tools needed to construct objects from wood. Supply the suggested tools, then demonstrate how each is used. Stress the safety precautions to observe. Ask the children to draft a set of rules for the care and use of tools.

Build an object from wood.   Provide different kinds of wood: soft pine, balsa, plywood, doweling. Encourage the children to develop their own ideas about what to construct. Show them how to plan a project by making a drawing of the finished product. Provide rulers to make exact measurements, emphasizing how important it is to understand mathematical concepts in order to have a good finished product. Have them list the materials they will need, then let them implement their project. Some possibilities are: boxes for storing small items, a puppet theater, games. They might also build boats, trucks, cars, airplanes, and a diorama setting for their models. Coordinate a woodworking project with map making by building a model of your neighborhood with wooden stores and houses.

Make a replica of a construction project.   Discuss different kinds of construction projects: home building, office complexes, freeway construction. Collect and display pictures of construction projects in progress and of finished buildings. Provide toy replicas of equipment needed to construct areas of a city: earth movers, trucks, cement mixers, etc. Encourage children to create a city in progress in the sandbox using houses from their woodworking projects.

Invite a carpenter to visit your class.   Ask him or her to bring some special tools used on construction projects. Discuss the use of each of the tools. Allow children to ask questions. They might ask: What are the qualifications for the job? What do you have to know to be able to do the job? What do you like about your job? What do you do each day?

Chef's Club

Purposes: Provide opportunities to explore career options

Work cooperatively to prepare and serve a snack for the group

Strengthen group decision-making skills

Practice measuring using fractions and whole numbers

Develop a bulletin board of people cooking at home and in restaurants.
Ask children to contribute pictures of their family cooking together or pictures
that they have found in magazines. Encourage them to discuss what is needed to
prepare a meal for a family or for the patrons of a restaurant.

Visit a restaurant.   Talk to the chefs. Tell children to observe the processes for
preparing meals. What is done ahead of time? What are the kinds of things that
have to be done just before serving a meal? Ask the chefs how or where they
learned to cook. What do they have to know to be a chef? What are the qualifications for the job? What is the hardest part of their work? What do they like best?

**Visit a bakery or factory that produces large quantities of a food prod-
uct.**   Tell children to notice the kinds of equipment needed to automate food
production. Find out if computers are used to program the machinery. Interview a
worker or supervisor. What are the qualifications for the job?

Prepare pizza for a snack.   Set up an assembly line to prepare the pizzas. Use
frozen bread dough, canned biscuits, English muffins, or bagels for the crust. At
station one, the bread dough or canned biscuits are rolled into rounds and placed
on a cookie sheet. At station two, seasoned tomato sauce is spread on the rounds.
(There are several kinds of pizza sauce available at any supermarket.) Station three,
grate the cheese and sprinkle it over the tomato sauce. Station four can add additional toppings such as olives, mushrooms, pepperoni, or cooked sausage. Station
five is responsible for putting the pizzas in the oven and watching them until done.
If large rounds of bread dough were used as the crust, the final station, six, must
figure how many pieces to cut each pizza into in order to serve the group.

Prepare a snack from a recipe that requires measuring.   In Chapter 14,
Figure 14–2 is a recipe for Navajo Fry Bread. Also, look for cookbooks with simple
recipes. The NAEYC book *More Than Graham Crackers* listed at the end of Chapter
14 has many recipes that are designed for children.

Set up a restaurant and kitchen.   Have children arrange an area of the
room with a table and chairs plus a kitchen area where food can be prepared. They
can create signs for the restaurant, decorate the table with flowers, and write a
menu. Supply them with aprons and a chef's hat. Add tableware and some cook-
ware. Some children can role-play being the chef while others can be the waiter
and the patrons.

Space Travel and Communication

Purposes: Foster curiosity about the solar system

Increase knowledge about the United States space program

Challenge preconceived ideas about outer space

Strengthen the ability to think creatively

Design a space alien.   Research which planets have conditions that might support life. As an example: Venus has an atmosphere that is brownish yellow and is made up primarily of carbon dioxide gas with clouds of sulfuric acid. The temperature is around 880° Fahrenheit (470° Celsius). Design a space alien who could live in those conditions. Either draw a picture of the alien or construct one from papier mâché or other materials.

Explore communication between astronauts and the ground.   Have children research the technology used to make earth-to-space communication possible. Sources children can write to for information are cited in Chapter 12. Obtain pictures of a communication room at Cape Canaveral. Provide used circuit boards, computer equipment, and telephones. Encourage children to set up a communication center where they can role-play interactions between earth and a spaceship.

Build a space shuttle or spaceship.   Provide children with large pieces of cardboard or large packing boxes. Encourage them to design and build a spaceship. They can paint the outside and equip the inside with places for the astronauts to work. Place the spaceship near the communication center so the children can talk back and forth.

Brainstorm space travel in the future.   Ask children to imagine what space travel will be like in the future. Will people go into space as easily as they fly across the country? Will spaceships land and stay for a period of time on other planets? What part would they like to play in space travel of the future? Ask them to write down their thoughts or draw a picture. Display the various responses.

Environmental Conservationists

Purposes: Develop awareness of environmental issues

Strengthen ability to plan and carry through a long-term project

Practice cooperative problem solving

Increase ability to communicate ideas

Create a bulletin board showing man's misuse of the environment. Examples are: burning rain forests, soil erosion because of logging, polluted streams or lakes. In conjunction with a study of weather, investigate how these practices affect not only the immediate environment, but the global environment. Ask children to brainstorm alternatives to these harmful practices. Write down their responses and include that information on the bulletin board.

Increase pollution awareness.   Have children write to companies that have the potential for polluting their communities. What are they currently doing to eliminate pollution? Are there additional plans as information becomes available and technology advances? What would the children do when they are adults to prevent environmental pollution?

Start an ecology club.   Let the children choose interest areas concerning the environment: ozone layer, smog, greenhouse effect, nuclear waste, solar energy, lasers, sound waves, and transistors. Have them research what these might be doing to the environment and what is being done to prevent further damage.

Compile a scrap book.   Have children collect newspaper or magazine articles on the destruction of our natural resources: rivers, forests, lakes, wilderness areas, animal habitats. Classify the information according to the kind of resource. Compile a large scrapbook of the articles and leave it in the reading corner for children to browse at leisure.

Analyze food packaging for potential harm to the environment.   Examples are candy wrappings that contain a plastic wrap inside a cardboard box. All sorts of foods are sold or packaged in styrofoam, which does not biodegrade. When the styrofoam breaks up, it can be eaten by wildlife. Plastic rings that hold six-packs of drinks can strangle birds and fish. Have children write to companies that make the products or publish an article in the child-care center newspaper.

Concerned Consumers

Purposes: Increase ability to infer results based on previous information

   Think creatively when finding new uses for household objects

   Communicate information and ideas to others

Survey packaging materials that are biodegradable or non-biodegradable. Explain to the children the meaning of the two words and ask them to think of examples that they might have in their kitchen at home. Group them in twos or threes and tell them that each group will survey an aisle in the grocery store. Take a trip to a nearby store. (Get permission from the store manager before planning this trip.) Provide children with paper, pencils, and clipboards or a book to write on. Assign each group an aisle of the store. Tell them to go slowly through the items on the shelves, noting things that are packaged in biodegradable and non-biodegradable packaging. Discuss the information they have gathered when they are back at the center. Can they think of better ways to avoid filling the environment with trash that will still be there many years into the future?

Sort items into biodegradable and non-biodegradable.   Collect items and ask children to bring in empty boxes, bags, or other materials that were used to package goods. Have them sort them into piles according to their degradability.

Survey the trash at the child-care center.   Have children collect the contents of the classroom wastebaskets into plastic bags. Sort the contents according to those that could be reused and those that can be sent to a recycling center. Ask for their suggestions on how to decrease the amount of trash. Have them prepare a list of suggestions to distribute to the school.

Test the biodegradability of several items.   Have children dig one hole for each item in an unused part of the playground. Pour some water in the hole and let it soak into the ground. Place one object in each hole, then cover it with dirt. Mark the places with small signs to show what is buried there. Some suggestions for items to bury are: newspaper, egg carton, tin can, plastic food carton, paper bag. Have them predict which items will deteriorate. Dig up the objects at the end of 30 days. How accurate were their predictions? Would some of the items degrade if left longer?

Recycle household objects.   Ask children to bring one object from home that would have been thrown away. Place all the objects on a table and ask children to think of things that could be done with each. Provide any additional materials they need to make useful items from the objects. Some things children might make are: sand shovels from plastic bottles; a paint applicator from roll-on deodorant bottles; a rocket from an oatmeal box; towers from painted cans of all sizes to add interest to block buildings. A large variety of objects can also be used to create sculptures or other art projects.

Advertising

Purposes: Develop critical thinking skills

Evaluate and challenge preconceived ideas

Increase ability to observe objectively

Communicate information to others

Develop children's awareness of how television shapes our buying habits. Ask children to think about commercials they remember from their television viewing. Talk about the claims made by the ads. Discuss the purpose of the ads. Did the ads make them want to buy the product?

To further children's awareness, tape a half-hour children's television show, then view it with the children. Have them keep track of the number of commercials and the amount of time devoted to them. Discuss their reactions to the commercials. Do they want to buy the product? Why or why not? Do they believe the claims? Are there distortions in the way the product is shown? Discuss how television creates illusions when showing products.

Ask children to bring from home something they bought or had their parents buy after seeing a television ad. Ask them to write an ad that is honest, but would make people want to buy the product. Have them read their ads, then post them on a bulletin board.

Set up a product testing lab.   Bring in several products that would be found in most households. Allow children to test and compare different brands of the product. For example, test two brands of paper towels, each claiming to absorb more water and to be the strongest. Ask children to decide how they can test those claims. (Pour the same amount of water on each and pull the edges.) Which held up without tearing? Another example: Certain cereals claim to contain more raisins per serving. Select two brands and pour out the contents into two large bowls. Have children count the number of raisins in each. Yet another example: two brands of chocolate chip cookies claim to have more chips per cookie. Ask the children how they can test that claim. (Dissolve the cookie in water, then extract the chips for counting.) Ask the children for other possibilities for testing, then implement those ideas.

Taste-test products children are familiar with through advertising. Select one product to compare such as crackers, cola, or canned fruit. Choose several brands of the product. Cover the outside of each of the items so they cannot be identified. Label each with a number or letter. Provide children with a cup, bowl, and a spoon. You will also need a serving spoon for fruit or other products that need to be spooned. Ask the children to take small portions of each item, then rate each product. Use a numerical scale or Best, OK, Not Good to show their assessment of each. Did they all agree which one was best or were there differences?

Solicit ads for newspaper publication.   Ask children to survey other adults at the center or their parents to see if they want to place an ad in the center's newspaper. Have the children write the ad copy and include any appropriate artwork. If a computer is available, there is a lot of clip art that can be used for this purpose. They can also cut and paste pictures on their ads for later photocopying.

Newspaper Publication

Purposes: Work cooperatively on a common task

Increase decision-making skills

Plan and organize a series of tasks

Increase writing and communication skills

Write, edit, and publish a newspaper.   Have the children plan the various tasks: reporter, editor, photographer, illustrator, cartoonists, and production staff. Discuss the length of the paper and when it will be published. Have them set a schedule for completing tasks. They can interview adults in the center, obtain interesting stories from other children, gather information from their parents, or write an editorial on a topic pertinent to the center. Produce the paper and distribute it to other classrooms.

Plan a trip to a local newspaper office.   Arrange to visit a newspaper office and schedule interviews with several employees. Prepare children by asking them to think of questions they would like to have answered. They might want to know how someone becomes a reporter or what are the most exciting parts of the job. How are other jobs they see being performed important to the final product? What are the best and most difficult parts of any of the job categories? Follow the visit with a discussion of the complex process of producing a newspaper and what kinds of jobs they might like to prepare for.

Scientist

Purposes: Increase awareness of the different fields of scientific study

Develop familiarity with devices that are used for research

Provide experience in using a variety of scientific tools

Stimulate curiosity about the sciences

Scientist for a day.   Provide a variety of tools that are used by scientists: microscope and prepared slides, telescope, metal detector, compass, barometer or rain gauge. Teach the children how to use the devices, then allow them to experiment freely. Ask them to imagine the kind of scientists who would use the devices and what kinds of information they may be able to find.

FIGURE 13–2   "This is a spaceship." Dustin, age 5

Visit a site where scientific devices are used.   Examples are: a weather station, a university research lab, a water treatment plant, a company that has a research component, or any other appropriate site in your community. Arrange to have an employee at the site tell the children how the devices fit into the overall purposes of the facility and the qualifications for workers.

Equipment to Have Available

Following is a list of equipment and materials that is probably minimally essential. Most of the items are things you might find at home. If not, try to add them gradually. Be sure that full-sized, good quality items are used. It is vital to the smooth functioning of your operation that all equipment and materials be stored and presented in good order. Put nails and screws into muffin pans. Use old cartons, wastebaskets, etc. for wood pieces. Plastic bags are good storage for just about anything. A pegboard is useful for hanging up tools (do not forget labels).

FIGURE 13–3a and b   Perhaps these children will have a career in acting.

Awl, blankets, blocks, bowls, brace and bit, C clamps, cardboard boxes, chalk, cookie cutters and sheets, cutting boards, files, first-aid kit, forks, glue, grater, hammers (11 to 13 ounces), knives, masking tape, measuring spoons, paper clips, pancake turner, pens and pencils, pitchers, planes, pliers, rasp, recipes, refrigerator, rolling pin, rulers, sawhorses, saws (coping, crosscut, and rip), scissors, screwdrivers (slot and Phillips), stove, styrofoam pieces, T square, tape measure, tarps, tin snips, toothpicks, vegetable brushes and peelers, vise, wallpaper samples, wire, wood, workbench, wrenches, and yardsticks.

FIGURE 13–4   *"When I grow up I want to be a teacher." Rachel, age 6*

When you can, add these:

- Books on construction; food preparation; transportation, etc.
- Computers and software
- Films and filmstrips on technology issues
- Games: Monopoly®
- Legos® to build castles or other structures
- Lincoln Logs® to construct buildings
- Old models and blueprints rescued from architect's offices
- Photographs
- Plaster of Paris; sand; a sandbox
- Tree branches with leaves

As you can see, the above is a representative list and more than ample for a beginning. You can add as needed. A great deal depends upon the interests of the children involved. It is often difficult to foresee what any one group (or individual) will respond to or enjoy.

Guidelines for Child-Care Staff Members

Encourage children to practice their skills as they participate in curriculum activities. Focus on the characteristics and skills referred to by Toffler. He said workers of the future will need to take an active role in decision making, resolve problems, and challenge preconceived assumptions. The list below includes Toffler's suggestions as well as some additional ones.

FIGURE 13–5   *"Feeding my bird." Elizabeth, age 10*

Future workers will probably need to be able to:

- Solve problems
- Work cooperatively
- Make decisions
- Understand spatial relationships
- Think creatively
- Read and speak fluently
- Practice safety procedures
- Plan for use of time and materials
- Operate complex equipment
- Use a variety of tools
- Be accurate and precise
- Be able to be retrained for a new career
- Evaluate and challenge preconceived ideas

Plan ahead when you invite speakers to visit your center. Prepare the speaker by suggesting topics that are of special interest to the children. Set a time limit. Ask the presenter to bring visual materials whenever possible: pictures, videos, tools, or instruments are some examples. Ask the children to think of questions they might want answered.

Plan just as carefully for visits to community workplaces. Visit the site yourself, determine what will be of interest to your group. Talk to the person in charge to plan exactly what the children will see. Prepare the children by describing what will happen on the visit. Follow up with a discussion when you are back at your center.

One of the exciting aspects of working with school-age children is that they are such avid learners. They want to explore the world outside of their own families, schools, or neighborhoods. They are eager to be competent and will work diligently to accomplish difficult tasks. You can capitalize on these characteristics when you plan your curriculum. In addition, you can be helping to prepare these young people for their future as adult workers in a complex global society.

Summary

Future workers will have to manage complex technology. In addition, they will need skills that allow them to take an active role in what happens at their work site. They will need to be able to: solve problems, work cooperatively, make decisions, understand spatial relationships, practice safety procedures, plan for use of time and materials, operate complex equipment, use a variety of tools, be accurate and precise, and challenge preconceived ideas. Practice in these skills can be built into the activities in a child-care center.

The theoretical concepts of industrial technology can best be presented to the school-age child through relatively simple activities. Some are suggested.

Lists of equipment and materials that support these activities are presented.

Invite speakers to visit your center to talk about their jobs. Prepare ahead of time by suggesting topics, limiting time, and asking children to think of questions to be answered.

Arrange field trips to community workplaces. Visit the site yourself, plan what the children will see. Prepare the group by telling them what will happen. Follow the visit with a discussion.

References

Doan, D. (1983). *Teaching problem-solving strategies.* Menlo Park, CA: Addison Wesley Publishing Company.

Toffler, A. (1990). *Powershift: Knowledge, wealth, and violence on the edge of the 21st century.* New York: Bantam Books, Inc.

Selected Further Reading

Blaw, L. (1994). *Super science.* Bellevue, WA: One From the Heart Educational Research.

D'Amico, J., & Drummond, K. (1996). *The science chef travels around the world—Fun food experiments and recipes for kids.* New York: John Wiley & Sons, Inc.

Douglas, F. (1992) *A chef.* New York: Greenwillow Books. Primary.

Douglas, F. (1991) *A carpenter.* New York: Greenwillow Books. Primary.

Gardner, R. (1994). *Science projects about chemistry.* Springfield, NJ: Enslow Publishers, Inc.

Horenstein, H. (1994). *My mom's a vet.* Cambridge, MA: Candlewick. Advanced.

Kalman, B. (1991). *Reducing, reusing, and recycling.* Canada: Crabtree Publishing Company.

Kenda, M., & Williams, P. (1992). *Science wizardry for kids.* Hauppauge, NY: Barron's Educational Series, Inc.

McVey, V. (1993). *Sierra club kids' guide to planet care and repair.* San Francisco: Sierra Club.

Vitkus-Weeks, J. (1994). *Television.* Parsippany, NJ: Crestwood House, Silver Burdett Press. Advanced.

Computer Software

Jobs for Me! (Mac IBM). Ontario: Logicus. Advanced.

Career-O-Rama (Mac MPC CD-ROM) Brunswick, ME: Wintergreen/Orchard House. Intermediate, Advanced.

Job City Series (Mac IBM Laserdisk). Altamonte Springs, FL: Techware Corp. Intermediate, Advanced.

Student Activities

1. Survey your child-care group concerning what they want to be when they grow up. Are their interests similar to or different from those discussed in this chapter?
2. Visit your community library. List available resources you could use in planning this curriculum area. Besides books, do they have videos, films, or recordings?
3. Plan a field trip to a work site in your community. Choose a company that uses computers to automate their production.
4. Discuss with your parents and grandparents any changes they have seen during their lifetime in regard to modes of travel and communication or advances in science or medicine. Find out what their lives were like without these technological advances. Share this information with a group of children.

Review

1. Why is it important to expose children to a variety of adult work roles?
2. When do children begin developing ideas about what they will be when they grow up?

3. List several activities that are related to map making.
4. Describe how to set up a production line for the preparation of pizza for snack.
5. Name two activities that will help children be aware of decreasing the amount of trash that is accumulated.
6. List five characteristics future workers will need.
7. Do you agree with Toffler's premise that future workers will have to take a more active role? Write several sentences supporting your answer.
8. List guidelines for planning and implementing a field trip to a community workplace.

CHAPTER 14

Getting Fit, Staying Fit

Objectives

After studying this chapter, the student should be able to:

- Discuss the physical health of American children
- Plan and implement age-appropriate nutritional activities
- Plan and implement age-appropriate fitness experiences
- State suggestions for caregivers when implementing a fitness program

How Healthy Are Our Kids?

Health-care providers, teachers, and child-care workers frequently see children who are obviously in poor health or who do not get needed medical treatment. These children are often listless and cannot concentrate. Some are thin, while others are overweight. Many cannot keep up with their peers during active play or games. These professionals know that good health and overall fitness are essential to children's development and achievement. Yet America's children are not healthy! Let's look at some of the facts about the status of American children.

The Institute for Aerobic Research in Dallas reported in 1987 that signs of arteriosclerosis are appearing in children as young as five years old. The 1984 findings of a national health and fitness study done by the U.S. Department of Health and Human Services had equally disturbing news. Only 5 percent of elementary-aged children qualified for the Presidential Award for Physical Fitness. More than half the children in the United States, 64 percent, tested below the 50th percentile on overall fitness.

In California, nearly a million children were tested in the spring of 1990. The result showed that California children were not fit. Only 16 percent of the fifth-grade students, 21 percent of seventh-grade students and 26 percent of ninth-grade students met four or more of the fitness standards.

The Children's Defense Fund also published some shocking statistics in its 1990 publication *S.O.S. America! A Children's Defense Budget.* They reported that one-quarter of our children have decayed, filled, or missing teeth.

As you read in Chapter 5, approximately 14 million children live in families with incomes below the poverty level. Many of these children have no health insurance coverage and consequently suffer from a variety of conditions (Children's Defense Fund, 1996). Many have inadequate nutrition, have poor academic performance, and suffer from chronic physical conditions.

Newacheck & Taylor (1992) found that 20 million children nationwide suffer from chronic health conditions. The most commonly reported are respiratory allergies and repeated ear infections. Although these seem mild, the fact that they are recurring interferes with children's total health and their ability to progress in school. Other health concerns in young children include communicable diseases, hearing and vision limitations, and ambulatory limitations. Among teenagers, early sexual behavior that leads to pregnancy or sexually transmitted diseases is a major problem. In addition, there is an increase of teenagers with drug or alcohol dependency.

You can do little about some of the above problems other than advocating more and better health-care resources in your community. However, you can have an impact on the small group of children in your child-care group. Provide them with experiences that foster attitudes and practices that will improve their well-being. You can also give them knowledge that will enable them to continue these throughout their lifetimes.

Since snack time is already a part of every session in after-school child care, it is a good place to start. Teach children what their bodies need to stay healthy. Then, help them select, plan, and prepare food for snacks. Encourage them to broaden their tastes and experience foods from other cultures.

Activities

Good Food, Good Health

Purposes: Increase ability to make informed decisions about food choices

Expand knowledge of nutritional requirements

Encourage participation in planning food for snacks

Teach children what their bodies need to stay healthy. Prepare a bulletin board that shows the food 4guide pyramid that is the latest recommendation by the U.S.

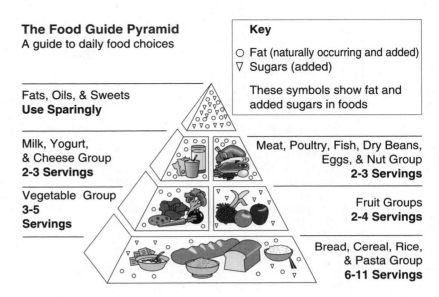

The Food Guide Pyramid
A guide to daily food choices

Key

○ Fat (naturally occurring and added)
▽ Sugars (added)

These symbols show fat and added sugars in foods

Fats, Oils, & Sweets
Use Sparingly

Milk, Yogurt,
& Cheese Group
2-3 Servings

Meat, Poultry, Fish, Dry Beans,
Eggs, & Nut Group
2-3 Servings

Vegetable Group
**3-5
Servings**

Fruit Groups
2-4 Servings

Bread, Cereal, Rice,
& Pasta Group
6-11 Servings

FIGURE 14–1   The U.S. Department of Agriculture Food Guide Pyramid

Department of Agriculture. Encourage the children to consider their own diet. How many food groups did they have for breakfast? How many are in today's snack? What are some things they could have for snack that would be nutritious? The food guide pyramid is shown in Figure 14–1.

Navajo Fry Bread

Purposes: Increase cultural awareness

Practice math concepts by measuring ingredients

Foster cooperation

Prepare a snack of Navajo fry bread. This is a snack that is representative of a culture and is nutritious as well. It can be prepared fairly quickly by hungry children. Assign two or three children to do the initial measuring and mixing. Divide the dough in half, allowing two more children to roll it out and cut it. Two more children can be assigned to fry the finished squares.

> **CAUTION:** Be sure to set up the preparation area to allow maximum safety. Place the electric frying pan on a table. Extend the cord from the pan to a convenient wall outlet, then push the table against the wall. The cord will be out of the way and children will not trip on it. Caution the children not to touch the hot pan and to use long-handled tongs to turn the bread. Supervise carefully when frying is taking place. See Figure 14–2 for the recipe.

Navajo Fry Bread

1 cup whole wheat flour
1 teaspoon baking powder
1/2 teaspoon salt
1/2 cup lukewarm water
8 to 10 tablespoons salad oil for frying
Sift the flour, baking powder, and salt together into a bowl. Stir in the water, then use your fingers to finish the mixing. Knead the dough with the heel of your hand, dusting it with flour if it gets sticky.
Roll out the dough to 1/4 inch thickness. Cut it into squares.
Pour the oil into an electric skilled. (Use just enough to coat the bottom of the pan.) When it is hot, but not smoking, quickly fry the squares of dough a few at a time. Using a long-handled slotted spoon, brown one side, then turn them over and brown the other. When browned and puffed up, remove from the pan and place them on a paper towel. Serve them with honey or jam.
The recipe makes about 24 fry bread squares.

Figure 14–2   Navajo Fry Bread

Fancy Five Sandwiches

Purposes: Reinforce knowledge of foods from the food guide pyramid
                Expand experiences with different foods
                Communicate information about choices to others

Provide the following foods from the food guide pyramid.

Bread: whole-wheat bread, wheat pita bread, whole-wheat tortillas

Fruits and vegetables: cucumbers, tomatoes, bananas, raisins, apples, sprouts

Meats and meat substitutes: peanut butter, hard-cooked eggs, sliced turkey

Milk: low-fat Swiss cheese, low-fat cheddar cheese, low-fat cottage cheese

Fats: low-fat mayonnaise or margarine.

Group the foods on trays labeled with their group name. Allow each child to make a sandwich using as many of the food groups as possible. During snack time have each child describe his sandwich and name the groups.

Taste Trip

Purposes: Increase cultural awareness and appreciation
                Expand food preferences

Select food from several different countries. Set them out on trays with labels indicating where they are from. Encourage children to taste several items, then write their reactions.

The following are some suggested foods, but visit your local supermarket to find others.

• From Haiti: mango; peel, slice, and add to fruit cups
• From Central and South America: burro banana; add to salads or fruit cups

FIGURE 14–3   A bulletin board about milk focuses on one of the food groups.

- From Hawaii: papaya; cut in half, seed, peel, and slice
- From Japan: Asian pear; eat raw or bake
- From Mexico: cactus pears; peel and eat or add to salads
- From New Zealand: feijoa, also called pineapple guava; peel and slice
- From New Zealand: kiwi fruit; serve in thin slices peeled or unpeeled
- From New Zealand: passion fruit; scoop out pulp and serve over yogurt
- From China: lichee fruit; buy in cans at most supermarkets
- From Mexico: jicama; peel and slice, serve with a seasoned cottage-cheese dip
- From East Indies or Mexico: mango; peel and slice
- From South America or Hawaii: pineapple; peel, core, and cut into chunks

Menu Planning

Purposes: Expand ability to make cooperative decisions

Practice mathematical calculations when determining how much
to buy

Plan snacks for a week. Appoint a committee to plan nutritious snacks for a week.
Instruct them to include items from at least two food groups. When they have
completed their menu, ask them to make a shopping list of required ingredients.

They may have to consult cookbooks or ask someone to help them determine quantities. If you have a cook at your center, he or she would be a good resource person. Schedule a trip to the supermarket to purchase the food. See the reading list at the end of this chapter for books that contain recipes. Also, a list of scrumptious snacks can be found in Figure 14–4.

Ice Cream in a Bucket

Purposes: Observe the physical changes that take place when the mixture freezes

Participate in a group effort to achieve a goal

Make ice cream in a bucket. Most children have never had the opportunity to make homemade ice cream and this is a unique experience. The recipe shown in Figure 14–5 gives the directions.

As a variation to this method, use one of the ice-cream makers that are on the market. There are several that are electric and one that operates with a handle that must be turned. The hand-operated freezer is ideal for making frozen yogurt. Merely mix crushed fresh fruit with plain yogurt. Add a small amount of sugar or honey, then pour into the container. Freeze according to the machine's directions.

Apple slices, peanut butter, raisins
Assorted raw vegetables with seasoned cottage-cheese dip
Banana slices—dip in honey, roll in nuts
Celery stuffed with peanut butter or cheese spread
Cheese balls—form balls with softened cheese, roll in chopped nuts
Cottage cheese with fruit
Deviled eggs—add yogurt, mustard, salt and pepper to the yolk
Fresh fruit gelatin—any fruit in season—do not use kiwi or fresh pineapple
Fruit kabobs—banana wheels, pineapple chunks, cherries, strawberries, orange wedges
Fruit shakes—blend fruit and nonfat dry milk in blender with a few ice cubes
Graham crackers, peanut butter and applesauce
Granola or Grape-nuts® sprinkled on yogurt
Ice cream with fruit—in milkshakes or in make-your-own sundaes
Nachos—tortilla wedges, refried beans, cheddar cheese. Heat in microwave oven until cheese melts.
Nut bread with cheese spread
Peanut butter on whole wheat bread with raisins, dates, apples, banana, applesauce, chopped celery, shredded carrots
Pizza—use pizza dough or English muffins, add pizza sauce, cooked ground meat, cheese, tomatoes, mushrooms, chopped bell peppers, olives
Tacos or burritos—fill with cheese, leftover meat, sliced tomatoes
Tiny meatballs made with ground meat, rice, and seasoning
Wheat toast with tuna salad or cheese, broiled to melt
Yogurt with fruit

FIGURE 14–4   Scrumptious Snacks

Ice Cream in a Bucket

You need:
a large plastic bucket
a one-pound coffee can with a plastic lid
2 cups of rock salt
Beat together in the coffee can:
   1 egg
   1/4 cup honey
   Add 1 cup milk
   1/2 cup cream
   1 teaspoon vanilla
   dash of salt
Be sure the coffee can is only half-full or the ice cream will spill over the sides as you freeze it.
Put a layer of ice in the bottom of the pail. Crushed ice freezes faster, but cubes will work also. Sprinkle the ice with part of the salt.
Put the lid on the coffee can and set the can on top of the ice. Pack more salt and ice in the pail around the sides of the can. Sprinkle layers of ice with salt as you fill the bucket. When the ice is almost to the top of the can, take off the plastic lid.
Stir the ice-cream mixture around and around with a big spoon, letting the can turn too. Keep on stirring and watching. Let the children take turns with stirring because it will take from 15 to 30 minutes for the ice cream to freeze to mush. You will probably want to eat it right away, while it is still soft. If you want to wait until it hardens, put more ice and salt around the can and let it sit for an hour or two.
This recipe will serve four to five children. You will probably want to make more than one batch. Also if you are concerned about possible salmonella bacteria in the raw egg, you can coddle it. Heat water to 140 degrees. Pour enough water into a cup to completely cover the egg. Let it stand for one minute. Any bacteria will be killed and the egg will not cook.

FIGURE 14–5   Ice Cream in a Bucket

Parent Demonstration

Purposes: Increase awareness of cultural meanings of food preferences
                 Expand food experiences to include those from other countries

Invite a parent to cook a favorite recipe that is representative of his or her culture. Demonstrate how the food is prepared and cooked. Let children taste the final product. Note: discuss the food with the parent before the presentation. Remind the person that it has to be something simple, that can be quickly prepared. Hungry children will not want to wait too long before tasting. Consider also the constraints of your facility. Where will the food be prepared? Will it be safe? Do you have an oven, a frying pan or whatever else will be required? Ask the parent to choose a food that is enjoyed by children.

For added interest ask a parent to demonstrate a dish that is specific to his or her culture. Have the parent explain whether this is a dish the family might eat frequently or if it is served on special occasions. Some possibilities are:

An Asian stir-fry dish. Provide chopsticks and ask the parent to demonstrate to the children how to use them.

Mexican burritos with homemade salsa

Japanese noodles and vegetables

Jewish potato latkes or cheese blintzes

Indian puri

Spanish sopapillas

Cookbook

Purposes: Cooperative effort to achieve a goal

Increase reading and writing skills

Plan and carry out a long-term project

Compile a book of the children's favorite recipes. The children may have to consult a cookbook or ask their parents for help with this. Use a computer or type-writer to type up the recipes. Make copies for each of the children in your group. Let each of them make a cover for their book.

Cook, Cook, Cook

Purposes: Reinforce knowledge of nutritional requirements for health and fitness

Practice in decision-making skills

Experience foods from different cultures

Involve children in cooking projects often. Each experience is an opportunity to reinforce good nutrition and the importance of making appropriate food choices. It is also an opportunity for children to broaden their tastes and to experience foods from different cultures.

Japanese Rice Balls

1 cup short-grain white rice
1½ cups water
salt

Put rice in a saucepan and add water. Soak for 30 minutes, then cook until all the water is absorbed. Let the rice cool with the pan covered for about 5 minutes or until it is cool enough to handle (already cooked, cold rice can be used if no stove is available). Tell children to wet their hands, then take a scoop of rice. Form the rice into a ball and make a hole in the middle. Place a pickled Japanese plum in the hole. If desired, the ball can be wrapped with a piece of Nori (seaweed).

Flour Tortillas

4 cups whole-wheat flour
1 teaspoon salt
⅓ cup vegetable oil
approximately 1 cup warm water

Mix the flour and salt: add oil, mix together with fingers. Stir in enough water to make a firm ball. Knead the dough until it is smooth, then let it rest for 20 minutes. Pinch off a golf-ball size piece of the dough. Roll it out on a floured board until it is 4 inches in diameter. Cook on an unoiled griddle for about 2 minutes on each side.

Navajo Fry Bread—Recipe can be found in Figure 14–2.

Equipment to Have Available

You will need some equipment for food preparation or cooking. If your center has a kitchen, most items will be available there. If not, accumulate the basics, then add to them as your children become more involved in their culinary projects. The number of each item that you require will depend upon the size of your group of children.

- Bottle and can opener
- Bowls, several sizes for mixing ingredients
- Cake pans, both sheet pans and layer pans, muffin tins
- Colander, strainer, flour sifter
- Cookie cutter, cookie sheets
- Cutting boards, plastic or wooden, large boards and individual size
- Eggbeaters, scrapers
- Fork, tongs, both long-handled
- Gelatin molds, both single and individual
- Grater, four-sided is best for children to hold
- Hot plate
- Knives, serrated for greater safety (if ends are pointed, round them with a tool grinder)
- Measuring spoons, liquid and dry measuring cups
- Pancake turner, spatula, wooden and slotted spoons
- Pastry brushes
- Potato masher
- Saucepans
- Rolling pin (you can also use pieces of dowel)
- Skillet (electric)
- Timer
- Vegetable peeler, apple corer

When you can, add the following:

- Corn popper
- Electric blender and mixer
- Electric food processor
- Ice-cream freezer
- Portable bake oven

Getting Fit, Staying Fit

The kinds of outdoor play experiences children have today are vastly different from the past. Many children live in urban areas in apartments where there is no space to play. Even in residential areas where there are yards, many children do not go outdoors because of fear for their safety or because they would rather sit indoors watching television. Even when children are outdoors, studies show they are not active enough to raise their heart rates for very long periods of time (Gilliam et al, 1981, 1982). Increased heart rate is one indicator of fitness.

Although an after-school child-care program provides a safe place where children can play outdoors, there is still a need to institute an exercise regimen. The fitness statistics described at the beginning of this chapter indicate that children are far from being fit. Many children do not conform to the standard of fitness described by the American Alliance for Health, Physical Education, Recreation, and Dance (AAHPERD) (1995). They describe fitness as a physical state of well-being that allows people to:

1. Perform daily activities with vigor.
2. Reduce their risk of health problems related to lack of exercise.
3. Establish a fitness base for participation in a variety of physical activities.

Their standards address several components: aerobic endurance, body composition (proportion of fat and lean), muscular strength, and flexibility. A good fitness program will address all of these. In addition, exercise can also relieve some of the tensions children feel because of the pressures of school or family problems.

Schedule exercise sessions before snack time. Always begin with warm-up activities. This serves two purposes: it limbers up the muscles in preparation for exercise and prevents possible injuries or strains. In each of the lists of exercises below, the first ones are the easiest. Start with a few from each category. Gradually add others or move on to more difficult exercises when the children have increased their fitness. Above all, make the sessions fun. Adding music at times helps to keep the pace going and increases the enjoyment.

In all of the exercises, an adult leads the exercise and models the proper movements.

Activities

Warm-up

Purposes: Preparation for exercise in order to prevent injuries or strain

Foster a sense of well-being that will increase the likelihood of continuing a fitness regimen

Start exercises with a warm-up. Do the following:

1. Head tilt. Stand with feet apart, hands on sides. Drop head forward, then arch head back as far as possible.
2. Head tilt, side to side. Stand with feet apart, hands at sides. Keeping shoulders stationary, drop head to one side then the other. Touch ear to shoulder.

3. Head turn. Stand with feet apart, hands at sides. Turn head to right as far as possible, then to the left.
4. Shoulder shrugs. Stand with feet apart, arms at sides. Tighten abdominal muscles while raising shoulders up to ears. Lower them and repeat.
5. Knee bends. Stand with feet apart and arms outstretched at shoulder height. Tighten abdominal muscles. Bend right knee while keeping the other leg straight out to the side. Reverse, bending left knee.
6. Torso bend. Stand with feet apart, hands at side. Keep legs straight while leaning to one side, then the other. Let hand slide down thigh. Stand straight, then repeat.

Arm and Hand Exercises

Purposes: Increase strength in arms and hands

Develop awareness of muscle action

Stand with legs together, bring left arm forward and up. Swing right arm back. Reverse process.

Stand with legs apart. Hold both arms together. Swing them down, then up, in a semicircle. Go from left to right, then from right to left.

Stand with legs apart, arms stretched out at shoulder level. Rotate arms in circles, first in one direction, then the other.

Stand with legs apart. Grasp a yardstick or three-foot-long piece of dowel at each end. Keep the legs straight while swinging arms from side to side.

Extend one arm from the elbow, keeping upper arm close to the body. Place a small rubber ball in the extended hand. Squeeze as hard as possible while counting to four. Change to other hand and repeat. As strength increases, continue the count up to eight.

Leg Exercises

Purposes: Increase strength in leg muscles

Cooperate with a partner

Develop group cohesiveness

Squat with feet flat and palms touching the floor. Push one leg straight back. Hold for a few seconds, then reverse.

Run in place, raising knees as far off the floor as possible. Vary this exercise by telling the children to jump, then land in a squat when they hear you clap. Another clap is a signal to jump and continue running in place.

Stand with feet together, hands extended to the front at shoulder height. Raise one leg at a time, trying to touch each hand.

Sit on the floor. Grasp one foot with both hands and pull it up to the nose. Repeat with other foot.

Lie on the floor on one side. Rest on the elbow and forearm with legs outstretched. Lift and lower one leg, keeping toes pointed straight. Turn to other side and repeat.

Lie on right side, body propped up by right elbow. Put left hand on the floor in front of body. Lift left leg a few inches, then swing it forward. Repeat several times. Turn to other side and repeat.

Squat on floor, with hands flat on the floor. Jump with both legs, extending feet straight out back. Return to a squatting position.

FIGURE 14–6   Playground equipment can help children stay physically fit.

Sit on floor with legs straight and apart. Point toes toward floor while clasping left knee with both hands. Push body forward toward knee as far as possible. Push several times, then straighten to sitting position again. Repeat with other leg.

Form children into pairs for this exercise. Each player places a ball on the ground or floor behind him. Partners join hands. One player in each pair sits on his ball while the other remains standing. As the seated player stands up, the partner lowers himself onto his ball. Alternate sitting several times.

A group of five or more children can participate in this exercise. Players stand in a circle, all facing in the same direction. The first player passes a ball over his head to the player behind him. The second player has to reach up for the ball, then pass it through his legs to the next player. Continue this alternation several times around the circle. You can also use two balls so each player has more turns to reach or bend.

Torso Exercises

Purposes: Increase torso flexibility and strength

                Work with a partner to achieve a goal

FIGURE 14–7   Healthy children have lots of energy.

Lie on the stomach with hands outstretched to the side. At the same time, raise legs and hands while arching back. Hold for a few seconds, then lie flat again. Repeat.

Two children can work together on this one. One child lies on floor with hands clasped behind the head. Raise the knees, but keep feet flat on the floor. Second child holds his partner's feet firmly on the floor. The partner tightens his abdominal muscles and pulls to a sitting position. Hold for a count of five, then slowly lower to a prone position again. They then change places.

Stand with feet apart. Stretch arms out to the side. Bend over and touch right foot with left hand. Keep right arm stretched up in the air. Return to standing position, then repeat with the other arm.

Equipment to Have Available

In addition to exercises, there are some simple pieces of equipment that will encourage children to participate in physical activities. They are not expensive and in fact, may already be in your school.

Jump ropes. Have several so more than one child can jump at a time. Have at least one that is long enough for two children to hold while others jump.

Beach balls, gigantic balls. Children can throw or roll on balls.

Nerf® balls. Use with paddles described in Chapter 10. Imagine a volleyball game played with a Nerf® ball and nylon paddles!

Hoops. Children can jump in and out. They can be laid in patterns on the floor so that children have to hop or jump from one to the other.

Frisbees®. Can be played by two or more children.

Balance beam. You can find a low beam in many school equipment catalogues. They are also simple to make. Children can walk across with eyes open or closed. Have them try to walk across holding a plastic or wooden egg in a spoon.

Guidelines for Child-Care Staff Members

Remember that cooking and eating food should be fun. Do not pressure children to taste unfamiliar foods. If you keep offering interesting varieties their curiosity will probably get the better of them. Also, they will see that others try out those strange things you bring to class and they may want to get involved.

Set up a cooking environment with maximum safety in mind. Position the cooking table against a wall, with the electrical cord behind the table and out of the way. Teach children the rules and how to accomplish the tasks safely. They are quite capable of cutting up vegetables without getting hurt or using an electric frying pan without getting burned. (The author has used both knives and frying pans with preschoolers without mishap.) Supervise closely and never leave an area where children are cooking.

Try not to impose your own food likes and dislikes on children. If you really hate a particular food, then do not include it. You may think you will be able to hide your dislike from the children, but they will sense it.

Be a good role model. Do everything you can to be healthy yourself. Demonstrate good eating habits by bringing only healthful foods to school.

Provide a variety of activities and materials that encourage active play. Tag games, ball games, jump rope, follow-the-leader, obstacle course are all possible physical activities that can be incorporated into the daily program.

Allow children to choose an activity according to their developmental capabilities or fitness level. A vertical ladder leading to a high piece of climbing equipment may be too difficult or intimidating to the youngest children. They might be able to master a short ladder leading to a low platform. Young children can hit a ball on a support, while older children may be ready to try hitting a ball when it is pitched to them.

Set up active play stations indoors and outdoors. Chapter 10 includes suggestions for active games to be played indoors. Begin with those and then add others of your own design. Install basketball hoops outdoors at different heights, provide places to toss balls at a target, a place to jump from, or cement areas for skating.

Allow ample opportunities for children to practice skills. This means having more than one ball or that group activities should be organized for a small number of children. Only one ball or large team games entail waiting idly for a turn with little chance to participate and practice.

Enjoy exercising yourself and children will enjoy it. Avoid any comparisons or competition. This is not a time to see who can do the most sit ups or jump the highest. Be careful not to use phrases such as "Let's see who can keep the ball in the air the longest." Simply say "Keep the ball in the air as long as possible."

Encourage parents to use health-care resources for themselves and their children. Find out what is available in your community, then share this information with parents.

Be an advocate for good health programs and policies for children. Join professional organizations that will lobby for health programs. Speak or write to local government officials about the need to protect children.

Volunteer for health-related events in your community. Include your child-care group when you can. Health fairs, running, or bicycling events are some examples.

The health of children is too important to be overlooked.

Summary

Health-care providers, teachers, and child-care workers all see children who are in poor health or need medical treatment. These children are listless, cannot concentrate, cannot keep up with their peers.

There are some shocking reports about the health of American children. Signs of arteriosclerosis are appearing in five-year-olds. Many children cannot meet minimum fitness standards. One-quarter of children have decayed or missing teeth.

As a child-care worker you can provide children with experiences that foster attitudes and practices to improve their health. You can also give them knowledge that will enable them to continue to be healthy throughout their lives.

One way to develop health consciousness is to begin with the foods children eat. Introduce them to the food guide pyramid, then help them plan and prepare nutritious snacks. Expose them to new foods and different methods of cooking.

Although children who are in child care spend time each day playing outdoors, there is still a need to focus on fitness. The AAHPERD definition of fitness includes: performing daily activity with vigor, reducing the risk of health problems related to lack of exercise, and establishing a fitness base for participation in physical activities. In order to achieve this degree of fitness, children and adults need to exercise.

A variety of exercises for specific parts of the body are described. In addition, there are some simple pieces of equipment that encourage children to engage in physical activity.

There are some suggestions for caregivers as you institute a good food program. Cooking and eating should be fun, so do not pressure children. Keep maximum safety in mind. Do not impose your own food likes or dislikes on children. Be a good role model by eating only healthful foods.

There are some additional guidelines for helping children to achieve fitness. Enjoy exercising yourself. Encourage parents to use health-care resources for themselves and their children. Be an advocate for good health programs in your community. Participate in health-related community events.

References

AAHPERD. (1995). *Moving into the future, national physical education standards.* Reston, VA: The American Alliance for Health, Physical Education, Recreation, and Dance.

Children's Defense Fund. (1996). *The state of America's children yearbook 1996.* Washington, DC: Children's Defense Fund.

Gilliam, T.B., Freedson, P.S., Greenen, D.L., & Shahraray, B. (1981). Physical activity patterns determined by heart rate monitoring in six-to-seven-year-old children. *Medicine and Science in Sport, 13*(1), 65–67.

Gilliam, T.B., MacConnie, S.E., Greenen, D.L., Pels, A.F., & Freedson, P.S. (1982). Exercise programs for children: A way to prevent heart disease? *The Physician and Sports Medicine, 10*(9), 96–108.

Newacheck, P., & Taylor, W. (1992). Childhood chronic illness: Prevention, severity, and impact. *American Journal of Public Health, 82*(3), 364–371.

Selected Further Reading

Cook, D. (1995). *Kids' multicultural cookbook.* Charlotte, VT: Williamson Publishing.

Harrison, J. (1993). *Hooked on fitness—Physical conditioning games and activities for grades K–8.* West Nyack, NY: Parker Publishing Company.

Rowland, T.W. (1990). *Exercise and children's health.* Champaign, IL: Human Kinetics Books.

Wanamaker, N., Hearn, K., & Richarz, S. (1979). *More than graham crackers.* Washington, DC: National Association for the Education of Young Children.

Warren, J. (1992). *Super snacks.* Everett, WA: Warren Publishing House. (Available from School Age Notes.)

Student Activities

1. Make either Navajo fry bread or ice cream in a bucket at home. Invite your family or friends to taste-test the results. Did they like the food? If not, why not?

Were there any difficulties you encountered that were not provided for in the recipe? How can you change the procedure to eliminate the problem?

2. Make a list of your own favorite foods. How many are healthful and how many might be considered junk foods?

3. Buy or borrow one of the pieces of equipment listed in this chapter. Try it out. How many activities can you think of to do with this equipment?

Review

1. Name two agencies that have done studies on fitness of American children. What were their conclusions?

2. Name the food groups in the food pyramid. State the recommended daily servings of each.

3. Describe an activity a parent might conduct in a child-care center.

4. Describe two activities that encourage children to try new foods.

5. Name ten pieces of equipment that you need for food preparation.

6. Define fitness.

7. Describe three exercises that strengthen leg muscles.

8. List four pieces of equipment that will encourage children to be active.

15

Getting Along With Other People

Objectives

After studying this chapter, the student should be able to:

- Plan activities that encourage effective conflict resolution
- Plan activities that increase self-esteem
- Plan activities that help children develop cooperative behavior

Antisocial Behavior and Development

In earlier chapters of this book you learned that middle childhood is a time when children refine their sense of self through mastery of a variety of skills. One of the most important skills acquired during this period is getting along with others. Children want to belong to a group and have friends. To achieve that goal they must be able to recognize that others have different points of view or different needs. In an increasingly diverse society that task becomes more difficult. You also learned that during this period children develop moral values, the standards that help them judge how to react to the moral dilemmas everyone faces at one time or another. In addition, they are learning what kinds of behavior their parents, their teachers, and society expects of them.

222

During the process of acquiring and testing these skills children often exhibit antisocial behaviors such as arguing, questioning authority, teasing other children, or resorting to name-calling. They form cliques, or gangs, to foster a sense of belonging through excluding others. These behaviors frequently lead to clashes and conflicts. No group of children is ever going to be without some conflicts and actually, conflict can be a motivator for change. The task for any adults who work with children is to help them learn to resolve disagreements through nonviolent means that are satisfying to both sides. Children can learn prosocial behaviors, cooperating with others to achieve mutual goals rather than focusing on achieving only their own personal goals. This results in increased self-esteem, and the environment in which they spend their before- and after-school time will be more peaceful and productive.

Conflict Resolution

Children often come to after-school programs tired or stressed from their day in school and altercations erupt over seemingly trivial situations. They can learn skills for resolving problems effectively as well as ways to communicate their needs to others. Chapter 7 discussed the steps to follow in a conflict resolution discussion. There are additional ways adults can help children.

Strategies

- Increase children's ability to read nonverbal cues from others. Sometimes a look or gesture is misinterpreted and an argument ensues. When an altercation takes place, encourage the participants to discuss what they saw and what they thought it meant. If there has been misunderstanding, help them to clarify their meaning. Does ignoring an invitation to play just mean "I didn't hear you" or does it mean "I don't want to play right now. Go away"? Does an angry look mean, "He's mad at me about something," or just that he had a bad day at school?
- Help children to see that others may have a different view. Use discussions to let all children express their own perspective or state their own needs. One way to accomplish this is to involve children in planning parts of the program. They may all have good ideas based on their own interests or what is most important to them. Each contribution should be accepted and valued even though it may not be put into action.
- Provide many opportunities for children to learn by trial and error. They have to practice conflict negotiation and ways to cooperate with one another.
- Encourage children who are having frequent conflict difficulties to draft a Conflict Plan. The plan might include a description of the kinds of conflicts, their usual behavior, and how they might change their behavior. The plan's final statement should be a future date to evaluate how it is working.

Activities

Silent Stories

Purposes: Practice in reading nonverbal cues

Increase understanding that others have different points of view

Have children work in pairs. Tell them to use nonverbal ways to tell their partner something about themselves. For instance, they can use gestures to tell their age or things they are interested in. Facial expressions can be used to indicate something that makes them mad or sad. Set a time limit of five or ten minutes. At the end of that time each tries to relate to the other what has been learned. Have them clarify any misinformation and discuss another way they might have conveyed the information.

Cultural Scenes

Purposes: Practice observational skills

Understand the similarities and differences in the ways families carry out familiar routines

Appreciate the similarities and differences in cultures

Ask three or four children from the same culture to enact a typical scene from their culture. Allow them time by themselves to talk about what they will do. Examples might be a dinner time routine, a visit from grandparents, or a birthday celebration.

The remainder of the group observes the enactment, paying attention to procedures and the things people say. When the enactment is finished, allow them time to ask questions of the participants.

Lead a discussion of their observations, focusing on how some of the audience saw things the others did not and how actions or words were interpreted differently.

Shopping Trip

Purposes: Practice in working together as a group

Develop decision-making skills

Resolve conflicts effectively

Divide your class into groups of three. Give each group a catalogue. Tell them they have a hundred dollars to spend buying presents for a boy and girl who are both nine years old. Explain that they all must agree on what to buy. Set a time limit. When they make their decision, they can cut out the pictures and paste them on a sheet of paper.

Have each group share their choices. Ask children about the problems they encountered and how they resolved them. Why did they make the choice they did?

Build a Tower

Purposes: Cultivate creativity

Develop leadership qualities

Encourage verbal and nonverbal communication

Divide your class into groups of three or four. Pass out twenty pieces of heavy paper and a roll of tape to each group. Tell them they are to construct a tower using only these supplies. (You can add another dimension by telling them they cannot talk while working on the project.) Set a time limit of ten or fifteen minutes.

Let each group show their tower. Discuss how they managed to complete their tower. Was one person the leader? Did anyone feel excluded? What kinds of nonverbal communications did they use? Is it easy or difficult to understand nonverbal messages?

Brainstorming

Purposes: Foster divergent thinking skills

Strengthen ability to negotiate conflicts

Amplify group cohesiveness

Tell children that many great inventions are the result of a group of people getting together to create something new. You might remind them that it takes numerous scientists and engineers to design and build space vehicles. Divide them into groups of four. Tell them they are going to invent a new bicycle. Give each group a piece of paper and tell them to designate one member to write down ideas. When they have several designs, ask them to choose one that should be built. Set a time limit of ten minutes.

Let each group relate their ideas to the entire group. Discuss the value or difficulties of creating as a group. How did they decide on the design that should be built?

Picture Problems

Purposes: Increase ability to understand (decode) nonverbal communications in pictures

Recognize and accept others' points of view

Practice in group decision making

Glue pictures of people in a problem situation onto the front of a large manila envelope. You can find pictures in magazines, coloring books, discarded books, posters. Have children work in groups of three. Give each group a picture and some paper. Ask them to reach an agreement about the problem portrayed in the picture, then write it down. Tell them to put their paper into the envelope then pass it on to the next group until all groups have looked at all the pictures. Allow three minutes for each picture.

Collect the envelopes. Read each of the descriptions. Discuss how different groups saw the problem differently.

Fighting Fair

Purposes: Practice in resolving conflicts effectively

Foster independence

Expand self-esteem

When two children get involved in a fight or argument, send them to a quiet corner of the room. Tell them they are to have a three-minute "timeout." During that time they are to work out a solution to their conflict. Set a three-minute timer. When the timer goes off, ask them to tell you their solution, then implement it. Praise them for success.

Self-Esteem

Self-image has two components, our perceptions of ourselves and the perceptions conveyed to us by others. Throughout a lifetime, self-image changes as physical abilities evolve, as cognitive functions change, and as interactions with others are refined. During middle childhood, self-image is tied closely to feelings of competence. Children compare themselves to their contemporaries in terms of physical abilities, academic success, and popularity with their peers. Their evaluations of themselves are sometimes realistic and at other times radically unrealistic. In addition, adult attitudes and behaviors play a significant role in how children feel about themselves. When adults react positively to them, children feel they are valued and therefore have self-worth.

How children feel about themselves has a direct effect upon their behavior. If they like themselves and see that others react positively to them, they behave in ways that gain further approval. If children have negative perceptions of themselves, they may use unpopular tactics to gain attention or to satisfy their needs. This solidifies their perception of themselves as someone who is unlikable or who cannot succeed. Therefore, it is essential that anyone who works with children convey attitudes that help, rather than hinder, children in the development of their identity and self-esteem.

Strategies

- Have a genuine interest in every child. Find opportunities to spend time with children individually. Get to know them, listen to them, and try to understand their concerns. Offer help when needed, but also support their own ability to find solutions to problems.
- Recognize every child's unique qualities and respect their differences. Eliminate any evidence of prejudice or bias in your own thinking or in the behaviors of the children. Ensure that all activities are nonracist or nonbiased.
- Support self-esteem by involving children in intrinsically meaningful activities. Plan challenging projects in which children and adults work together, where children develop skills and gain knowledge. As they acquire skills and feel more competent, children gain in their assessment of their own self-worth.
- Conduct group meetings that allow all children to ask questions, express concerns, discuss problems, or make plans. During group meetings, there should be a free exchange with no "put-downs." Each contribution should be shown respect and consideration, and children should learn to consider all sides of an issue.

- Provide many ways for children to be successful. Offer a variety of activities appropriate for children at different developmental levels. In that way, all children will be able to choose, according to their needs, some activities that are easy for them and others that offer a challenge. Writing and illustrating a simple story is a fairly easy task for nine- or ten-year-olds. Older children might tackle the more difficult task of writing a play complete with dialogue.

Activities

Greetings

Purposes: Foster respect and recognition of each child's unique qualities

   Develop a feeling of belonging to a group

Welcome each child who comes into your group. Every day, when children enter your room, greet them and spend a minute or so chatting. If any children enter during a group time, stop, greet them, then help them find a place in the group. Tell them what the group has been doing. Continue the contacts when children are ill. Telephone them at home to find out how they are feeling and when they will return.

Interior Decoration

Purposes: Cultivate feelings of responsibility for and control over their environment

   Strengthen ability to negotiate differences in ideas, needs, and preferences

In a group meeting, discuss plans for making the room their own. Ask for ideas about what they want to have in "their room." Write down all the ideas either on a chalkboard or a large piece of paper. If needed, suggest some additional ideas they might like to add: a class mural, a rearrangement of the furniture, a room sign or logo, or decorative containers for storage. Ask for discussion of which are the most important ideas or the most feasible, then vote on the ones to be implemented. Tell them that the plan will be reevaluated at a specific time in the future.

Getting to Know You

Purposes: Develop friendship skills

   Increase awareness of similarities and differences between people

Encourage children to get to know others in the classroom. Make a class roster with children's names and pictures. Or make a class book with a page for each child. Information on the page can include a picture, the names of family members, the child's birthday, his likes and dislikes, or whatever he chooses to say about himself. Leave the book in a place where classmates and parents can look through it.

   For a more extensive project, have the children make an individual book all about themselves. The purpose of this book is to provide helpful information for the adults who work with these children. (See the Appendix for reproducible pages that can be used for this purpose.)

Puppet Talk

Purposes: Foster development of language skills

Increase organizational skills

Provide an outlet for the expression of ideas and feelings

Explore fairy tales and stories from other cultures

Set up a puppet stage. Provide books of fairy tales, fables, or stories from other cultures. Assist children in writing scripts using the stories from the books as the framework or a story of their own devising. Make available materials and instructions for making puppets. Chapter 11 has some suggestions for making puppets.

TV Talk

Purposes: Foster development of language skills

Increase each child's feelings of self-worth

Provide a setting where children can interview their classmates. Secure a microphone or make one. Use a piece of wooden dowel for the handle. Make two slits in the form of a cross on a tennis ball. Slip the ball over the end of the dowel. If you wish you can spray it with black paint. When the microphone is ready, help the children structure an interview. Suggest a few questions they can ask, then allow them to devise their own format. It may also help if you suggest they watch television interviews.

Silhouettes

Purposes: Strengthen ability to work together

Develop appreciation for similarities and differences

Increase feelings of self-esteem

Have children work in pairs. Tape large pieces of paper onto a wall. Darken the room and provide a bright light. (A strong, steadily held flashlight or a high-intensity lamp will work.) Ask one person to sit sideways in front of the paper while the partner outlines a facial silhouette. Children can sign and color their silhouette. Display the portraits.

Getting to Know Me

Purposes: Increase self-esteem

Understand how people are alike and different

Communicate each person's uniqueness to others

Develop appreciation for others' individual traits

Ask children to bring things from home that are special to them and that represent who they are. These may be things they like to collect, photos of special people, or mementos of special occasions in their life. The objects must be small enough to fit into a shoe box.

FIGURE 15–1   *"My dad." Vince, age 7*

Provide each child with a box and distribute materials they can use to decorate their box. Wallpaper pieces, wrapping paper, construction paper, collage materials, paint, marking pens, and pictures from magazines are just some examples.

Allow time at group meetings to have each child show the items from his box and explain why they have special meaning to him.

Family Tree

Purposes: Increase self-esteem

Develop appreciation for family differences

Increase communication with family members

Develop pride in one's family

Instruct children to gather as much information as possible about their family. Who are their parents' parents? How about their grandparents' parents? How many aunts, uncles, cousins can they discover? Help them to draw up a family tree. They can include names or pictures of the people.

Older children can use the computer software program listed an the end of this chapter to gather family information.

Cooperation

Cooperation with others does not come easily to children. As infants, toddlers, and young preschoolers, they are intensely egocentric. During those years their main concern is satisfying their own needs and achieving their own goals with

FIGURE 15–2   *Children want to get along with each other.*

little focus on the needs of others. Gradually, during middle childhood, cognitive development enables children to see others more clearly and they begin to understand that others have needs too. When others' needs conflict with their own they learn to compromise and cooperate in order to have friends. They also find they can achieve common goals by working together. Key factors in helping children to learn cooperative behaviors are supportive parents and well-qualified staff members in child care.

Strategies

- One of the most powerful strategies adults can use for teaching children to be more cooperative is modeling, or what parents call "setting a good example." When children see adults helping others, being kind or compassionate, and assisting others to achieve their goals, they are shown how it can be done. They have a model to follow when confronted with situations in their own daily activities. Conversely, children will also imitate selfishness, cruelty, and noncooperative behaviors they observe in adults.
- Another important strategy is emphasizing cooperation rather than competition. During middle childhood, children are striving to succeed at whatever they attempt and constantly compare themselves to others. They want to be the "best, the first, the fastest." Some competitiveness is inevitable, since many of the sports that are popular among youngsters are based on someone winning and someone losing. It cannot be avoided, but it can be minimized by child-care staff members. Each child can be recognized for his or her participation during the game, rather than praising only the winner. In addition, there should also be games that are not predicated upon someone emerging as the winner. Several of the games that are described in Chapter 10 require cooperation and there is no real victor.

- Space for school-age child care should be designed to accommodate groups of varying sizes. When children play in close proximity to others, they are forced to make some compromises or to engage in negotiations concerning the use of space or materials. Space should not be so limited, however, that children feel crowded for that causes tension and squabbling. Within the workspace, materials should be close at hand, adequate in number for all to share, and stored in an uncluttered manner. In this way, children can work comfortably and with fewer conflicts.

- Staff members can help children develop more cooperative behavior by leading discussions about sharing, fairness, taking turns, and negotiating when working together. They can use examples from daily occurrences or hypothetical situations. As an example, fairness is an important issue for school-age children and conflicts occur frequently. A sensitive child-care leader will use these situations to discuss what happened, why a situation may have seemed unfair, or what could be done differently next time. It is also important to help children become aware of the fact that sometimes one child or another has needs that may seem to take precedence over his own. Equity does not always mean fairness, but implies that each child's needs will be met to the greatest extent possible. Equity should be part of the philosophical approach to school-age care.

    In child-care groups where there are children of different age levels or children with special needs, there are many opportunities to help children be more cooperative. Capable children can be encouraged to take on responsibilities commensurate with their abilities for helping younger or special-needs children with activities, games, projects, or even homework. Both children and adults gain from this arrangement.

- The program of a child-care center should include activities that require children to work cooperatively together toward a common goal. A good example is the production of a play. An entire group could work on this kind of project with some children writing the script, others making costumes, taking roles, designing stage sets, or directing the final presentation. Another example is producing a newsletter. Children have to work together to gather news, write articles, decide upon format, print, and distribute the paper. Both of these projects require a great deal of discussion, negotiation, and compromise and can be effective techniques for helping children to develop those skills.

Activities

Sculpture

Purposes: Provide opportunity for sharing ideas

Increase ability to work under time pressure

Strengthen problem-solving skills

Divide the class into groups of three. Give each a pile of toothpicks, some glue, a piece of styrofoam, and some small corks. Tell them they are to make a single sculpture. The ground rules are that they each get to help decide what to make and to participate in the construction. Set a time limit. (You can also use other objects: clay, Tinkertoys, beads, etc.) Have each group share their sculpture.

Discuss how they decided what to make. What were the problems they encountered? How did they resolve the problems?

Storytelling

Purposes: Develop language skills, both talking and listening

Create a group fantasy with a beginning, a middle, and an end

Tell the children they are going to write a story together. Use a tape recorder to record it. Designate one child to start the story with a few sentences, then point to another child to continue. Allow any child to pass if he or she chooses not to add to the story. Set a time limit for bringing the story to an end.

Rewind the tape and listen to the story. Ask the children what they thought of their tale. Would it have been different if just one person told it?

Y'All Come Up

Purposes: Increase awareness of others' feelings

Foster group cohesiveness

Practice problem solving

This game is the opposite of "King of the Hill." One child stands at the top of a hill, then one by one asks others to join. The object is to get everyone onto the hill without anyone falling off. (If no hill is available, use a very low table.)

Discuss what they had to do to keep everyone together at the top of the hill. How did it make them feel to be included? How did it make them feel if they fell off and could not be included?

Class Caring Project

Purposes: Increase cooperative behavior

Foster feelings of empathy for others

Involve the entire class in planning and implementing a caring project. It can be raising money for a worthy cause, getting involved in a community cleanup drive, or visiting a retirement home. Allow them to research community needs, then choose a project. Have them plan ways to implement their ideas. Encourage them to assign tasks and coordinate ways to follow through. When the project is completed, evaluate what they learned, what they might have done differently.

These, then, are some of the ways you can encourage children to feel better about themselves and learn to function effectively in a group. However, in spite of all your efforts, you may find that there are still some children who are troublesome to themselves and their peers. These children may need some extra thought and care.

Summary

Middle childhood is a time when children refine their sense of self through mastery of a variety of skills: getting along with others, understanding others' point of view, developing moral values, and learning what behaviors are acceptable to parents, teachers, and society. During the process of testing these skills, children often exhibit antisocial behaviors. Children can learn to resolve conflicts effectively with the help of adults. Adults can help children by providing opportunities for them to practice the skills they need.

Self-image has two parts, our perceptions of ourselves and the perceptions conveyed to us by others. How children feel about themselves has a direct effect on their behavior. Adults can strengthen children's self-esteem by being interested in every child, recognizing each child's unique qualities, involving children in meaningful activities, allowing time for discussions of problems or concerns, and finding many ways for children to be successful.

Cooperation with others does not come easily to children. Gradually, during middle childhood, children learn to understand that others have needs and that they must compromise and cooperate in order to have friends. Adults can be a strong force in helping children learn to be more cooperative by modeling or "setting a good example." Cooperation, rather than competition, should be stressed and games should be included that are not predicated upon someone winning. The child-care environment should include space where groups of varying sizes can work together without crowding. Group discussions can help children find alternative ways of interacting with others at activities that require children to work together.

Selected Further Reading

Canter, L., & Petersen, K. (1995). *Teaching students to get along: Reducing conflict and increasing cooperation in K–6 classrooms.* CA: Lee Canter & Associates.

Curry, N.E., & Johnson, C.N. (1990). *Beyond self-esteem: Developing a genuine sense of human value.* Washington, DC: National Association for the Education of Young Children.

Derman-Sparks, L., & the A. B. C. Task Force. (1989). *Anti-bias curriculum: Tools for empowering young children.* Washington, DC: National Association for the Education of Young Children.

Dinwiddie, S.A. (1994). The saga of Sally, Sammy, and the red pen: Facilitating children's social problem solving. *Young Children, 49*(5), 13–19.

Gutwirth, V. (1997). A multicultural family study project for primary. *Young Children, 52*(2), 72–78.

Honig A.S., & Wittmer, D.S. (1996). Helping children become more prosocial: Ideas for classrooms, families, and communities. *Young Children, 51*(2), 62–70.

Slaby, R.G., Roedell, W.C., Arezzo, D., & Hendrix, K. (1995). *Early violence prevention: Tools for teachers of young children.* Washington, DC: National Association for the Education of Young Children.

Wittmer, D.S., & Honig, A.S. (1994). Encouraging positive social development in young children. *Young Children, 49*(5), 4–12.

Computer Software

Family Tree Maker (IBM Windows MPC CD-ROM) Novato, CA: Broderbund/Banner Blue. Advanced

Student Activities

1. Choose one of the conflict resolution activities described in this chapter. Try it out with several friends or classmates. What problems did you encounter? How do you think the process would have been different with children?
2. Interview a caregiver. What methods does he or she use to promote cooperation? How does this person help children to resolve conflicts?
3. Work with one of your classmates to test whether your perception of yourself is the same or different from how others see you. First, write down five words that describe your partner. Next, write five words that describe yourself. Compare your partner's list with your own. Did each of you agree when describing the other? How close was your self-evaluation to the way your partner described you? How does this activity contribute to your understanding of the complexity of self-image in children?

Review

1. State the skills children need in order to get along with others.
2. Why do children argue, question authority, tease other children, or resort to name-calling?
3. Why is it important for children to learn to read nonverbal cues from others?
4. State three strategies that can help to prevent conflicts between children.
5. Describe one activity that helps children learn to resolve conflicts effectively.
6. What are the two components of self-esteem?
7. One of the strategies for helping children increase their self-esteem is to involve them in projects where children and adults can work together. How does this affect how they feel about themselves?
8. Cooperation does not come easily to children. Why not?
9. In what ways can adults minimize competition among school-age children?
10. Describe one activity that helps children acquire the ability to cooperate with others.

16

Using Community Resources

Objectives

After studying this chapter, the student should be able to:

- Discuss the advantages and disadvantages of using community resources
- Describe a variety of activities appropriate for seniors and children
- List activities for which teen volunteers are suited
- Describe ways to use resources outside the child-care center
- State ways to make a volunteer program effective

How Community Resources Can Support Development

Teachers and caregivers sometimes greet the idea of using community resources to enrich their curriculum with mixed reactions. Some cite the general hassle involved in recruiting and training volunteers. Others say they cannot get out into the community because of transportation problems. Some point to the fact that except for summers, the time children spend at the center is too limited. Some caregivers say it is difficult because of the wide age differences of the children they serve. All these are valid reasons, but should not deter you. The problems can be resolved. You may find the benefits to the children will be well worth the effort.

School-age children are ready and eager to learn about the world outside their immediate environment. When they go to kindergarten, they take that first step

235

away from their home and out into the community. Most find it a fascinating place and are eager to find their own place out in the world. Developmentally they are ready. They have good muscular control and want to try out their skills in new ways. Cognitively, they have a good memory and a much longer interest span. Coupled with this, they can postpone rewards allowing them to work on projects that take a long time to complete. They are ready to consider different ways of thinking or doing things. They find not everyone lives or thinks as they do. When presented with alternatives, they like to consider the options. In addition to all the above characteristics, school-age children have a high energy level. They need lots to do and challenges to meet.

Bringing the Community to Your Center

One of the ways you can involve your children in the community is to invite residents or representatives from agencies and organizations to participate in activities at your center. This method has a distinct advantage in that it eliminates transportation problems and does not entail travel time. An added advantage is that your school becomes known and this may be helpful if you have to do fundraising. What is most important, however, is that both children and outside adults benefit from this relationship.

Intergenerational Programs

As a nation, our population is aging. People are living longer and many older persons are still healthy and active. They are looking for meaningful ways to use their energies. Oftentimes in our contemporary society, there are children who either do not know or do not live close to their own grandparents. When senior volunteers spend time with children, both can benefit from the relationship. The adults will feel they still can make a difference in someone else's life. The children will enjoy increased self-esteem because there is someone who listens to them and cares about them. Both can learn to appreciate the similarities and differences that exist between the generations.

Child-care centers can use the talents of older adults who come from a variety of jobs and professions. Artists, teachers, musicians, scientists, gardeners, veterinarians, cooks are just a few who have knowledge and skills that can be shared with children. These people can do what grandparents do: plan special activities, demonstrate how to do things, go on outings together, celebrate holidays and special occasions.

Recruit older persons through the following:

- Active living centers
- Community centers

- Groups for active seniors
- Parks and recreation departments
- Senior centers
- Retirement communities
- Churches
- Special-interest groups: hobby clubs or computer users
- Subsidized housing complexes for persons over fifty-five
- Senior citizens service agencies (county or city)
- Notices in volunteer information columns of newspapers

You can also write to organizations for seniors to find groups in your community. Try:

American Association of Retired Persons
1909 K Street NW
Washington, DC 20049

Gray Panthers
215 South Juniper Street, Suite 601
Philadelphia, PA 19107

Activities for Seniors and Children

The following is a list of just a few things older adults can do with children. You can develop others based upon the needs of your particular center or the talents of the adults available to you.

Tutoring

Assist individual children with math, English, or homework.

Many retired teachers want to maintain contact with children, but do not want the structure of a classroom setting. They might find helping in a child-care center to their liking. Children will appreciate help with school work and someone who will listen while they practice conversing in English.

Science Experiences

Demonstrate scientific phenomena: electricity, chemistry, weather.

Plan and conduct hands-on science activities for the children. Schedule hands-on activities to follow a demonstration. Any of the activities described in Chapter 12 or contained in the books on the reading list for that chapter would be suitable.

Share an interest in exotic plants (orchids, cacti, tropical plants, etc.).

Work with children to make exhibits for a school science fair. Invite other school groups and parents to see the results.

Cultural Awareness

Demonstrate musical instruments specific to a culture. Let children play them.

Cook and taste ethnic foods. Use traditional cooking pots and implements.

Teach dances of native peoples. Make costumes and plan a performance of dances.

FIGURE 16–1   Both children and adults benefit from an intergenerational program.

Display toys and games used by children in different cultures. Tell how they are used. Let children try them out.

Read children's books from different countries in the native language, then translate. Discuss how the stories reflect life in that country.

Show children folk arts or crafts. Teach children how to create some typical folk objects.

Share with children how holidays and special occasions are celebrated in their native country.

Develop a network of pen pals from different countries. Help children write letters to a pen pal.

Collections

Share special collections: rocks, shells, fossils, insects, stamps. Work with children to classify and organize their own collection.

Act as an adviser to a club based on collections.

Chess, Checkers

Teach children how to play, organize tournaments. Be an adviser for a club.

Plan and conduct a tournament. Consider a tournament between adults and children.

Cooking

Prepare a variety of foods with children: bread, ice cream, muffins.

Share favorite recipes or recipes passed down from family members. Prepare holiday specialties.

Help children put together a book of recipes for foods they and their families especially enjoy.

Reading

Read stories to children. Children love hearing stories read to them in groups or one-on-one.

Listen while children read. Discuss the story or ask questions about the story. "What happened when . . . ?" or "What if . . . ?"

Take individual children on a trip to the library. Browse together, then choose books to take back to the center.

Puppet Making

Help children make puppets then put on a puppet show. This can be a long-range project beginning with writing a script, making the puppets, planning the production, then performing.

Life Stories

Tell children about their own childhood. Many children cannot conceive of a world without the modern conveniences they take for granted. A good storyteller can paint a picture of life in "the old days."

Share photo albums of their own childhood with children. Show themselves as babies, as "school-agers," as teens.

Help children compile their own life story. Older children will be able to write theirs. Younger children can portray their history through photographs and drawings or collages.

Art Projects

Work on special art projects. Teach children new techniques for creating art: airbrush painting, mold making, using charcoal for drawing. Accompany children on a tour of the studio of an artist who uses one of these techniques.

Help children plan and paint a mural. This can either be a child-only project or a joint project between adult and children. Each could contribute something to the finished product.

Field Trips

Accompany children on trips to museums, plays, factories. Extra adults provide better supervision, but older adults can share their knowledge with children as well.

Woodworking

Teach children proper use of power tools and hand tools. Supervise woodworking projects.

Accompany children to a furniture-manufacturing site.

Computer Assistance

Teach the use of a computer. Play games with children, help them write stories, help them write letters to pen pals.

Work with children to produce a monthly newspaper. Show them how to gather news, go with them to interview interesting community people. Use a word-processing program to write the stories. Use a desktop publishing program to arrange the stories into a newspaper layout. Print the paper and distribute it to parents, staff, and other child-care groups.

Gardening

Teach children the basic needs of plants. Help them to prepare, plant, and maintain a garden.

Plant a vegetable garden and harvest vegetables. Prepare vegetables for a snack: raw vegetables and a dip or zucchini bread.

Bicycle Maintenance

Teach children how to repair and maintain their own bikes.

Teach safety rules to observe when riding a bike.

Photography

Teach children the basics of using a camera. If possible, help children to develop their own pictures.

Help children put together an exhibit of their photographs for a parent bulletin board.

Needlework

Teach children how to knit or crochet. Help them create simple garments: a scarf, hat, small blanket.

Teach children embroidery stitches. Help them to create a pillow cover, place mat, wall hanging.

Help children make a simple hand loom. Teach them how to weave place mats, wall hangings, pot holders.

Accompany children to needlework shops to see the variety of materials available. Purchase materials needed for a project.

Activities Using High-School and College Students

Although many young people can do the things suggested for older persons, they may have a different approach. They also may be better suited for some activities. The following are some activities young people may be especially suited for.

FIGURE 16–2   *"Me being a Black Belt." Ricky, age 9*

Sports

Teach children proper techniques for playing popular sports: tennis, basketball, baseball, soccer, golf, swimming, gymnastics. Practice with individual children who need help in perfecting their skills.

Organize a game with another child-care center, possibly at a nearby park.

Drama

Work with children to write, produce, and perform a play. Children can make their own costumes, design and construct scenery, set up proper lighting.

Dance

Teach children how to dance ballet, tap, clogging, current popular dances.

Help children choreograph a dance. Perform for other children or parents.

Conversation

Talk with and listen to children. Teens may be able to help children express their worries, their fears, or to discuss their problems.

Field Trips

Accompany children on active field trips: park, zoo, beach, nature walk.

Exercise

Teach children some basic exercises such as those suggested in Chapter 14.

Cultural Awareness

High-school exchange students can tell about life in their homeland: their play activities, school, their family.

Games

Play table or language games with children. Monopoly®, Clue®, Trivial Pursuit®, Scrabble®, Life®, or card games can be enjoyed by children and teens. Teens will contribute their own enthusiasms for language games such as telephone, taking a trip, twenty questions, or charades.

Community Agencies, Organizations, and Businesses

You may decide you do not want volunteers who come to your school, but would rather schedule periodic activities that use facilities in your community. Nearly every area will have some resources that would interest children. Check your neighborhood, call government offices, talk to other caregivers. If you have lived in the area for a long time, where did your parents take you when you were a child?

Museums

Natural history museums are an excellent source of persons to do presentations or conduct tours at the museum. Consider presentations on local history, plants, or animals indigenous to the area.

Children's discovery museums are marvelous places for a field trip. These are places where children can touch, manipulate, and participate in a variety of activities.

Art museums may conduct tours especially designed for children. Most large museums have a docents program, volunteers who know a great deal about the art in the galleries. Sometimes a tour is followed by a session in which the children can create their own art.

Library

Many libraries have a children's librarian who will help children choose books. They may also have reading incentive programs: a reward for children who read a specified number of books.

Libraries often have film series that are suitable for young children.

Businesses

Some businesspeople may be willing to conduct a tour of their facility, then answer questions or tell children how to prepare themselves for that line of work. A newspaper office, dairy, radio station, a computerized office might interest children.

Fire Station

Take a tour of the facility. Discuss requirements for becoming a firefighter.

Some departments have fire-prevention programs featuring Smokey the Bear and could do a presentation.

Police Station

Take a tour of the facility. Discuss requirements for qualifying to be a member of law enforcement.

Some departments have drug prevention programs and could do a presentation.

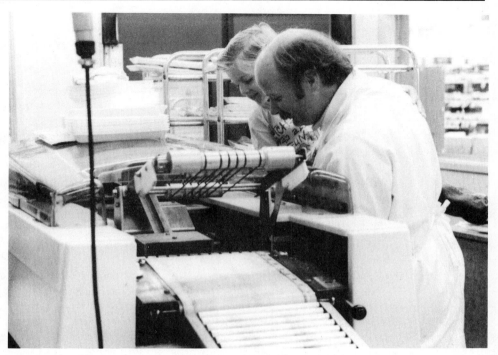

FIGURE 16–3   Local businesses may be willing to conduct tours of their facilities.

Wildlife Refuge

A few communities have areas set aside for endangered animal species or plants. Some conduct nature walks. Others may have plant propagation workshops where children help plant seeds or transplant native plants or trees.

Community Facilities

Find out if your children can use a local riding stable, swimming pool, or public tennis courts.

All of the above activities will enhance your child-care curriculum immeasurably. However, you may still be thinking that it is all too much trouble. There are some ways to resolve problems that schools and child-care centers have found helpful.

Guidelines for Using Volunteers

It is important to have an organized method of managing a volunteer corps. Volunteers will be more valuable if they know what they are expected to do, if they are trained and supported as they work with you, and if they know they are appreciated. Time and effort spent in setting up this kind of program will pay off in the long run. Your volunteers are more likely to stay with you longer. They will contribute to your curriculum rather than being an additional burden.

Prepare a booklet of information that clearly states expectations for volunteers. Spell out what their job is, what their hours will be. Let them know who will be supervising them and to whom they can go when problems arise.

Check your local licensing requirement regarding fingerprinting volunteers. If necessary, tell volunteers where it can be done.

Assign volunteers to simple, specific tasks at first. Start with having them work with one child alone at an activity. As you learn more about each person's abilities and strengths, you can gradually allow greater responsibility.

Plan and conduct an orientation for each volunteer. Develop a program that gives a general overview of your center, its goals and philosophy. Suggest ways of interacting with children. State rules that apply to the children and to themselves.

Ask for a specific time commitment from each volunteer. Since a lot of effort goes into making a volunteer program successful, it is important to avoid constant change in its members. Have each volunteer say how much time and for how long a period they can commit themselves to your program.

Provide ongoing supervision and training. Additional training as volunteers become more familiar with your program will enhance their self-esteem and make them more committed.

Evaluate and provide feedback periodically. Remember that volunteers are not getting paid for their time. To make it worthwhile, they must feel they are appreciated and that they are learning.

Have realistic expectations for your volunteers. Remember that they may not always be available when you need them. Older persons sometimes have health problems, young people have many other demands on their time.

You may have to make some adaptations to your environment in order to foster an effective intergenerational program. Consider the following changes to accommodate both older adults and teenagers in your setting.

Place small sofas or wide armchairs in a quiet corner. This will invite an adult or teen and one or two children to sit together to read or talk.

Install an extra-wide swing in the playground. The favorite place for many children of past generations was in the porch swing with grandpa or grandma. Not many have that experience today, but a wide swing can bring a little of that atmosphere to your playground. Children will also enjoy swinging with a teenager who may be a little daring and swing them fast.

Provide at least one table high enough for an adult or a teenager. Let children sit on stools so they can work with the adult at this table on art projects, science experiments, writing, or whatever they wish.

Provide a place where children can leave a message for the adult or teenager. Most volunteers are not there on a daily basis, but children may want to write them a note about something that happened or just leave a special drawing. This can be an important avenue for developing a relationship.

Provide a place where the adults or teens can keep their own belongings.

Removing Barriers to Community Participation

At the beginning of this chapter, it was indicated that many caregivers have mixed reactions to the use of community resources. They cite a variety of reasons. There are some solutions that other programs have found successful. They are:

- Use public transportation—buses or trains.
- Walk to places that are close to the child-care center.
- Rent or use donated buses and vans from churches (these are usually not used by the church during the week.)
- Take small groups at a time, using public transportation or private cars.
- Divide groups according to age levels of children and take trips to different sites.
- Use senior volunteers to take small groups or individual children for a walk into the community.
- Have parents pick up their children at the place being visited—park, swimming pool, library.

    REMINDER: Before you take any children on trips outside your child-care facility, you must obtain written permission from their parents. You should also check with your insurance agent to be certain that the form of transportation you will use is covered by your policy.

Intergenerational contact is not a new concept. In past generations young children were often cared for by older brothers and sisters, aunts, uncles, and grandparents. Each age level contributed to the child's knowledge of what growing up means. Each age level was a model children could imitate. Today's children who live in nuclear and mobile families miss that experience. Using volunteers can recreate that kind of environment. It is well worth the effort in terms of benefits to the children and to the volunteers themselves.

Summary

Teachers and caregivers are sometimes reluctant to use community resources. They say the problems are difficulty in recruiting and training volunteers, transportation problems, short time children spend at the center, and that children are at such different age levels.

One way to involve children in the community is to invite individuals or representatives of agencies to visit the center. Using older persons as volunteers is one method that has been successful in some programs. A variety of activities for seniors and children are possible depending upon the talents and interests of the volunteers.

Teenage volunteers can do many of the same things older persons can, but there may be some for which they are better suited. Teens can participate in more active experiences such as sports, dance, and exercise.

Community agencies, organizations, and businesses may have resources for activities that will interest children. Museums, libraries, police, and fire departments may have programs. Businesses might be willing to conduct tours of their facility.

An organized method of managing volunteers will make the program more effective. Prepare a manual of information, start volunteers doing simple, specific tasks with children. Have an orientation, provide ongoing supervision, and give the volunteer feedback about performance. It is also important to have realistic expectations for your volunteers.

You may have to alter your physical environment to make the most effective use of volunteers. Have places where adult and child can sit together and a high table that is comfortable for an adult. Provide a place where children can leave messages for volunteers and where adults can keep their belongings.

Remove barriers to community participation by using public transportation or walking to nearby sites. Rent church-owned vehicles that are unused during the week. Take small groups at a time. Use senior volunteers to take individual children into the community. Have parents pick up children at the place being visited.

Selected Further Reading

Community involvement. (1982, September–October). *School Age Notes, 3*(1).

Lyons, C. (1985, Spring). Older adults in intergenerational programs: The other side of the story. *Beginnings, 2*(1), 3–5.

Schine, J., & Campbell, P. (1989). Young teens help young children for the benefit of both. *Young Children, 44*(3), 65–69.

Seefeldt, C., Jantz, R., Serock, K., & Bredekamp, S. (1979). *Young and old together: A training manual for intergenerational programs.* Urbana, IL: U.S. Educational Resources Information Center, ERIC Document 210 089.

Seefeldt, C., Warman, B., Jantz, R., & Galper, A. (1990). Young and old together. Washington, DC: National Association for the Education of Young Children.

Wolf, D. (1985, Spring). Creating settings for multi-age caregiving. *Beginnings, 2*(1), 27–30.

Young and old together, a resource directory of intergenerational programs. (1986). Prepared by Parenting and Community Education, California State Department of Education.

Student Activities

1. Talk to an older person in your family about his or her childhood. How different was it from your own growing years? In what ways might this information help you to understand that older person better?

2. Visit a senior center in your community. Find out if they have any volunteer programs. If they do, ask what seniors hope to get out of participating in their community. If the center does not have a volunteer program, ask why.
3. Plan one activity either a teenager or older person could do with a group of nine-year-olds. List the materials that would be needed and describe any special procedures.

Review

1. Caregivers are often reluctant to use community resources. List the reasons discussed in this chapter.
2. State five places to recruit senior volunteers.
3. Describe five activities in which seniors can share their cultural heritage with children.
4. Name two activities that are especially suited for teens and school-age children.
5. State the resources that often are available through museums.
6. This chapter listed seven things you can do to make a volunteer program more effective. What are they?
7. In what ways can you change the environment of a child-care center to make it easier for volunteers to interact with the children?
8. This chapter stated seven ways to remove barriers to community participation. What are they?

Appendix

All About Me

_____

Name

Adapted from material written by JoAnn Kosko Simmons.

Full name _____

I want to be called: _____

Parent(s) _____

Address _____

_____

Phone Number _____

Vital Stats!

Then

Date of birth: _____

Place of birth: _____
      (city, state)

_____
      (hospital)

Weight at birth: _____ pounds, _____ ounces. Length at birth: _____ inches

Hair color at birth: _____

Eye color at birth: _____

Now

Height now: _____ feet _____ inches

Hair color now: _____ Eye color now: _____

About My Family . . .

Members of my family include: _____

_____

_____

_____

_____

I am told that I look like _____

Here are some pictures of: _____

ME   MY FAMILY

My Friends

The person I consider my best friend is _____

My newest friend is _____

The qualities that I admire in friends are: _____

My Memories

My first memory of my childhood was: _____

_____

The first birthday that I remember was: _____

_____

My first memories of school include: _____

_____

Some of the things that I would like you to know about me are: _____

_____

I think I am: _____

_____

Thoughts About School

What is your favorite school subject? _____

What is your least favorite subject? _____

Do you like to read? Why or why not? _____

_____

What do you like to read? _____

_____

What is the best book you ever read or had read to you? _____

Do you usually have homework assignments every day? _____

How much time do you usually need to spend completing your homework?

_____

Do you occasionally need help with some subjects? _____

Do you have any special interests or things you like to do? _____

Would you be willing to share your interests with your classmates? _____

If you could plan a day in your after-school program, what would be included?

_____

If you could invite two famous people to join our class for a day, they would be:

_____ and _____

Favorite Things

Favorite food: _____

Favorite meal: _____

    Prepared by: _____

Favorite color: _____

    Second favorite color: _____

Favorite group (musical): _____

Favorite song: _____

Favorite board game: _____

Favorite sport to play: _____

Favorite sport to watch: _____

Favorite TV show: _____

Second favorite TV show: _____

Favorite hobby: _____

Favorite season: _____

My Goals

This year, I want to be able to: _____

For Parents

Some things that I would like you to know about my child include: _____

_____

He/She has the following talents: _____

He/She has the following strengths as a student: _____

He/She has experienced some difficulty with the following subject(s) in school:

_____

_____

My child learns best by: _____

My thoughts on homework are: _____

_____

Other information you should know about my child: _____

_____

A funny/amusing anecdote I would like to share about my child would be the time that: _____

_____

I would be willing to share my talents/skills with the class for the purpose of enrichment. My talents/skills include: _____

_____

I would like to get involved with my child's after-school experience in the following way(s): _____

_____

The most convenient time(s) for me to do so are: _____

Should a problem arise with my child, I would like you to handle it in the following manner: _____

_____

If you need to contact me, the best time to do so would be:

_____ at work _____-_____-_____ Between _____ and _____

_____ at home _____-_____-_____ After _____ No later than _____

(signature) _____

(date) _____

Index